PRINCIPLES OF HEALTH INSURANCE COVERAGE

PRINCIPLES OF HEALTH INSURANCE COVERAGE

Prem Nagpal

CYBER TECH PUBLICATIONS
4264/3, Ansari Road, Daryaganj, New Delhi-110002 (India)
Ph.: 011-23244078. Fax: 011-23280028
E-Mail: cyberpublicationsdelhi@yahoo.com

PRINCIPLES OF HEALTH INSURANCE COVERAGE

Prem Nagpal

First Edition 2009

Published by :

G.S. Rawat for **Cyber Tech Publications**
4264/3, Ansari Road, Daryaganj, New Delhi-110002 (India)
Ph.: 011-23244078. Fax: 011-23280028
E-Mail: cyberpublicationsdelhi@yahoo.com

Printed at : Asian Offset Printers

Preface

In theory, the introduction of private health insurance can contribute to increasing the aggregate costs of health care in several different ways. Most of the arguments in favour of increasing health care costs due to private health insurance have to do with some disparity in the information available to parties involved in transactions in the health care and health insurance markets.

In interactions between health care providers, such as doctors and patients, it is a given that the former have much better information about their patients' health status and future course of treatment than the latter. This, together with the prospect of being ill and accompanying psychological costs and loss of earnings, makes the demand for health care fairly dependent on the course of treatment recommended by a physician. One consequence is that in a regime of pure indemnity insurance, providers have an incentive to provide more care than may be medically appropriate. For the same reason, the patient or, insurers for that matter, may be less willing to question the qualifications of the doctor as to his or her expertise.

—Author

CONTENTS

1

HEALTH INSURANCE IN INDIA: CURRENT SCENARIO

INTRODUCTION

The health care system in India is characterised by multiple systems of medicine, mixed ownership patterns and different kinds of delivery structures. Public sector ownership is divided between central and state governments, municipal and Panchayat local governments. Public health facilities include teaching hospitals, secondary level hospitals, first-level referral hospitals (CHCs or rural hospitals), dispensaries; primary health centres (PHCs), sub-centres, and health posts. Also included are public facilities for selected occupational groups like organized work force (ESI), defence, government employees (CGHS), railways, post and telegraph and mines among others. The private sector (for profit and not for profit) is the dominant sector with 50 per cent of people seeking indoor care and around 60 to 70 per cent of those seeking ambulatory care (or outpatient care) from private health facilities. While India has made significant gains in terms of health indicators-demographic, infrastructural and epidemiological, it continues to grapple with newer challenges.

Not only have communicable diseases persisted over time but some of them like malaria have also developed insecticide-resistant vectors while others like tuberculosis are becoming increasingly drug resistant. HIV / AIDS has of late assumed extremely virulent proportions. The 1990s have also seen an increase in mortality on account of non-communicable diseases arising as a result of lifestyle changes. The country is now in the midst of a dual disease burden of communicable and noncommunicable diseases.

This is coupled with spiralling health costs, high financial burden on the poor and erosion in their incomes. Around 24% of all people hospitalized in India in a single year fall below the poverty line due to hospitalization (World Bank, 2002). An analysis of financing of hospitalization shows that large proportion of people; especially those in the bottom fourincome quintiles borrow money or sell assets to pay for hospitalization (World Bank, 2002)

This situation exists in a scenario where health care is financed through general tax revenue, community financing, out of pocket payment and social and private health insurance schemes. India spends about 4.9% of GDP on Regional Overview in South-East Asia health (WHR, 2002). The per capita total expenditure on health in India is US$ 23, of which the per capita Government expenditure on health is US$ 4. Hence, it is seen that the total health expenditure is around 5% of GDP, with breakdown of public expenditure (0.9%); private expenditure (4.0%).

The private expenditure can be further classified as out-of-pocket (OOP) expenditure (3.6%) and employees/ community financing (0.4%). It is thus evident that public health investment has been comparatively low. In fact as a percentage of GDP it has declined from 1.3% in 1990 to 0.9% as at present. Furthermore, the central budgetary allocation for health (as a percentage of the total Central budget) has been stagnant at 1.3% while in the states it has declined from 7.0% to 5.5%.

In light of the fiscal crisis facing the government at both central and state levels, in the form of shrinking public health budgets, escalating health care costs coupled with demand for health-care services, and lack of easy access of people from the low-income group to quality health care, health insurance is emerging as an alternative mechanism for financing of health care.

HEALTH INSURANCE

Health insurance in a narrow sense would be 'an individual or group purchasing health care coverage in advance by paying a fee called premium.' In its broader sense, it would be any arrangement that helps to defer, delay, reduce or altogether avoid payment for health care incurred by individuals and households. Given the appropriateness of this definition in the Indian context, this is the definition, we would adopt. The health insurance market in India is very limited covering about 10% of the total population. The existing schemes can be categorized as:

(1) Voluntary health insurance schemes or private-for-profit schemes;

(2) Employer-based schemes;

(3) Insurance offered by NGOs / community based health insurance, and

(4) Mandatory health insurance schemes or government run schemes (namely ESIS, CGHS).

Voluntary health insurance schemes or private-for-profit schemes In private insurance, buyers are willing to pay premium to an insurance company that pools people with similar risks and insures them for health expenses. The key distinction is that the premiums are set at a level, which provides a profit to third party and provider institutions. Premiums are based on an assessment of the risk status of the consumer (or of the group of employees) and the level of benefits provided, rather than as a proportion of the consumer's income.

In the public sector, the General Insurance Corporation (GIC) and its four subsidiary companies (National Insurance Corporation, New India Assurance Company, Oriental Insurance Company and United Insurance Company) and the Life Insurance Corporation (LIC) of India provide voluntary insurance schemes. The Life Insurance Corporation offers Ashadeep Plan II and Jeevan Asha Plan II. The General Insurance Corporation offers Personal Accident policy, Jan Arogya policy, Raj Rajeshwari policy, Mediclaim policy, Overseas Mediclaim policy, Cancer Insurance policy, Bhavishya Arogya policy and Dreaded Disease policy (Srivastava 1999 as quoted in Bhat R & Malvankar D, 2000)

Of the various schemes offered, Mediclaim is the main product of the GIC. The Medical Insurance Scheme or Mediclaim was introduced in November 1986 and it covers individuals and groups with persons aged 5-80 yrs. Children (3 months-5 yrs) are covered with their parents. This scheme provides for reimbursement of medical expenses (now offers cashless scheme) by an individual towards hospitalization and domiciliary hospitalization as per the sum insured. There are exclusions and pre-existing disease clauses. Premiums are calculated based on age and the sum insured, which in turn varies from Rs 15 000 to Rs 5 00 000. In 1995/96 about half a million Mediclaim policies were issued with about 1.8 million beneficiaries (Krause Patrick 2000). The coverage for the year 2000-01 was around 7.2 million.

Another scheme, namely the Jan Arogya Bima policy specifically targets the poor population groups. It also covers reimbursement of hospitalization costs up to Rs 5 000 annually for an individual premium of Rs 100 a year. The same exclusion mechanisms apply for this scheme as those under the Mediclaim policy. A family discount of 30% is granted, but there is no group discount or agent commission. However, like the Mediclaim, this policy too has had only limited success. The Jan Arogya Bima Scheme had only covered 400 000 individuals by 1997.

The year 1999 marked the beginning of a new era for health insurance in the Indian context. With the passing of the Insurance Regulatory Development Authority Bill (IRDA) the insurance sector was opened to private and foreign participation, thereby paving the way for the entry of private health insurance companies. The Bill also facilitated the establishment of an authority to protect the interests of the insurance holders by regulating, promoting and ensuring orderly growth of the insurance industry. The bill allows foreign promoters to hold paid up capital of up to 26 percent in an Indian company and requires them to have a capital of Rs 100 crore along with a business plan to begin its operations.Currently, a few companies such as Bajaj Alliance, ICICI, Royal Sundaram, and Cholamandalam among others are offering health insurance schemes. The nature of schemes offered by these companies is described briefly.

- Bajaj Allianz: Bajaj Alliance offers three health insurance schemes namely, Health Guard, Critical Illness Policy and Hospital Cash Daily Allowance Policy.
  - The Health Guard scheme is available to those aged 5 to 75 years (not allowing entry for those over 55 years of age), with the sum assured ranging from Rs 100 0000 to 500 000. It offers cashless benefit and medical reimbursement for hospitalization expenses (preand post-hospitalization) at various hospitals across India

(subject to exclusions and conditions). In case the member opts for hospitals besides the empanelled ones, the expenses incurred by him are reimbursed within 14 working days from submission of all the documents. While pre-existing diseases are excluded at the time of taking the policy, they are covered from the 5th year onwards if the policy is continuously renewed for four years and the same has been declared while taking the policy for the first time. Other discounts and benefits like tax exemption, health check-up at end of four claims free year, etc. can be availed of by the insured.

* The Critical Illness policy pays benefits in case the insured is diagnosed as suffering from any of the listed critical events and survives for minimum of 30 days from the date of diagnosis. The illnesses covered include: first heart attack; Coronary artery disease requiring surgery: stroke; cancer; kidney failure; major organ transplantation; multiple sclerosis; surgery on aorta; primary pulmonary arterial hypertension, and paralysis. While exclusion clauses apply, premium rates are competitive and high-sum insurance can be opted for by the insured.

* The Hospital Cash Daily Allowance Policy provides cash benefit for each and every completed day of hospitalization, due to sickness or accident. The amount payable per day is dependant on the selected scheme. Dependant spouse and children (aged 3 months-21years) can also be covered under the Policy. The benefits payable to the dependants are linked to that of insured. The Policy pays for a maximum single hospitalization period of 30 days and an overall hospitalization period of 30/

60 completed days per policy period per person regardless of the number of confinements to hospital/nursing home per policy period.

- ICICI Lombard: ICICI Lombard offers Group Health Insurance Policy. This policy is available to those aged 5-80 years, (with children being covered with their parents) and is given to corporate bodies, institutions, and associations. The sum insured is minimum Rs 15 000/-and a maximum of Rs 500000. The premium chargeable depends upon the age of the person and the sum insured selected. A slab wise group discount is admissible if the group size exceeds 100. The policy covers reimbursement of hospitalization expenses incurred for diseases contracted or injuries sustained in India. Medical expenses up to 30 days for Pre-hospitalization and up to 60 days for post-hospitalization are also admissible. Exclusion clauses apply. Moreover, favourable claims experience is recognized by discount and conversely, unfavourable claims experience attracts loading on renewal premium. On payment of additional premium, the policy can be extended to cover maternity benefits, pre-existing diseases, and reimbursement of cost of health check-up after four consecutive claims-free years.
- Royal Sundaram Group: The Shakthi Health Shield policy offered by the Royal Sundaram group can be availed by members of the women's group, their spouses and dependent children. No age limits apply. The premium for adults aged up to 45 years is Rs 125 per year, for those aged more than 45 years is Rs 175 per year. Children are covered at Rs 65 per year. Under this policy, hospital benefits up to Rs 7 000 per annum can be availed, with a limit per claim of Rs 5 000. Other benefits include maternity

benefit of Rs 3 000 subject to waiting period of nine months after first enrolment and for first two children only. Exclusion clauses apply (Ranson K & Jowett M, 2003)

- Cholamandalam General Insurance: The benefits offered (in association with the Paramount Health Care, a re-insurer) in case of an illness or accident resulting in hospitalization, are cash-free hospitalization in more than 1 400 hospitals across India, reimbursement of the expenses during pre-hospitalization (60 days prior to hospitalization) and post-hospitalization (90 days after discharge) stages of treatment. Over 130 minor surgeries that require less than 24 hours hospitalization under day care procedure are also covered. Extra health covers like general health and eye examination, local ambulance service, hospital daily allowance, and 24 hours assistance can be availed of.

Exclusion clauses apply. Employer-based schemes Employers in both the public and private sector offers employer-based insurance schemes through their own employer-managed facilities by way of lump sum payments, reimbursement of employee's health expenditure for outpatient care and hospitalization, fixed medical allowance, monthly or annual irrespective of actual expenses, or covering them under the group health insurance policy. The railways, defence and security forces, plantations sector and mining sector provide medical services and / or benefits to its own employees. The population coverage under these schemes is minimal, about 30-50 million people.

Insurance Offered by NGOs / community-based Health Insurance

Community-based funds refer to schemes where members prepay a set amount each year for specified services. The premia are usually flat rate (not income-related) and therefore not progressive. Making profit is not the purpose of these funds, but rather improving access to services. Often there is a problem with adverse selection because of a large number of high-risk members, since premiums are not based on assessment of individual risk status. Exemptions may be adopted as a means of assisting the poor, but this will also have adverse effect on the ability of the insurance fund to meet the cost of benefits.

Community-based schemes are typically targeted at poorer populations living in communities, in which they are involved in defining contribution level and collecting mechanisms, defining the content of the benefit package, and / or allocating the schemes, financial resources (International Labour Office Universities Programme 2002 as quoted in Ranson K & Acharya A, 2003). Such schemes are generally run by trust hospitals or nongovernmental organizations (NGOs).

The benefits offered are mainly in terms of preventive care, though ambulatory and in-patient care is also covered. Such schemes tend to be financed through patient collection, government grants and donations. Increasingly in India, CBHI schemes are negotiating with the forprofit insurers for the purchase of custom designed group insurance policies. However, the coverage of such schemes is low, covering about 30-50 million (Bhat, 1999). A review by Bennett, Cresse et al. (as quoted in Ranson K & Acharya A, 2003) indicates that many community-based insurance schemes suffer from poor design and management, fail to include the poorest-of-thepoor, have low membership and require extensive financial support. Other issues relate to sustainability and replication of such schemes. Table provides an overview of some non-profit social insurance schemes. Some of the schemes are described below (Ranson K & Jowett M, 2003).

Some examples of community-based health insurance schemes are discussed herein.

- Self-Employed Women's Association (SEWA), Gujarat: This scheme established in 1992, provides health, life and assets insurance to women working in the informal sector and their families. The enrolment in the year 2002 was 93 000. This scheme operates in collaboration with the National Insurance Company (NIC). Under SEWA's most popular policy, a premium of Rs 85 per individual is paid by the woman for life, health and assets insurance. At an additional payment of Rs 55, her husband too can be covered. Rs 20 per member is then paid to the National Insurance Company (NIC) which provides coverage to a maximum of Rs 2 000 per person per year for hospitalization. After being hospitalized at a hospital of one's choice (public or private), the insurance claim is submitted to SEWA. The responsibility for enrolment of members, for processing and approving of claims rests with SEWA. NIC in turn receives premiums from SEWA annually and pays them a lumpsum on a monthly basis for all claims reimbursed. (Ranson K & Acharya A, 2003).
- Another CBHI scheme located in Gujarat, is that run by the Tribhuvandas Foundation (TF), Anand. This was established in 2001, with the membership being restricted to members of the AMUL Dairy Cooperatives. Since then, over 1 00 000 households have been enrolled under this scheme, with the TF functioning as a third party insurer.
- The Mallur Milk Cooperative in Karnataka established a CBHI scheme in 1973. It covers 7 000 people in three villages and outpatient and inpatient health care are directly provided.
- A similar scheme was established in 1972 at Sewagram, Wardha in Maharashtra. This scheme

covers about 14 390 people in 12 villages and members are provided with outpatient and inpatient care directly by Sewagram.

- The Action for Community Organization, Rehabilitation and Development (ACCORD), Nilgiris, Tamil Nadu was established in 1991. Around 13 000 Adivasis (tribals) are covered under a group policy purchased from New India Assurance.
- Another scheme located in Tamil Nadu is Kadamalai Kalanjia Vattara Sangam (KKVS), Madurai. This was established in 2000 and covers members of women's self-help groups and their families. Its enrolment in 2002 was around 5 710, with the KKVS functioning as a third party insurer.
- The Voluntary Health Services (VHS), Chennai, Tamil Nadu was established in 1963. It offers sliding premium with free care to the poorest. The benefits include discounted rates on both outpatient and inpatient care, with the VHS functioning as both insurer and health care provider. In 1995, its membership was 124 715. However, this scheme suffers from low levels of cost recovery due to problems of adverse selection.
- Raigarh Ambikapur Health Association (RAHA), Chhatisgarh was established in 1972, and functions as a third party administrator. Its membership in the year 1993 was 72 000.

Social Insurance or mandatory health insurance schemes or government run schemes (namely the ESIS, CGHS) Social insurance is an earmarked fund set up by government with explicit benefits in return for payment. It is usually compulsory for certain groups in the population and the premiums are determined by income (and hence ability to pay) rather than related to health risk. The benefit packages are standardized and contributions are earmarked for spending on health services The government-run schemes include the Central Government Health Scheme (CGHS) and the Employees State Insurance Scheme (ESIS).

CENTRAL GOVERNMENT HEALTH SCHEME (CGHS)

Since 1954, all employees of the Central Government (present and retired); some autonomous and semi-government organizations, MPs, judges, freedom fighters and journalists are covered under the Central Government Health Scheme (CGHS). This scheme was designed to replace the cumbersome and expensive system of reimbursements (GOI, 1994). It aims at providing comprehensive medical care to the Central Government employees and the benefits offered include all outpatient facilities, and preventive and promotive care in dispensaries. Inpatient facilities in government hospitals and approved private hospitals are also covered. This scheme is mainly funded through Central Government funds, with premiums ranging from Rs 15 to Rs 150 per month based on salary scales. The coverage of this scheme has grown substantially with provision for the non-allopathic systems of medicine as well as for allopathy. Beneficiaries at this moment are around 432 000, spread across 22 cities.

The CGHS has been criticized from the point of view of quality and accessibility. Subscribers have complained of high out-of-pocket expenses due to slow reimbursement and incomplete coverage for private health care (as only 80% of cost is reimbursed if referral is made to private facility when such facilities are not available with the CGHS).

EMPLOYEE AND STATE INSURANCE SCHEME (ESIS)

The enactment of the Employees State Insurance Act in 1948 led to formulation of the Employees State Insurance Scheme. This scheme provides protection to employees against loss of wages due to inability to work due to sickness, maternity, disability and death due to employment injury. It offers medical and cash benefits, preventive and promotive care and health education. Medical care is also provided to employees and their family members without fee for service. Originally, the ESIS scheme covered all power-using non-seasonal factories employing 10 or more people. Later, it was extended to cover employees working in all non-power using factories with 20 or more persons. While persons working in mines and plantations, or an organization offering health benefits as good as or better than ESIS, are specifically excluded. Service establishments like shops, hotels, restaurants, cinema houses, road transport and news papers printing are now covered. The monthly wage limit for enrolment in the ESIS is Rs. 6 500, with a prepayment contribution in the form of a payroll tax of 1.75% by employees, 4.75% of employees' wages to be paid by the employers, and 12.5% of the total expenses are borne by the state governments. The number of beneficiaries is over 33 million spread over 620 ESI centres across states. Under the ESIS, there were 125 hospitals, 42 annexes and 1 450 dispensaries with over 23 000 beds facilities. The scheme is managed and financed by the Employees State Insurance Corporation (a public undertaking) through the state governments, with total expenditure of Rs 3 300 million or Rs 400/-per capita insured person.

The ESIS programme has attracted considerable criticism. A report based on patient surveys conducted in Gujarat (Shariff, 1994 as quoted in Ellis R et a, 2000) found that over half of those covered did not seek care from ESIS facilities. Unsatisfactory nature of ESIS services, low quality drugs, long waiting periods, impudent behaviour of personnel, lack of interest or low interest on part of employees and low awareness of ESI procedures, were some of the reasons cited.

Other Government Initiatives

Apart from the government-run schemes, social security benefits for the disadvantaged groups can be availed of, under the provisions of the Maternity Benefit (Amendment) Act 1995, Workmen's Compensation (Amendment) Act 1984, Plantation Labour Act 1951, Mine Mines Labour Welfare Fund Act 1946, Beedi Workers Welfare Fund Act 1976 and Building and other Construction Workers (Regulation of Employment and Conditions of Service) Act, 1996.

The Government of India has also undertaken initiatives to address issues relating to access to public health systems especially for the vulnerable sections of the society. The National Health Policy 2002 acknowledges this and aims to evolve a policy structure, which reduces such inequities and allows the disadvantaged sections of the population a fairer access to public health services. Ensuring more equitable access to health services across the social and geographical expanse of the country is the main objective of the policy. It also seeks to increase the aggregate public health investment through increased contribution from the Central as well as state governments and encourages the setting up of private insurance instruments for increasing the scope of coverage of the secondary and tertiary sector under private health insurance packages. The government envisages an increase in health expenditure as a % of GDP from existing 0.9% to 2.0 % by 2010 and an increase in the share of central grants from the existing 15% to constitute at least 25% of total public health spending by 2010. The State government spending for health in turn would increase from 5.5% to 7% of the budget by 2005, to be further increased to 8% by 2010.

The National Population Policy (NPP) 2000, envisages the establishment of a family welfare-linked health insurance plan. As per this plan, couples living below the poverty line who undergo sterilization with not more than two living children would be eligible for insurance. Under this scheme, the couple along with their children would be covered for hospitalization not exceeding Rs 5 000 and a personal accident insurance cover for the spouse undergoing sterilization. The Institute of Health Systems (IHS), Hyderabad has been entrusted the responsibility of operationalizing the mandate of the NPP 2000. The initial scheme proposed by the IHS was discussed at a workshop in June 2003. The consensus at the meeting was that the scheme, needed further improvement prior to its implementation even as a pilot project. In keeping with the recommendations of the Tenth Five Year Plan and the National Health Policy (NHP) 2002, the Department of Family Welfare is also proposing to commission studies in eight states covering eight districts, to generate district-specific data, which is essential for conceptualization of a reasonable and financially viable insurance scheme.

The current plan-the Tenth Five Year Plan (2002-07)-also focuses on exploring alternative systems of health care financing including health insurance so that essential, need-based and affordable health care is available to all. The urgent need to evolve, implement and evaluate an appropriate scheme for health financing for different income groups is acknowledged. In the past, the government has tried to ensure that the poor get access to private health facilities through subsidy in the form of duty exemptions and other such benefits. Social health insurance for families living below the poverty line has been suggested as a mechanism for reducing the adverse economic consequences of hospitalization and treatment for chronic ailments requiring expensive and continuous care.

In the budget for the year 2002-2003, an insurance scheme called Janraskha was introduced, with the aim of providing protection to the needy population. With a premium of Re 1/-per day, it ensured indoor treatment up to Rs 3 000 per year at selected and designated hospitals and outpatient treatment up to Rs 2 000 per year at designated clinics, including civil hospitals, medical colleges, private trust hospitals and other NGO-run institutions. A few states have started implementing this scheme under pilot phase.

In the budget for the period 2003-2004, another initiative of community-based health insurance has been announced. This scheme aims to enable easy access of less advantaged citizens to good health services, and to offer health protection to them. This policy covers people between the age of three months to 65 years. Under this scheme, a premium equivalent to Re 1 per day (or Rs 365 per year) for an individual, Rs 1.50 per day for a family of five (or Rs 548 per year), and Rs 2 per day for a family of seven (or Rs 730 per year), would entitle them to get reimbursement of medical expenses up to Rs 30 000 towards hospitalization, a cover for death due to accident for Rs 25 000 and compensation due to loss of earning at the rate of Rs 50 per day up to a maximum of 15 days. The government would contribute Rs 100 per year towards the annual premium, so as to ensure the affordability of the scheme to families living below the poverty line. The implementation of this scheme rests with the four public sector insurance companies.

The government also offers assistance by way of Illness Assistance Funds, which have been set up by the Ministry of Health and Family Welfare at the national level and in a few states. State Illness Assistance Funds exist in Andhra Pradesh, Bihar, Goa, Gujarat, Himachal Pradesh, Jammu and Kashmir, Karnataka, Kerala, Madhya Pradesh, Maharashtra, Mizoram, Rajasthan, Sikkim, Tamil Nadu, Tripura, West Bengal, NCT of Delhi and UT of Pondicherry. A National Illness Assistance Fund (NIAF) was set up in 1997, with the scheme being reviewed in January 1998.

Through this, three Central Government hospitals and three national-level institutes have been sanctioned Rs 10 00 000 each at a time from the NIAF to provide immediate financial assistance to the extent of Rs 25 000 per case to poor patients living below the poverty line and who are undergoing treatment in these hospitals / institutions. Thereafter the scheme has been extended to few other institutes across the country and provides Rs 25 000-Rs 50 000 per case.

Health Insurance Initiatives by State Governments

In the recent past, various state governments have begun health insurance initiatives. For instance, the Andhra Pradesh government is implementing the Aarogya Raksha Scheme since 2000, with a view to increase the utilization of permanent methods of family planning by covering the health risks of the acceptors. All people living below the poverty line and those who accept permanent methods of family planning are eligible to be covered under this scheme. The Government of Andhra Pradesh pays a premium of Rs 75 per acceptor. The benefits to be availed of, include hospitalization costs up to Rs. 4000 per year for the acceptor and for his / her two children for a total period of five years from date of the family planning operation. The coverage is for common illnesses and accident insurance benefits are also offered. The hospital bill is directly reimbursed by the Insurance Company, namely the New India Assurance Company. The Government of Goa along with the New India Assurance Company in 1988 developed a medical reimbursement mechanism. This scheme can be availed by all permanent residents of Goa with an income below Rs 50 000 per annum for hospitalization care, which is not available within the government system. The non-availability of services requires certification from the hospital Dean or Director Health Services. The overall limit is Rs 30 000 for the insured person for a period of one year.

A pilot project on health insurance was launched by the Government of Karnataka and the UNDP in two blocks since October 2002. The aim of the project was to develop and test a model of community health financing suited for rural community, thereby increasing the access to medical care of the poor. The beneficiaries include the entire population of these blocks. The premium is Rs 30 per person per year, with the Government of Karnataka subsidizing the premium of those below poverty line and those belonging to Scheduled Castes/ Scheduled Tribes. This premium entitles them to hospitalization coverage in the government hospitals up to a maximum of Rs 2 500 per year, including hospitalization for common illnesses, ambulance charges, loss of wages at Rs. 50 per day as well as drug expenses at Rs 50 per day. Reimbursements are made to an insurance fund which has been set up by the NGO / PRI with the support of UNDP.

The Government of Kerala is planning to launch a pilot project of health insurance for the 30% families living below the poverty line. The scheme would be associated with a government insurance company. Currently, negotiations are under way with the IRA to seek service tax exemption. The proposed premium is Rs 250 plus 5% tax. The maximum benefit per family would be Rs 20 000. The amount for the premium would be recovered from the drug budget (Rs 100), the PRI (Rs 100) and from the beneficiary (Rs 62.50) while the benefits available would include cover for hospitalization, deliveries involving surgical procedures (either to the mother or the newborn). Instead of payment by the beneficiary, Smart Card facility would be offered. This scheme would be applicable in 216 government hospitals.

Concerns, Challenges and the Way Ahead

The preceding sections of this paper present the health insurance scenario in India. Given the situation, there are few issues of concern or barriers towards implementing a social health insurance scheme in India. These are enumerated below along with the possible way ahead.

India is a low-income country with 26% population living below the poverty line, and 35% illiterate population with skewed health risks. Insurance is limited to only a small proportion of people in the organized sector covering less than 10% of the total population. Currently, there no mechanism or infrastructure for collecting mandatory premium among the large informal sector. Even in terms of the existing schemes, there is insufficient and inadequate information about the various schemes. Data gaps also prevail. Much of the focus of the existing schemes is on hospital expenses. There continues to be lack of awareness among people about health insurance. In spite of existing regulation in some States, the private sector continues to operate in an almost unhindered manner. The growth of health insurance increases the need for licensing and regulating private health providers and developing specific criteria to decide upon appropriate services and fees.

Health insurance per se, suffers from problems like adverse selection, moral hazard, cream-skimming and high administrative costs. This is coupled with the fact that in the absence of any costing mechanisms, there is difficulty in calculating the premium. There is also a need to evolve criteria to be used for deciding upon target groups, who would avail of the SHI scheme/s and also to address issues relating to whether indirect costs would be included in health insurance. Health insurance can improve access to good quality health care only if it is able to provide for health care institutions with adequate facilities and skilled personnel at affordable cost.

Given this scenario, the challenge, then, for Indian policy-makers is to find ways to improve upon the existing situation in the health sector and to make equitable, affordable and quality health care accessible to the population, especially the poor and the vulnerable sections of the society. It is in a way inevitable that the state reforms its public health delivery system and explores other social security options like health insurance. Implementing regulations would be one, but by no means the best mechanism to contain provider behaviour and costs. This can only be done by developing mechanisms where government and households can together pool their funds. This could be one way of controlling provider behaviour. There is an urgent need to document global and Indian experiences in social health insurance. Different financing options would need to be developed for different target groups. The wide differentials in the demographic, epidemiological status and the delivery capacity of health systems are a serious constraint to a nationally mandated health insurance system.

Given the heterogeneity of different regions in India and the regional specifications, one would need to undertake pilot projects to gather more information about the population to be targeted under an insurance scheme and develop options for different population groups. Health policy-makers and health systems research institutions, in collaboration with economic policy study institutes, need to gather information about the prevailing disease burden at various geographical regions; to develop standard treatment guidelines, to undertake costing of health services for evolving benefit packages to determine the premium to be levied and subsidies to be given; and to map health care facilities available and the institutional mechanisms which need to be in place, for implementing health insurance schemes. Skillbuilding for the personnel involved, and capacity-building of all the stakeholders involved, would be a critical component for ensuring the success of any health insurance programme.

The success of any social insurance scheme would depend on its design, the implementation and monitoring mechanisms which would be set in place and it would also call for restructuring and reforming the health system, and developing the necessary prerequisites to ensure its success.

Economic and Political Weekly July 10, 2004

According to the World Health Organisation, greater than 80 per cent of total expenditure on health in India is private (figure for 1999-2001 [World Health Organisation 2004]) and most of this flows directly from households to the private-for-profit health care sector. Most studies of health care spending have found that out-of-pocket spending in India is actually progressive, or equity neutral; as a proportion of nonfood expenditure, richer Indians spend marginally more than poorer Indians on health care. However, because the poor lack the resources to pay for health care, they are far more likely to avoid going for care, or to become indebted or impoverished trying to pay for it. On average, the poorest quintile of Indians is 2.6 times more likely than the richest to forgo medical treatment when ill [Peters, Yazbeck et al 2002].

Aside from cases where people believed that their illness was not serious, the main reason for not seeking care was cost. The richest quintile of the population is six times more likely than the poorest quintile to have been hospitalised in either the public or private sector [Mahal, Singh et al 2000]. Peters et al (2002) estimated that at least 24 per cent of all Indians hospitalised fall below the poverty line because they are hospitalised, and that out-of-pocket spending on hospital care might have raised by 2 per cent the proportion of the population in poverty [Peters, Yazbeck et al 2001]. Given this context, health insurance appears to be an equitable alternative to out of pocket payments. In recent years, community health insurance (CHI) has emerged as a possible means of: (1) improving access to health care among the poor; and (2) protecting the poor from indebtedness and impoverishment resulting from medical expenditures. The World Health Report 2000, for example, noted that prepayment schemes represent the most effective way to protect people from the costs of health care, and called for investigation into mechanisms to bring the poor into such schemes (World Health Organisation 2000). Various other terms are used in reference to community health insurance, including: 'micro health insurance' [Dror et al 1999], 'local health insurance' [Criel 2000] and 'mutuelles' [Atim C 2001]. We define CHI (along the same lines as [Atim 1998]) as "any not-for-profit insurance scheme that is aimed primarily at the informal sector and formed on the basis of a collective pooling of health risks, and in which the members participate in its management."

CHI schemes involve prepayment and the pooling of resources to cover the costs of health-related events. They are generally targeted at low-income populations, and the nature of the 'communities' around which they have evolved is quite diverse: from people living in the same town or district, to members of a work cooperative or micro-finance groups. Often, the schemes are initiated by a hospital, and targeted at residents of the surrounding area. As opposed to social health insurance, membership is almost always voluntary rather than mandatory. Internationally, there is a shortage of empirical evidence to assess whether or not CHI schemes have improved access and financial protection among the poor. Enthusiasm for such schemes was fuelled in part by studies showing disproportionate increases in utilisation among the poorest with the implementation of insurance [Yip and Berman 2001] or mandatory prepayment schemes [Diop, Yazbeck et al 1995] in developing countries. But studies of voluntary CHI schemes have yielded less promising results. The studies and reviews that have been undertaken suggest that many schemes are short-lived and fail even to meet the goals they set for themselves [Bennett, Creese et al 1998].

Often, the schemes enrol relatively small populations (of 1,000 people or less) thus limiting the extent to which there can be pooling and resource transfers (International Labour Office (Universitas Programme) 2002). Furthermore, CBHIs have tended to exclude the poorest among their target populations, in part because they generally charge a flat (or uniform) premium that is unaffordable to the poorest. Under the three schemes reviewed by Preker et al [Preker, Carrin et al 2001] in Rawanda, Senegal and India, even among the insured, low income remained a significant constraint to health care utilisation.

The purpose of this paper is to describe Indian CHI schemes, and where data are available, their impact-it is intended to serve as an update on earlier work by one of the authors [Ranson 2003]. In India, community health insurance has a long history. The earliest such scheme was started in Kolkata in 1952 as part of a student's movement. The Student's Health Home (SHH) caters to the students in the schools and universities of West Bengal. Currently there are more than 20 documented CHI programmes, of which five were initiated in the past three years. Based on visits to twelve of the schemes, the authors describe the context in which they are operational, their design and management, the administrative challenges faced by them, and their impact. The names and locations of the programmes included in this summary are given in the accompanying table.

2

COMMUNITY HEALTH INSURANCE IN INDIA

AN OVERVIEW

Community health insurance is an important intermediate step in the evolution of an equitable health financing mechanism such as social health insurance in Europe and Japan. Social health insurance in these countries, in fact, evolved from a conglomeration of small 'community' health insurance schemes. Historically, during the peak of the industrial revolution workers' unions developed insurance mechanisms which were eventually transformed. Community health insurance programmes in India offer valuable lessons for policy-makers. Documented here are 12 schemes where health insurance has been operationalised. The two following articles describe in some detail two successful community health projects.

UNDERLYING OBJECTIVES

Most of the insurance programmes have been started as a reaction to the high health care costs and the failure of the government machinery to provide good quality care. The objectives range from "providing low cost health care" to "protecting the households from high hospitalisation costs." BAIF, DHAN, Navsarjan Trust and RAHA explicitly state that the health insurance scheme was developed to prevent the individual member from bearing the financial burden of hospitalisation. Health insurance was also seen by some organisations as a method of encouraging participation by the community in their own health care. And finally, especially the more activist organisations (ACCORD, RAHA) used community health insurance as a measure to increase solidarity among its members-"one for all and all for one."

CONTEXT

Almost all the 12 CHIs are based in rural or semi urban areas, working among the poor. This ranges from tribal populations (ACCORD, Karuna Trust, RAHA), dalits (Navsarjan Trust), farmers (MGIMS, Yeshasvini, Buldhana, VHS), women from self help groups (BAIF, DHAN) and poor self-employed women (SEWA). The size of the target population (i e, the population from which they aim to draw members) ranges from a few thousands to 25 lakh (Yeshasvini trust). Most of them (eight of the twelve) use existing community based organisations to piggyback the health insurance programme. While in some it is the existing self help groups (SHGs), e g, DHAN, BAIF; in others it is a union (SEWA, ACCORD and Navsarjan). In two others it is the cooperative movement (Yeshasvini and Buldhana). These community-based organisations have been a useful platform to explain the principles of health insurance to the community, for collecting premium and for managing claims and reimbursements. And most important, they have instilled a sense of ownership of the insurance programme among the community.

In India, there appears to be three basic designs, depending on who is the insurer. In Type I (or HMO design), the hospital plays the dual role of providing health care and running the insurance programme. There are five programmes under this type. In Type II (or Insurer design), the voluntary organisation is the insurer, while purchasing care from independent providers. There are-two programmes under this type. And finally in Type III (or Intermediate design), the voluntary organisation plays the role of an agent, purchasing care from providers and insurance from insurance companies.

This seems to be a popular design, especially among the recent CHIs, with five of the 12 adopting this. The insurance companies are mostly the GIC subsidiaries, e g, National Insurance Company, the New India Assurance Company, the United India Insurance Company, etc. Of late private insurance companies like the Royal Sundaram, and ICICI Lombard have been involved with CHI programmes. As most of these programmes serve the rural poor, the premiums also have been low; in the range of Rs 20 to Rs 60 per person per year. Only three programmes had premiums higher than Rs 100 per person. The premium is usually paid as a cash contribution once a year during a definite collection period. Two schemes (RAHA and MGIMS) allowed the community to pay equivalents in kind. The community and their representatives as well as the staff of the voluntary organisation helped with the collection of the premium, e g, at Yeshasvini, the premium collection is organised through the existing cooperative infrastructure.

Enrolment to the insurance programme ranged from a thousand to seventeen lakhs (Yeshasvini). At most of the schemes, the unit of enrolment is the individual and membership is voluntary. While some of the schemes encourage family membership by providing a family package/ rate (e g, DHAN, Vimo SEWA and VHS), none requires enrolment of the whole household. However, several of the schemes do enrol groups rather than individuals-enrolment in these same schemes is to some extent 'mandatory', and they come to resemble social insurance schemes as a result.

At Karuna Trust, for example, the cost of the premium is entirely subsidised for the poorest among the target population-the BPL-SC/ST-who are automatically enrolled in the scheme. Some of the self-help groups at DHAN purchase insurance for all SHG members (generally 15 to 20) out of profits earned by the SHG (i e, certain SHGs have chosen to make the scheme mandatory). At SHH, once a school or institution registers, then it becomes mandatory for all the students to pay the premium.

As stated earlier, while some of the CHI schemes limited the benefit package to only ambulatory care, the twelve studied by the authors all provided inpatient care. Some also provided out patient care as well as outreach services. It is observed that the community prefers to have both outpatient and inpatient care. Most schemes had important exclusions like pre-existing illnesses, self-inflicted injuries, chronic ailments, TB, HIV, etc. One scheme covered only surgeries, all other medical conditions being excluded. While most of the schemes reimbursed direct costs of treatment (consultation, medicines and diagnostics), one scheme (Karuna Trust) also reimbursed loss of wages for the patient. Some CHIs had also added other benefits, e g, life insurance, insurance against personal accident and/or asset insurance into the package to make it more attractive to the community.

In the Type I CHIs, there is a cashless system of reimbursement. However, in the other two types, usually it is a fixed indemnity with patients having to settle bills and then getting it reimbursed 2-6 months later from the NGO. The exception was the Yeshasvini scheme, which, though a Type III scheme, had managed to negotiate a cashless system with the private sector by using the services of a Third Party Administrator (TPA). Most of the CHIs have a fixed upper limit, ranging from Rs 1,250 to Rs 1,00,000 per patient per year.

Most of the providers are from the private sector-either for profit or not-for-profit hospitals. Only one CHI (the Karuna Trust) had a public sector provider. In the Type I schemes, where the insurer is also the provider, there is an attempt to maintain quality and keep costs down. For example at ACCORD, the hospital largely uses only essential and generic drugs. However, in the Type II and Type III schemes, where the provider is mostly the private sector, we did not find any evidence of cost containment or quality checks. Yeshasvini was the exception, where they have managed to negotiate capitation fees for each surgery. At SEWA, there is an ongoing initiative to empanel select hospitals (primarily government and trust hospitals) judged to be providing a high standard of care.

As stated earlier, most of the schemes are administered by the community, their representatives or by the voluntary organisation staff. This helps keep costs down. Usually they handle the following activities:

Creating awareness among the community; collecting premium (at ACCORD, the sangam leaders collect the premium and hand it over to the NGO); monitoring for fraud (DHAN has an insurance committee comprising of SHG members who scrutinise every single claim); submitting claims; and channelling the reimbursements (at BAIF, the reimbursements are sent to the local SHG who while handing over the amount to the patient, reinforces the benefit of insurance). All these activities help in increasing the efficiency of the scheme. Also it helps build a sense of ownership among the community and increases accountability. One of the weaknesses of the CHIs is the lack of technomanagerial expertise. This is reflected in the fact that most of them do not have inbuilt mechanisms to prevent adverse selection or moral hazard. Due to the asymmetry of information, it is possible that only the sick enrol in these schemes (adverse selection). Simple measures like a larger enrolment unit, a mandatory enrolment, a definite collection and waiting period are measures to prevent this. While all (except VHS) have a definite collection period, other measures are usually not used. SHH to a certain extent overcomes adverse selection by using the institution as an enrolment unit.

Similarly, because of the insurance programme, the behaviour of the patient or the provider may change (moral hazard). Capitation fee structures, standard treatment guidelines and copayments are some strategies to prevent this. The only measure consistently used by most CHIs to reduce the patient induced moral hazard is co-payments and deductibles.

The absolute number of enrolees varies tremendously, from only 909 at BAIF (scheme is only in its second year) to as many as seventeen lakhs at the Yeshasvini programme. The average subscription rate varies from 10 to 50 per cent of the target population. Except at Vimo SEWA, there has been no study as to why the rest of the target population are not subscribing, but during the interviews, some of the reasons for not paying were elicited. These included: (1) No immediate benefit; (2) premium too high; (3) "we are well, why should we pay in advance? When we fall sick, we shall pay"; (4) large families-this is specially since most of the CBHI's unit of membership is the individual; (5) "(Insurance scheme) Hospitals are far away and so we have to pay a lot to access hospitalisation. Better use the premium money to go to a nearby doctor"; and (6) "we pay every year, but do not get any benefit out of it. So we have decided not to pay anymore".

There is tremendous variation in terms of claims submitted annually for inpatient care, ranging from only 1.4/1,000 insured per annum to more than 240/1,000 insured per annum. Among schemes with the highest rates of utilisation, adverse selection appears to be responsible for the high rates.

Among schemes with low rates of utilisation, it appeared that not enough had been done to address non-financial barriers to accessing health care.

The indirect costs of health care are not addressed by the schemes (Karuna Trust being an exception), and in many of the schemes, the direct costs are only covered up to a 'cap' or 'ceiling' (as at DHAN, RAHA and SEWA). Even at those schemes that do not have a cap (e g, SHH), non-financial barriers may prevent people from utilising the scheme (e g, distance, lack of knowledge about the scheme, limited awareness of health/illness, etc.)

In terms of their ability to protect individuals and households against the catastrophic costs of health care, the schemes again seem to vary considerably. Those that provide the greatest degree of protection have the following characteristics:

(1) Cover 100 per cent of the direct costs;

(2) cover all (or at least some) of the indirect costs;

(3) cover all kinds of illness (e g, all nonelective causes of hospitalisation, including complications of delivery, chronic illnesses); and

(4) provide benefit right at the source of health care, i e, with no period during which the patient has to cope with the costs of care.

Thus, it was generally the Type I schemes, which provide health care directly, and usually with no upper limit to the financial benefits, that provided the greatest degree of protection.

An important question is about the financial viability of these 'small' schemes. Of the 12 studied, four (BAIF,

DHAN, Buldhanha and Yeshasvini) are run purely on funds raised from the community. All the Type I schemes have supplemented the locally raised resources with external resources (either from the government or donors). These external resources range from 20-40 per cent of the total reimbursements. Only two have relied exclusively on external resources. Unfortunately, it was difficult to get accurate financial estimates of the administrative costs, especially since a lot of this is subsidised by the community.

Financing health care has always been a very difficult exercise. Even in rich countries like the US, there does not seem to be enough for all. It becomes all the more challenging in a lowincome country like India. While the Constitution of India promises to provide adequate health care to the population, successive governments both at the state and the centre have failed in many ways to do so.

This is probably one of the reasons why the majority of the public turns to the private sector for their health care needs Another equitable method of health financing is the social health insurance-seen in most European countries. Given the low percentage of workers in the formal sector, this appears to be a distant dream. However, these European (and Japanese) social health insurances have actually evolved from a conglomeration of small 'community health insurance schemes'. Historically, during the peak of the industrial revolution, worker's unions developed health insurance mechanisms to protect their members. This gradually developed into today's social health insurance [Ogawa et al 2003; Barnighausen T et al 2002]. Thus community health insurance can be seen as an important intermediate step in the evolution towards an equitable health financing mechanism.

The community health insurance programmes in India offer valuable lessons for the policy-makers and the practitioners of health care. While many state that the poor in India cannot understand the complexities of health insurance and will not accept any insurance product, we hereby document 12 schemes where health insurance has been operationalised. It is clear that what is required is a good product. Some of the conditions that have allowed these schemes to succeed are:

- An effective and credible community based organisation (or NGO). This is absolutely necessary as it is the foundation on which health insurance can be built. The CBO helps in disseminating information about health insurance and more importantly helps in implementing the programme with minimum costs.
- An affordable premium-this is very important. While most health insurance products (even for the poor) have premiums in the range of Rs 100 plus per member per year, we find that people are willing to pay only in the range of Rs 20 to 60 per person per year. This is significant, and needs to be taken into account by the insurers if they want their products to penetrate the rural market.
- A comprehensive benefit package is necessary to convince the community of the benefits of health insurance. Most of the CHIs documented, especially the Type I schemes have provided a comprehensive package and this is one of the main reasons why people have enrolled in their schemes. Unfortunately, most of the Type III schemes (except for Karuna Trust) have been forced to introduce exclusions by the insurance companies. While most insurance companies introduce exclusions, based on economic reasons, one has to look at health insurance within a public health context. Diseases like TB, HIV and mental illnesses have significant public health

importance and should be covered. Similarly it is ironic that while the country has invested tremendously- in safe deliveries, most health insurance products do not cover it. And finally as India enters an epidemiological transition and will have to encounter chronic diseases like diabetes and hypertension, it becomes imperative that these diseases are included in the benefit package.

- A credible insurer is imperative for people to have faith in the product. This is where the NGOs and the CBOs score as they have a relationship with the community and so the people are willing to trust them with their money. Insurance companies need to learn from this important lesson and would need to approach the rural sector keeping this in mind.
- And last but not the least, the administration load of the scheme on the community should be minimal. Unnecessary documentation lead to frustration. In one of the schemes a community member mentioned that she had to pay more to get the certificates than she got in reimbursement. This is where the Type I and Type II schemes score over the others.

Many would dismiss community health insurance as a drop in an ocean. It may appear insignificant, given the scale of the problem in India. But, one needs to look at it in context. One of the main lessons from these case studies is the fact that a good community based organisation can help develop an effective community health insurance programme.

And India is teeming with such organisations-be it the trade movement, or the cooperative movement. So upscaling should not present a problem if one uses these existing institutions. Already there are examples of community health insurance being introduced in the dairy cooperative sector

(Mallur, Karnataka and Anand, Gujarat); the head loaders union (Mathadi trust in Mumbai), shop owner's union (Palakad, Kerala). The possibilities are endless, if approached properly.

However, one needs to mention a word of caution. The main pitfall in developing community health insurance is to find an appropriate provider. The Indian private health sector is unregulated and unaccountable [Bhat 1999]. In this context, introducing health insurance can lead to uncontrolled cost escalation without the promise of quality [Ranson and John 2001]. So it becomes imperative that while considering community health insurance, one should seriously consider mechanisms to introduce measures for cost containment, assuring quality and ensuring standard treatment practices. And this is where the CBO (or NGO) can play a crucial role, by countering the power of the providers.

The CBO could negotiate with the providers and develop a package that is conducive for the patients and the CHI." Yet another issue is the legality of these schemes, given the new Insurance act (IRDA Act 1999). Currently the act does not acknowledge the presence of these schemes and their role in the larger insurance market. This could also be the reason why many of the newer schemes have linked up with the formal insurance companies-to legitimise their activity. But in the process, they may have lost on the flexibility and innovations necessary for a successful CHI.

The other issue that needs to be addressed is that of financial sustainability. The very fact that many of them have been operational for more than a decade, itself is proof that it may be a sustainable form of health financing. While accurate financial data about the schemes were not available easily, rough estimates show that they are able to raise about 60 to 100 per cent of their resources.

This has important policy implications, as it gives an indication towards the amount subsidy required to make these schemes viable. And given the fact that most of these schemes target the poor, it is important that the government comes forward to subsidise this equitable health financing mechanism.

In a country with one of the highest out of pocket health care expenditure in the world, it is imperative that some measures be instituted to protect the poor. We suggest that community health insurance could be an interim strategy to finance the health care of the people; till a more formal social health insurance is in place. We also suggest that this is a feasible alternative given that community based organisations and movements exist in India. What is required is to regulate the providers and to legislate so that the community health insurance programmes find a space within the Indian insurance context.

3

HEALTH POLICY CHALLENGES FOR INDIA

INTRODUCTION

India's Achievements in Health: Great Progress and Persistence of Problems Over the last few decades, the Indian population has experienced great advances in its health situation. For instance, life expectancy at birth increased from 50 years in 1970 to an estimated 62 years in 1995 and is possibly even greater now. Infant mortality rates have fallen as well, from 137 per 1,000 live births in 1970 to 69 per 1,000 live births in 1991 (World Bank 1995). These are substantial improvements, but much remains to be done, relative to some its neighbors as well in terms of reducing differences in performance across states and socioeconomic groups.

For instance, China has done much better, with its life expectancy at birth hovering around 70 years, and India's neighbour, Sri Lanka, has a life expectancy of nearly 73 years (World Bank 1997). Both countries have much lower infant mortality rates as well, and in the case of Sri Lanka, less than one-quarter that of India. Again, Kerala has infant mortality rates below those in China, but states such as Madhya Pradesh, Orissa and Rajasthan have infant mortality rates of well over 100 per 1,000 live births in rural areas (Dreze and Sen 1995; Mahal, Srivastava and Sanan 2000). Similarly, in rural India, the infant mortality rates among the top-two income quintiles are nearly 34-50 percent lower than the rates reported for the bottom two quintiles.1 Substantial differences in life expectancies at birth are present across states and socio-economic groupings (Dreze and Sen 1995).

Another issue of concern is the growing prevalence of chronic illness in the Indian population, such as obesity, heart disease, diabetes, hypertension and the like. This has partly to do with changing dietary habits, from coarse grain to energy rich diets of meat, milk products, and sugar. It has also to do with an urban population growing at an average annual rate of growth of 3.2 per cent and sedentary lifestyles often characteristic of it (National Institute of Urban Affairs (NIUA) 2000, Popkin, Horton, Kim, Mahal and Shuigao 2001). Thus, the prevalence of diabetes rates were nearly three times higher among urban residents than among rural residents in 1995-96, the prevalence of heart disease 70 per cent higher, and the prevalence of hypertension more than double. With the urban population expected to grow further in the future, the emergence of chronic illnesses will have significant consequences on the financial costs of providing health care, as many illnesses are extremely expensive to treat (Mahal 2000a).

THE CASE FOR GOVERNMENT INTERVENTION IN THE HEALTH SECTOR

At any point in time, an individual's health status depends on a range of factors. These obviously include the endowment of health that an individual started out with-genetic aspects, as well as parental health. It will also depend on choices that various individuals, or their guardians make. These choices may relate to lifestyle factors, such as smoking and alcohol intake, frequency of exercise, the quality of nutrition, as well as on the access to good quality medical care when sick. The health status will also depend on exogenous events, such as the contraction of infectious diseases. The latter may, in turn, be dependent on the availability of clean water, sanitation facilities, the immunisation status of the individual, and so on. Economists often describe these relationships through the device of a "health production function" (Phelps 1997). Good health, in addition to the initial endowment, is determined by individual preferences, the socioeconomic circumstances that help shape those preferences (such as marital status, cultural and religious factors and education), incomes, and the prices of different items consumed by an individual, including health inputs and the quality of such inputs.

By influencing these choices the government may play quite a substantial role in improving health. For instance, many of the decisions that individuals take about health depend on the information that they possess about potential health impacts. To the extent that information is a public good, markets may fail to provide all the information relevant to healthy lifestyle choices to individual agents. Governments also intervene in situations where illnesses are very expensive to treat. Those who fall sick face the consequence of significant financial costs of treatment in the absence of insurance, with possible catastrophic effects on living standards. It is true that catastrophic illness, whose incidence is often uncertain for an individual, creates a demand for insurance among those who can afford it. Such insurance is, however, underprovided by the market.

By providing subsidised health services, or health insurance, the government can influence the consumption of health care by those in need of it while mitigating the inequity enhancing effects of illness. Government intervention is also desirable on account of the asymmetry of information that prevails in the market for medical care-with doctors (perceived to be) having much better information about the status of a sick person than the person himself. This creates an incentive for doctors to provide more services to patients than may be medically necessary, and lower quality care. For these reasons, protecting children and adults against infectious diseases, promoting better quality of care, and ensuring that families and individuals do not face inordinate financial risks related to catastrophic illnesses, form key objectives of public health policy (see, for example, Lok Sabha 1985).

In influencing the choices that make for better health and lowered financial burden of ill health, the society is typically faced with three key challenges. The first has to do with controlling the cost incurred in the provision of health interventions that it supports-be it care, health care regulation, or provision of insurance--given that resources are limited and face competing demands for their use. The second is to achieve an equitable distribution of the financial burden of ill health and morbidity. This is a direct consequence of the fact that societies are concerned not just about improvements in "average health" but also, especially, about the health and economic welfare of the socially and economically marginal groups in society. A third issue is to ensure the quality of medical care that is provided, because of its central importance to people who need care, and also because of its direct link to the cost-effectiveness of care provision. 1.2. Cost, Equity, and Quality of Medical Care in India: The Existing Situation In light of the previous discussion, it is of interest to check whether the existing Indian health system adequately addresses the three challenges mentioned earlier. In particular we ask: (1) How costly and "cost-effective" is the Indian health system? (2) How equitable is it from the point of view of the burden of health care spending? And (3) does it provide high quality care?

Costs and Cost-Effectiveness of Care Provision

Three approaches can be used to examine the costs and cost-effectiveness of health care provision at the national level. We can look at aggregate achievements in health and compare these to the actual amounts spent on health, relative to those in other countries, while controlling for potential confounding variables. One example of this approach is to estimate the relationship, say between life expectancy and health expenditures per capita, and to then compare the efficacy of health expenditures across countries in terms of the gains in life expectancy at birth per dollar/rupee spent. This, unfortunately, is not a straightforward exercise, since life expectancy at birth is linked to levels of living and past health expenditures as well, data for which are not readily available for most countries, except in the case of developed ones. Moreover, the relationship is likely to be confounded by the fact that life expectancy at birth may itself influence health expenditures and per capita incomes, so that any careful estimation exercise would have to consider the problem of simultaneity (Bloom, Canning and Graham 2000).

A second approach is to examine health expenditures in each country and assess whether these are too "high" or too "low", relative to the average expenditures figures for all countries, or to some predicted value from a regression linking health expenditures to say, per capita income. This approach takes as its starting point that, on an average the world expenditures on health are appropriate relative to any given level of per capita income, although individual countries may depart from this norm, in one direction or the other.

A third approach is to verify whether the existing composition of health spending in the country of interest could be modified so as to yield an increase in health outcome measures such as disability adjusted life years (DALYs), while leaving the magnitude of total health spending unchanged. If such realignment of resources were possible in India, one could argue that the country is spending "too much" on the existing level of health care. For the purpose of this brief introduction, we focus mainly on the second approach, while providing suggestive ideas for the other two.

Consider the first method of comparing health outcomes with aggregate health spending. According to the most recent estimates, the aggregate of public sector and private sector health spending amounted to nearly 5.6 per cent of the gross domestic product (GDP) of India (World Bank 1997).4 These estimates are certainly much higher, as a proportion of GDP, of aggregate health expenditures among India's neighbours such as Bangladesh with 2.4 per cent, China with 3.8 per cent, Pakistan with 3.5 per cent, and Sri Lanka with 1.9 per cent, respectively (World Bank 1997).5 Given that both Sri Lanka and China are doing significantly better than India in terms of indicators such as infant mortality rate and life expectancy at birth, this indicates that health spending in India is not as costeffective as among some of its neighbours.

We also compared India's health spending to what would be suggested by its income level, based on a regression of health expenditures per capita as a proportion of GDP, on income per capita. Using data on these variables for 109 countries, we find that India's estimated spending per capita in circa 1995 was about US$19.5, nearly 25 per cent higher than what the regression would predict.6 This too, would point to Indians spending a "little too much" on health care, despite being low in absolute terms, when compared to the United States (US$3,828) and other developed countries. The key point here is that the health expenditures are high relative to what would be expected of a country at its level of development and health achievements. One possible reason could be that Indians are spending relatively more on curative care, compared to the more cost-effective preventive care (World Bank 1995, p. viii).

This last idea points to the possibility of realigning health expenditures in India so as to yield greater benefits say in terms of measures such as quality and disability-adjusted life years (World Bank 1993). For instance, the poor utilisation of primary health facilities in India is partly owing to the low levels of quality of care that is provided in such facilities. These, in turn, are caused by and manifested in absenteeism among doctors and other medical personnel, lack of availability of drugs-themselves a consequence of poor incentives and low levels of accountability (World Bank 1995).

Equity in the Burden of Health Spending

The public sector in India offers heavily subsidised medical care to its citizens through a large network of government-operated facilities, to which access is ostensibly free. However, it is unable to cater to the needs of large sections of the population, since the bulk of total health spending-75 per cent of the total-is accounted for by out-of-pocket expenses of households (World Bank 1995).

The extremely large burden of health care spending on households is problematic since it raises the possibility of a disproportionate economic burden on the poor sections of Indian society. In fact, a recent study by van Doorslaer et al. (1997) for OECD countries demonstrates that out-of-pocket payments for health are the most inequitable among the class of resources that could be used to finance health services-other, more equitable, examples being, social insurance taxes, direct taxes, and the like. Table 9.1 presents information on the distribution of the burden of out-of-pocket spending on inpatient and outpatient care by households, by per capita expenditure quintiles, from the

52nd round of the National Sample Survey (NSS). Given that the ratio of out-of-pocket spending as a proportion of mean expenditure is higher in the richer quintiles, it would seem that the financial burden of health care is not too inequitably distributed.8 There are, however, at least three reasons for caution.

First, measures of out-of-pocket spending on health do not take into account the losses owing to foregone income that result from poor health. If lost income were also to be included in our calculus, the financial burden of health increases quite substantially for the lower quintiles. Data in Table 9.1 illustrate this clearly-the numbers in parentheses show the ratio of out-of-pocket spending plus income losses from ailments to mean per capita expenditure in each quintile. Indeed, the burden of care from lost income is substantially higher (comprising 50 per cent to 70 per cent of out-of-pocket spending) for the poorest 20 per cent in comparison with the richest 20 per cent (16 per cent to 28 per cent of out-of-pocket spending.)

Second, the burden of out-of-pocket spending does not include the adverse effects on long-term health that might result from not seeking care in time. The poorest groups not only report fewer illnesses, but they obtain treatment for a smaller proportion of those reported, compared to the richest groups. This fact clearly emerges from the 1995-96 health survey undertaken by the National Sample Survey Organisation (NSSO 1998). The proportion of ailments that the poor get treated for is also lower in comparison to the rich. For instance, the people in the poorest rural quintile left about 25 per cent of their reported ailments untreated, compared to 10-15 per cent in the case of the richest quintile. The corresponding numbers for urban areas were 17 per cent and 9 per cent, respectively. The treatment data, together with the data on the financial burden of health spending, suggest a problem of access to health facilities for people living in rural areas as well. A third aspect of concern is the distribution of public health subsidies.

Despite a considerable desirable for "equity" in public policy documents, a recent study shows that public subsidies on health are distributed quite unequally across different socioeconomic groups in India (Mahal et al. 2000). At the all-India level, the share of the richest 20 per cent of the population in total public sector subsidies is nearly 31 per cent, nearly three times the share of the poorest 20 per cent of the population.

The inequality was greater among the rural residents, where the share of the top 20 per cent in public subsidies was nearly four times that of the poorest 20 per cent. Urban areas enjoyed greater equality, in addition to enjoying a greater than proportional share in total subsidies. Mahal et al. (2000) find that 31 per cent of public subsidies on health accrued to urban residents, somewhat higher than their share in the total population of about 25 per cent.

There were substantial differences in the degree of inequality, with southern states such as Kerala, Tamil Nadu and Andhra Pradesh, and the western states of Maharashtra and Gujarat enjoying a much more equal distribution than the states of northern India.

Some of this inequality in the allocation of public health subsidies can be explained by income-related differences in utilisation patterns of public facilities, with the rich using more care, if health care is a normal good. Moreover, large subsidies to the rich may be a sine qua non for continued public support to the health sector. If, however, promoting equity is a key objective of the state, there is no doubt that substantial scope for improvement remains, whether in terms of inter-state equity, or within state distributions of public subsidies.

Quality of Care

A third key element of the health care system is the quality of care that its users are able to obtain. Quality refers to at least two different things. First, the level of competence with which an examination and/or treatment protocol is implemented-be it medical examinations, diagnostic tests, the quality of administered drugs and medical care generally. This type of technical quality is likely to depend on a host of factors including the level of medical training, market pressures to acquire requisite training, continuing education, infrastructure, and the regulatory set-up. Second is personal quality that has to do with provider attitudes towards patients, overall surroundings in which health care is provided, and the degree of attention that a patient receives (Harvard Team, The 2000).

QUALITY OF MEDICAL INPUTS IN INDIA

There is an extensive literature summarizing the poor quality of health care currently available to seekers of health care in India. Consider first the care provided by the public sector. Patients, both rich and poor, tend to overwhelmingly favour the private sector over the "free" services provided by the public sector, when it comes to ambulatory care Administrative Staff College of India (ASCI) 1996; Mahal et al. 2000; World Bank 1995). This is corroborated by studies noting large shortfalls in personnel, equipment, and medicines in public facilities reported in primary health centres and sub-centres (Naylor et al. 1999; World Bank 1995). The situation is no better for workers with access to facilities under the Employees State Insurance Corporation (ESIC), well known for their unresponsive staff and poor equipment quality (ASCI 1996; Wadhawan 1987).

Unfortunately, the private sector also faces problems with respect to the quality of health care it provides. One study in Maharashtra found a large number of doctors who practised modern medicine without being qualified to do so, several hospitals that did not have even the basic infrastructure and personnel to carry out their functions, and operated without any licenses or registration (Nandraj and Duggal 1996). Other studies of private medical hospitals in Kolkata and Mumbai further confirm the poor state of private sector facilities, apart from highlighting the frequency of medically unnecessary procedures carried out on patients (Nandraj, Khot, and Menon 1999).

These problems with quality have to do with a lack of well-defined laws, and where such laws exist, their poor enforcement, whether on account of judicial delays or because of low levels of self-regulation by the medical community. Typically, the legislation with respect to medical personnel involves the setting up of bodies (or councils) that oversee the maintenance of quality in new entrants to the profession, maintenance of membership records of the profession and, through codes of conduct and sanctions, maintenance of standards among existing members. Although quite widespread and covering all the Indian states, the record of these councils in ensuring continued good behaviour is quite poor (Jesani, Singhi and Prakash 1997). Moreover, there is other evidence of problems in that many practitioners of traditional systems practice modern (allopathic medicine) without any sanctions. There is no premium on continuing education or examination on those who already possess a medical degree.

The problem with quality control legislation is somewhat more acute in the case of health infrastructure. Until recently, the only relevant legislation was the Nursing Home Registration Act in a small group of states such as Delhi, Maharashtra and Bengal (Nandraj, Khot and Menon 1999). The focus of these laws is primarily on registration of facilities, although the Delhi legislation specifies quality standards for these facilities (Nabhi Publications 2000, p. 12). In any event, the enforcement of even these laws has been poor; records of private facilities are generally incomplete and the few existing studies typically find substandard facilities, understaffing and low quality of care provision. There was no law with respect to diagnostic centres until recently (in fact, the Delhi Shops and Establishments Act specifically excludes medical facilities (Nabhi Publications 2000)). Now, however, at least in a proposed Delhi Private Medical Establishments "Act" (Aggarwal and Chaudhri 1998) would also seek to impose quality standards on diagnostic centres limited, of course, to the state of Delhi.

Consumer Protection Laws and their Implementation

Even if quality related regulations against errant doctors and medical centres are not satisfactorily enforced by the government, quality can still be maintained if there exist a suitable set of laws on consumer protection, provided at least these are reasonably well implemented.

The two most common avenues for relief in the arena of medical care are the Consumer Protection Act and various civil courts (see, for example, Reddy 1997). Unfortunately, the Indian court system is not very effective, and by all accounts is characterised by lengthy delays and a massive backlog of cases.10 It is thus not surprising that the various consumer commissions established under the Consumer Protection Act (COPRA) of 1986 have begun playing a key role in protecting consumer rights, in spite of their relatively recent origin. The main rationale for COPRA was it offering a quicker and cheaper way for consumers to address their grievances. A number of cases related to insurance and medical negligence have reached these courts (Aggarwal and Chaudhri 1998, Vats 1997). Recent evidence suggests that problems with backlogs have begun to occur in consumer courts as well, owing to an inadequacy of judges and the increase in the burden of cases (Bhat 1996a). Effective enforcement of malpractice laws against errant doctors has also been hampered by doctors' unwillingness to depose against their peers (Bhat 1996b; Jesani, Singhi and Prakash 1997).

Policy Challenges

Clearly major concerns exist in all three areas of health policy that have been highlighted earlier-in the overall costs of care, financial equity and the quality of care. A sustained improvement in these areas would play a significant role in advancing the primary goal of health policy-health, itself. The government could essentially adopt one of two methods to address these issues.

The first option is to do nothing at all beyond what it has already done. This, unfortunately, does not imply an unchanged situation. First, the Indian health sector would have to contend with the emergence of the private health insurance sector, given the passage of the Insurance Regulatory and Development Authority (IRDA) Bill. Second, over the longer run, it would have to contend with an aging population and the increasing burden of expensive chronic illnesses, such as cancer, diabetes and heart disease, with substantial implications for the health budgets of the poor and of the government.

In section 2 we assess the potential impact of the entry of private health insurance on the objectives of cost-containment, financial equity, and quality. The existing regulatory regime relating to private health insurance in India is also evaluated, and suggestions made for appropriate changes in it to ensure that private health insurance works to promote the various (intermediate) goals of health policy. We do not focus on the problem of the increasing prevalence of chronic illness, mainly because that calls for a whole new study, but note that it will serve only to highlight even further the importance of cost-containment, equity and health insurance.

If, as one suspects, the spread of the private health insurance sector, even a well-regulated one, is unable to address all of these policy challenges effectively, then other options will need to be considered. In its search for alternatives, India, in fact, is in the fortunate situation of being able to learn from a number of health system experiments that have taken place in different countries around the world. Some of the more interesting case studies have been the United Kingdom, Netherlands, Germany, Israel, Canada and Singapore.

4

AN ASSESSMENT OF ITS IMPACTS AND REGULATORY ISSUES

INTRODUCTION

The passage of the Insurance Regulatory and Development Authority (IRDA) Bill in the Indian Parliament marked the last phase in the move towards the privatisation of the insurance sector in India (Asian Age 1999, Government of India 1999a). Up till then, the provision of various types of formal insurance had been under the exclusive control of the public sector (Government of India 1999a-c). The Bill allows for the entry of private sector entities in the Indian insurance sector, including health insurance, and envisages the creation of a regulatory authority that would oversee the operations of various players in the insurance market (Government of India 1999a).

Whether the regulatory steps envisaged in the IRDA Bill, including especially the provision for entry of private firms, will influence the progress towards achieving India's health policy goals, and the likely direction that this effect will take is assessed here. The relevant policy goals for this purpose are assumed to be a health care system that is: not too costly, of good quality, and with an equitably distributed burden of health care spending.13 Apart from indicating the implications of private health insurance for India, this section will also examine regulatory tools that can be utilised to address its adverse implications (if any) and takes account of its existing regulatory structure.

Private Health Insurance and Cost, Quality and Equity in Health Care

This section examines the theory and the evidence linking private health insurance to: (a) the aggregate cost of providing health care; (b) the quality of care provided by the health sector; and (c) equity in the financial burden of care and the distribution of public health subsidies.

Private Health Insurance and Aggregate Costs of Health Care

In theory, the introduction of private health insurance can contribute to increasing the aggregate costs of health care in several different ways. Most of the arguments in favour of increasing health care costs due to private health insurance have to do with some disparity in the information available to parties involved in transactions in the health care and health insurance markets.

In interactions between health care providers, such as doctors and patients, it is a given that the former have much better information about their patients' health status and future course of treatment than the latter. This, together with the prospect of being ill and accompanying psychological costs and loss of earnings, makes the demand for health care fairly dependent on the course of treatment recommended by a physician. One consequence is that in a regime of pure indemnity insurance, providers have an incentive to provide more care than may be medically appropriate. For the same reason, the patient or, insurers for that matter, may be less willing to question the qualifications of the doctor as to his or her expertise (Arrow 1963, pp. 371-3).

The transaction between the insurer and the insured in the health market suffers from an asymmetric information problem as well. Once insured, an individual faces a reduced incentive to take precautions against poor health, much as a person with house fire insurance is likely to take less precaution in storing hazardous materials in her house. A sick person may also feel less compelled to control her consumption of health care and expensive diagnostic examinations if medical care costs are covered by insurance. The arguments outlined above hold true for any type of insurance regime, public or private, so it is unclear on this basis alone whether costs are likely to be higher in a private insurance system in comparison to public sector dominated financing.

However, public sector operated insurance schemes, which typically involve dual functions of financing and provision of services involve a myriad restrictions on health care utilisation, especially referral to higher order care and overall budgetary limits. In India, government employees covered under the Central Government Health Scheme (CGHS) cannot obtain reimbursements for private care unless appropriate referrals have been obtained from authorised medical practitioners or the Director of CGHS. A similar set of rules hold for the state supported Employees State Insurance Scheme (ESIS) for workers employed in the organised sector in India. Whether these schemes curtail use of expensive medical care depends on the presence of an effective referral process that curtails the usage of public facilities, or private care if permitted under the public scheme. Under the CGHS, only about 6 per cent of the total expenditure is accounted for by outside/private referrals suggesting that the process for external referrals may be effective in India (Garg 1999, p. 34). However, this appears not to be the case for referrals within the public system where the utilisation patterns are biased towards public hospitals as against primary care facilities (World Bank 1995 and Mahal et al. 2000).

Managed care institutions, such as health maintenance organisations (HMOs) that have emerged in the private sector in other countries, combine the roles of the provider and the insurer and can, therefore, serve to cut costs. The cost-cutting mechanisms could include stricter referral processes, payments based on diagnostically related groups, capitation payments, and other methods of managing utilisation of health care services (Einthoven 1997; Phelps 1997). In the United States such systems covered nearly 60 per cent of the population in 1995, with the population coverage having expanded at rates of 12 per cent per annum during the previous decade (Einthoven 1997). Similar institutions can be found in many other countries including Israel, and on a miniscule scale, in India (Gupta et al. 1992; Chinitz 1995). There is some evidence to suggest that the emergence of HMOs has led to cost-containment in the United States (Phelps 1997).

To the extent that private insurance in the form of managed care can yield low-cost outcomes in comparison to a fee-for-service system, the relevant issue for policy makers and regulators is to devise methods to promote its emergence. At one level, such institutions might be thought to be a logical market outcome given their lower costs and no obvious declines in consumer satisfaction relative to fee-for-service systems. However, the experience of the United States suggests that such an outcome is not a fait accompli. HMOs faced stiff resistance from medical associations and legislatures until the 1970s and subsequently, much of this resistance was to do with the prevailing "guild free choice" model that supported the idea of free choice of health care providers by consumers (Einthoven 1997, pp.198-9). HMOs got a boost in the United States when laws were passed requiring employers to offer at least one HMO option to their employees and when the government began offering its own employees the option of such plans (Einthoven 1997, pp.212-3). Further evidence on this issue is available from the health reform experience of Chile where ISAPREs (private insurers) have functioned mainly as pure third-party payers (Baeza 1998; Ferreiro 1999).

A third form of information asymmetry common to insurance markets is the fact that individuals are likely to know much more about their health status and future needs than insurers. People expecting to incur significant health expenditures in the near future will figure disproportionately among those who choose to get insured. This causes profitoriented private insurance companies to adopt procedures that are often expensive to weed out bad risks via risk selection. In Chile, for instance, whereas the population over 60 years accounts for 9.5 per cent of the country's population, the share of the 60 yearplus group in the population insured with private insurers was only 3.2 per cent, with the rest being covered by the public sector (Baeza 1998, p.18). Similarly, the average family size in Chile is four members, whereas the average among ISAPRE members is only 2.3 (Ferreiro 1999).

The "administrative" costs resulting from this risk selection can be quite high and usually passed on to customers in the form of higher loading charges. Those unable to obtain insurance at the higher premiums may then go back to the free public health system if the public system is open to all, or to out-of-pocket payments. In sum, overall health care costs would be higher than under a comparable public insurance system where membership into the insurance scheme may be compulsory for designated groups, unless outweighed by the inefficiencies of a public sector bureaucracy. Regulatory methods to prevent risk selection must, per force, face up to the problem of adverse selection given its implications for the financial viability of an insurance company. Thus, market outcomes that lead to insuring large groups are desirable so that there is little to suspect a preponderance of poor risks in the applicant pool. Indeed, larger groups face lower administrative costs. In the United States, loading charges (defined as (premiums/claims) less 1) typically range from 40 per cent for individual insurance to 5-8 per cent for group insurance. In India, insurance plans offered by the General Insurance Corporation (GIC) offer discounts over individual premium rates that range from 15 per cent to 67 per cent for groups of size 50 thousand or more. Regulations that cap total overhead expenditure of insurance companies likely promote the administratively cheap group insurance business (Government of India 1999d).

Employment based group insurance can also be promoted by insurance contributionlinked tax benefits given to employers without corresponding tax liabilities for the employees (but not if premiums are paid by employees), as in the United States (Phelps 1997, pp.349-54). In India, however, tax benefits can accrue both to employers and employees depending on who pays the premium. In this setting employer paid premiums may still be desirable as a means to promote group insurance if corporate tax rates are higher than personal income tax rates or if there are returns to scale to employers from administering group insurance.

In developing countries, there is one other information-related factor that could lead to high health care costs--the financial health of health insurance companies. In the absence of minimum capital reserves and incomplete epidemiological information about the population, there is a risk that insurance companies could be guessing wrong and charging premiums that are much lower in comparison to the benefits offered in a competitive environment. The problems would be exacerbated if get-rich quick companies were to invest their premium income in high-risk assets that are not aligned to insurance claim liabilities. The importance of health insurance and the dependence upon it of a significant (and often politically powerful) cross-section of the population means that the government is unlikely to accept even short-run scenarios where the companies can become bankrupt.25 As a consequence the government or the insurance sector may incur additional amounts in expensive bailout packages for sick health insurance firms, creating a disincentive for individual firm managers to perform financially, since their downside risks are covered to some extent.

Worldwide, governments have sought to address these concerns by setting a minimum set of conditions relating to management and personnel, actuarial analyses, solvency, working capital and investment profile; and a system for dealing with liquidations/takeovers. In most cases, there is a national level regulator to oversee the implementation of these conditions.

Aggregate Cost Implications of Private Insurance: Cross-country Evidence

Cross-country data is examined here to check if increased health spending per capita is associated with increased private insurance, all else remaining the same. Information on per capita income, health care expenditures and private and public insurance coverage for about thirty-one developed and developing countries is used for this purpose. Of course, a macroassessment of the cost impact of the private insurance sector using national level data is not straightforward since it is likely to be confounded by income effects, the type of public insurance available, the nature and implementation of regulations and the like. Our preliminary analysis does not rule out the possibility that private insurance may have a much smaller impact on health spending than one would suspect. The magnitude of the coefficient suggests that health spending per capita is positively associated with the proportion of population covered by private insurance. Indeed, a onepercentage point increase in the proportion of population covered by private insurance is associated with a 7.8 per cent increase in the costs of health care per capita. Health spending, however, depends on many factors including income. Increased income may also lead to increased demand for insurance, both public and private. Increased incomes may also lead to greater out-of-pocket health spending. Thus, at the very least, the regression analysis would have to control for the overall level of insurance (and/or income) in examining the impact of private health insurance. Doing so reduces the coefficient on the proportion of population covered by private insurance to statistical insignificance at the 5-per cent level and its magnitude becomes small in absolute terms.The results remain unchanged even if we control for the type of health insurance coverage in operation-that is, whether it is an alternative, or merely a supplement to an existing system of public health insurance.

Is this result reasonable? The United States is often held as an outstanding example of a country with "very high costs" of health care, a fact that is often linked to its predominantly private health insurance system. In particular, the United States has a high spending on health per capita (US$3,828 in 1995) in comparison to other OECD countries, such as France (US$2,600), Japan (US$2,947), and especially the United Kingdom (US$1,205) and Canada (US$1,814) (World Bank 1997). On the other hand, it is worth noting that with some notable exceptions such as United Kingdom, the rate of growth of health care costs in the United States has often fallen below that of many of the OECD countries. California, a state with a long experience in managed care, experienced even lower rates of growth in health costs during the 1980s and 1990s. On the flip side, it is worth noting that even though the coefficient on the proportion of population covered by private insurance is statistically insignificant, it is by no means small in terms of its implied effects on health spending. Indeed, holding income to be the same, an increase in the share of private health insurance from negligible levels to 50 per cent of the total population would increase the health expenditure per capita by as much as 35 per cent (not percentage points).

Quality of Health Care

In a free market, with no uncertainty about the outcomes of treatment, one can expect higher quality treatment to be undertaken (subject to the usual constraints) as fully informed consumers choose the most effective doctors and medical facilities ignoring the rest. However, a major problem in the health care market is precisely the uncertainty about outcomes on the part of the consumer of services. Alternatively, institutions might develop to label/certify doctors and health care facilities, without necessarily excluding them from service provision, so as to address this problem of lack of information with the consumer (see Phelps (1997) for examples from the United States). In this case, one would expect greater demand for certified personnel and facilities and the gradual sidelining of others not so certified. This depends on the extent to which the consuming public is capable of taking informed decisions and whether it considers the certifications credible. Finally, there could be licensure that excludes everyone other than those meeting certain standards from practicing medicine.

The contribution of an insurance scheme, whether public or private, to improving the quality of health care depends on whether the scheme is able to influence the process of labeling or licensure of medical personnel and facilities or the entry of highly skilled individuals in the health sector.

The increased provision of private insurance may increase the demand for health care and so push up its price. While this would improve opportunities for high-quality individuals who might have otherwise sought employment in other sectors, it would also increase the supply of low-skilled individuals into the health sector, unless appropriate screening takes place. Thus a mere increase in returns to health care provision in this sector may not increase average quality and may even reduce quality at the margin. This is already occurring in the guise of doctors with degrees in Indian systems of medicine practising modern (allopathic) medicine (Nandraj and Duggal 1996). Insurance companies could contribute to enhancing quality if, for example, they put quality-determined restrictions on the nature of expenses they would reimburse.26 In the case of HMOs and other managed-care institutions, they could empanel only those doctors who meet certain qualifications and treatment guidelines (Einthoven 1997). By enhancing the returns of such doctors over that of others they could increase the demand for such qualifications over time. The same could presumably be done for institutions, such as hospitals and diagnostic centres. By restricting the use of unnecessary expensive care through guidelines for referrals and hospital stays, managed care could also promote costeffective treatment guidelines.

Many of the steps that appear necessary may well occur in a market, without any prompting by regulatory authorities. There are, however, three areas of concern. First, arguments that hold for HMOs need not also hold for indemnity based insurance. In the case of indemnity insurance, an expansion in coverage if accompanied by an increase in demand for care induced by physicians and lack of resistance to it by private insurers and patients could lead to enhanced use of expensive care and diagnostics without any change in health outcomes. It also does not follow that an indemnity system would cater only to highly skilled personnel and institutions, especially if consumers of health care are unable to readily distinguish among plans and premiums charged by managed care institutions and indemnity-type insurance. Indeed indemnity type insurance might appear more consumer friendly by not putting restrictions on whom to consult and get treated by.

Even otherwise, effective competition from managed care organisations might be slow to emerge if there is resistance from associations of medical personnel, consumers and employers. The formation of panels and exclusive contracting with doctors, characteristic of managed care may be problematic if there are pre-existing laws against restrictive pricing practices. For instance, the General Insurance Corporation (GIC) is exempt from the provisions of the Monopoly and Restrictive Trade Practices (MRTP) Act (Government of India 1999h, pp. 5-8). To the extent that preferential treatment for panel doctors associated with HMOs can be interpreted as a form of restrictive trade practice, the MRTP Act would hinder the development of managed care in India, apart from giving GIC an unfair advantage in the insurance market.

Second, insurers in managed care type systems may sacrifice quality of care in exchange for lower costs by empanelling lower quality (and cheaper) doctors and facilities if there is a low level of quality awareness among consumers and if laws against malpractice do not exist or are poorly enforced. One way around this would be regulation that promotes uniform benefits packages and information provision to consumers of care. Third, if private health insurance leads to increased incomes among private providers of care, it may affect the quality of medical personnel available in public sector facilities, if replacements are not readily available. High returns in the private sector would lead to their exit from relatively low paying public sector jobs as well as reduce the number of new entrants into public sector jobs and there is some anecdotal evidence that this is already taking place.

Equity Implications of Private Health Insurance

The entry of private health insurance companies could worsen the distribution of the burden of health care spending for two reasons. First, private companies may find it profitable to undertake risk selection so as to insure low risk individuals and exclude the high risk ones from insurance. This imposes a large financial burden on people who are likely to get sick and most in need of risk protection. In Chile, the ISAPREs (private managed care) insure a disproportionately large number of people in the economically well-off groups, leaving the worst-off to the public insurance system (Baeza 1998). In this sense, private insurance enhances inequity unless there is access to public services of reasonable quality as a last resort. If private insurance and subsequent private care expansion attract doctors and other skilled medical personnel away from public health facilities, it would imply the worsening of the quality of care available to precisely those who are denied this insurance. Second, if entry of private insurance raises the overall costs of health care for reasons discussed previously, patients who cannot afford to buy insurance would have to pay larger out-of-pocket amounts.

As against this, an expansion in private insurance could lead the better-off groups to consume high quality private care, thereby improving access to (somewhat) lower quality public sector facilities for the worse-off groups (see, for example, Besley and Coate 1991; Gertler and Sturm 1997). However, this requires the assumption that a shift out of public care by the rich is not only large but will also leave the magnitude of public expenditures unaffected. In a recent paper we simulated the effect of the spread of private health insurance on the usage of public facilities by the richest 20 per cent in the Indian population. Our main conclusion is that these effects are likely to be very small given that the rich benefit from substantial subsidies provided by the public sector, unless the quality differentials between the private and public sectors are very large and private insurance cheap (that is, with low administrative costs) (Mahal 2000b).

Internationally, the empirical evidence favours the view that inequality will worsen with private insurance. A recently completed study of OECD countries found that private insurance as a means of financing health care has fairly large adverse redistributive effects across income groups in countries where it plays a major role, such as the United States and Switzerland (van Doorslaer et al. 1999).

From a regulator's standpoint, steps to address inequality enhancing effects of private insurance may include limiting the number of insurance packages offered, together with some controls on prices, or linking the expansion of insurance business to a certain proportion of insurance business being undertaken among backward areas and communities. But this may end up harming the health and subsequent growth of the health insurance industry itself.

Health Insurance Regulation

The main lessons from theoretical and empirical literature are essentially the following. In an ideal world with well-informed consumers who can evaluate alternative health care and insurance packages, with proper legal protection and affordable care, private insurance may not be harmful for cost and quality, although its impact could still be adverse from an equity point of view. The previous section also suggests that there are specific things the government could do to yield better outcomes. These include: steps to ensure financial stability of insurers, enhance consumer protection, control risk selection and strengthen legislation complementary to health insurance, such as malpractice law and accreditation. This section focuses on regulation that relates specifically to insurance and compares the standard approach worldwide with the regulatory system in India.

Health Insurance Regulation: "Model" versus the Situation in India

In line with the preceding discussion, we will focus on the following five topics: (1) Financial requirements (for entry, operation and exit) (2) Consumer protection (3) Risk selection/fairness (underwriting, rating standards) (4) Benefits (5) Regulatory agency: overview. In each case, there is a general description of existing (or recommended) practices in other countries followed by a brief discussion of the relevant regulatory features in India.

Financial Stability

The key issue here is to balance the requirements of financial stability with that of enhanced competition, since very strict financial standards may leave few insurers in the market place and extreme competition of the "cut-throat" variety may lead to financial instability and bankruptcies (see, for example, Ranade and Ahuja 2000).

a. Capital and Solvency Requirements

The current regulatory practice is for insurers to meet minimum capital requirements and surplus (over liabilities) requirements, the latter known as the solvency margin. The first establishes a floor for insurers wishing to enter the market and remaining there. The second takes into account the insurer's size and risk profile. For example, the larger its estimated liabilities, the greater will be the surplus requirement. This is obviously a better indicator of the company's solvency than a system relying solely on some fixed minimum capital requirement.

In the United States, the trend is towards using a "risk-based capital standard" (RBC). The RBC formula takes consideration of possible risks from lower asset values, higher rates of morbidity and mortality, lower interest risk, and other business risks. In the European Union, the "solvency margin" is calculated as the higher of the claims basis (23-26 per cent of average claims in the last 3-7 years) or the premium basis (16-18 per cent of retained premiums).30 A reduction is allowed for reinsurance, up to a maximum of 50 per cent of the solvency margin (European Community (EC) 1999). The limit on using reinsurance for calculating solvency margins is to avoid creating incentives for the insurer to take on more risk.

The Indian regulatory structure under the IRDA Bill has similar features. Under the 1938 Insurance Act, the solvency margin (assets less liabilities) was given as a percentage of retained/net premiums (gross premiums less reinsurance payments), of the order of 20 per cent (Government of India 1999d). The IRDA Bill of 1999 provides for a minimum lower bound of Rs. 50 crores for the solvency margin along with a requirement of 20 per cent of net premiums, or 30 per cent of the average of net incurred claims in the three preceding years (Government of India 1999d, p. 28). This is in addition to an entry requirement of a minimum capital of Rs 100 crores.31 In this sense, many of the provisions of the IRDA Bill parallel the regulatory features of other countries and become even more alike as the regulatory authority acquires greater experience. As in other countries there are a number of restrictions on the nature of investments that can be undertaken by an insurance company in India and the Insurance Act of 1938 sets these out in more detail in sections 27B and 28B (Government of India 1999d; Tapay

1999). The IRDA Bill also prohibits the investment of funds outside of India (inserted as Section 27C in the Insurance Act of 1938).

b. Accounting and Auditing

A second condition has to do with periodic reviews of an insurer's financial condition, including audits, submission of annual reports and so on. In the United States, insurance regulators have broad powers of changing the management and financial practices should the need arise (Chollet and Lewis, p.88). Establishing and evaluating the solvency status of an insurer requires a uniform set of accounting procedures and methods by which contracts issued by an insurer can be translated into assets and liabilities. Under the Insurance Act of 1938 and the IRDA Bill the controller of insurance (now the Insurance Regulatory Development Authority) has wide powers just as in the United States and elsewhere. These include auditing by qualified actuaries, periodic submission of reports, appointing directors or taking over management, requesting information and even shutting down the operations of the insurance company through a court order (Government of India 1999d,e).

c. Organisationsal Restrictions

In many countries, insurers cannot undertake additional business that is not directly linked to insurance as, for example, banking. The main regulatory concern is that insolvency of one business may cause the insolvency of the other (Chollet and Lewis, 1997). An argument against this restriction is that given banks, insurance companies and stock markets essentially are markets that deal with risk, an artificial separation may neither be desirable in the interests of efficiency, nor feasible (Ranade and Ahuja, 2000). Restrictions may also include specifying some desirable citizenship or residency status, ownership in the insurance company, and experience with similar business elsewhere. Similar restrictions can be found in the Insurance Act, 1938, although there is no linkage to any specific industry or sector (Government of India 1999c).

d. Exit and Guaranty Fund

Exit rules are to ensure orderly exits from the market. The insurer who plans to leave the industry may have to give a timely notice to the regulator and submit plans for payment of all liabilities prior to the exit date. In the event of company insolvency, the practice often is that all insurers participate (contribute to) in the formation of a guaranty fund. The means of participation could be taxes on insurance premiums of the insurers. Generally, the fund does not pay out the full liabilities but only some portion of it to the insured. This is to address any problems of moral hazard on the part of insurers. While there is extensive discussion of liquidation of a company (voluntary or court ordered) under the Insurance Act of 1938, there is no mention of a guaranty fund under Indian law.32

Consumer Protection by the Regulatory Agency

Generally, insurance regulation with regard to consumer protection revolves around (a) the marketing and language of insurance contracts; and (b) the relationship between insurers and providers.

a. Marketing and Language of Insurance Contracts

This category covers the language of insurance contracts so that it is easy to understand along with the terms used-benefits package, premium rate, deductibles, and so on. It also includes regulation relating to unfair trade practices, such as misrepresentation, discrimination, inducements, and failure to maintain records. Moreover, qualifications of insurance agents and their mode of functioning may also fall in this category. Tapay (1999) documents a case where the United States government prohibited agents from specifically looking for healthy patients to enroll. The Insurance Act of 1938 addresses directly only two concerns relating to consumer protection. It does so first by detailing the procedure by which insurance agents are licensed including the requirement that they have not been previously convicted of "...criminal breach of trust, or cheating or forgery..." or of participating in "...fraud, dishonesty, or misrepresentation..." (Government of India 1999d, p. 62). Second, it imposes limitations on commissions that agents can be given or the incentives they can offer to clients while selling insurance (Government of India 1999d, pp.56-60). The IRDA Bill gives authority to the regulator to specify a code of conduct for agents but no further specifics are provided. It also allows for a tariff advisory committee to oversee premium rates, insurance plans and to prevent discrimination (Government of India 1999c, p. 9).

There is additional legislation that addresses consumer protection more forcefully. Indian consumers also have access to consumer courts under the Consumer Protection Act of 1986, protections under contract and tort law in the Code for Civil Procedure, and the Arbitration and Conciliation Act of 1996, but suffer from poor enforcement.

b. Relationship between Insurers and Providers

The primary objective of regulating this relation is to ensure that health care providers remain professionally independent of the insurers in a managed care system and not under undue pressure to avoid recommending expensive treatments. In the United States, regulations permit any provider to join a plan if he accepts its payment conditions, and also allows him to work with patients outside their plan (the provider cannot be locked in by managed care organisations).

Unfortunately, consumer protection laws in India have little to say on the relationship between the insurer and the provider. It may be that some of the practices described above could potentially fall into some version of "unfair trade practices" which belong in the realm of the Monopoly and Restrictive Trade Practices (MRTP) Act (Government of India 1999h). At the present time, there is no case law to support or dispute this assertion. The bulk of the existing case law deals with fraudulent claims or delays in clearing claims by the insurer.

Risk Selection/Fairness

Regulation in this area has taken two main forms in the United States: (a) restriction of underwriting/risk selection; and (b) restriction on prices based on health status.

a. Underwriting Restrictions

These restrictions may involve a guaranteed issue of certain plans (or all plans) to all applicants, without regard to their risk profile. A variation on this may be guaranteed renewal where the insurer can underwrite applicants at the time of first issue but not on subsequent renewals. In case only a few select plans are subject to this restriction it will be the case that these plans will become much more expensive, if the risk composition of the plan determines its price. Of course, if all plans were subject to this restriction there would be the problem of adverse selection. Ways to get around this would be the exclusion of "pre-existing" conditions, or having open enrollment only at certain times of the year.

A variation of the restrictions noted in the previous paragraph is the portability requirement. These are often used along with pre-existing exclusion restrictions. For example, as long as a reasonable continuity is maintained in coverage a second insurer cannot impose a pre-existing exclusion on a person who has already exhausted a similar exclusion with another insurer. Other restrictions could relate to insurer requests for medical history, application forms for insurance coverage, and so on.

b. Community Rating and Rate Review

Community rating is the requirement that premiums be based on some broad geographic or demographic criterion rather than on individual health status. This is likely to be somewhat inefficient since it involves a degree of cross-subsidy across participants. Another approach to this is controlling the premium rates directly by requiring government approval for rate levels and increases. The normal method to do this is by examining "loss ratios"-the proportion of claims to premium income--and putting a bound on them.

By restricting risk selection, the expectation is that insurers will compete in quality and prices. However, this may be particularly problematic in countries newly opened to the private insurance sector, as problems of adverse selection could overwhelm the small number of companies who first enter the market.

As in the previous section, there is currently no legislation in India that has specifics on underwriting restrictions. However, a tariff advisory committee and the IRDA have the power to issue guidelines relating to non-discrimination and the "...control and regulation of rates, advantages, terms and conditions..." (Government of India 1999c, p. 9; Government of India 1999d).

Benefits

With regard to benefit packages there are two issues of interest: (a) a minimum package of services available to everyone; and (b) catastrophic insurance.

a. Uniform Minimum Benefits Package

Given a uniform minimum benefits package that is accessible to all applicants, insurance companies would have a tendency to offer additional products to appeal to low risk applicants, or indulge in underwriting. Both options would increase costs and promote inequity-the latter by way of higher administration costs as well as increased premiums for the relatively more risky, and the former in terms of higher premiums for the sick. Thus, it would seem that the regulation on benefits package ought to accompany some sort of market "managing" regulation in the sense of Einthoven (1997) or Medici et al. (1997) that creates large buyers in the insurance market. The presence of large buyers could help enforce rules among insurers, in exchange for the volume of business they can bring. Examples of this are the social insurance schemes of the type in Netherlands and Israel (Chinitz 1995; West 1997; Ham 1997). In each case, a (uniform) basic package of services is provided by a set of sickness funds with compulsory enrolment in at least one of them. Funds from a central source follow the individual and there is some riskadjusted capitation payment to curtail risk selection. As a consequence, there is increased likelihood of competition in quality and less of risk selection.

b. Catastrophic Insurance and Emergency Care

These can only be covered through reinsurance of various kinds in view of the rarity with which they occur. Unfortunately, in developing countries, private reinsurance is typically difficult to obtain because of the poor quality of actuarial data on rare events (Chollet and Lewis 1997, p.94). Reinsurance could be promoted in the form of more relaxed solvency margin requirements as in the European Community.

There is no legislation in India relating to benefits packages of either type. The only pertinent statement is in the Insurance Act of 1938 stating that the Tariff Advisory Committee (and the Insurance Regulatory and Development Authority under-the IRDA Bill will oversee rates, benefits and other activities of insurers. The IRDA Bill, however, allows both the entry of re-insurers in the Indian insurance market and relaxed solvency margin requirements (Government of India 1999c).

Regulatory Authority: Overview

There are two issues of relevance here: (a) What are the main functions of this authority? (Who does what?) (b) How will the authority be funded?

a. Main Functions

The two main functions relate to market standards (including consumer protection) and to overseeing solvency and financial regulation. In the United States, the states have the primary responsibility for regulating insurance, including solvency and financial standards. In the European Union, supervisors in each country enforce country-specific market standards, but the financial standards are similar for all EU countries (Tapay 1999).

b. Funding

Funding could be obtained from sources such as a premium tax (about 2 per cent of annual premiums in the United States), allocation from general funds to the insurance department, a "dedicated funding system" whereby fees, fines and other income generated by it are placed in a separate fund.

Unlike the previous two sections, the Insurance Act of 1938 and the IRDA Bill of 1999 have much to say on the nature and functions of the regulatory authority. In some cases, the authority is wielded directly by the so-called "controller of insurance" or the IRDA. In other cases, it is committees predominantly composed of insurers and headed by the controller. As per the Indian Constitution, the authority to regulate insurance is centralised in the IRDA and the central government, with little control by Indian states.35 As to funding, the IRDA has the authority to levy fees or other charges to carry out its functions and can have access to grants from the central government.

The general picture that emerges is that legislation (existing and proposed) concerning health insurance in India is fairly comprehensive even in comparison to a model set of regulations when focusing on auditing, financial controls, investment guidelines and licensing regulations. There is much less regulatory focus, however, on the consumer of insurance products and on overall goals of health policy in the form of regulation that curbs risk selection, protects consumers, promotes HMOs and the like. To be sure, both the Insurance Act of 1938 and the IRDA Bill are sufficiently comprehensive (ambiguous!) to allow increased focus on these issues, yet problems remain. For instance, regulating the relationships between insurers and providers or controlling rates could have implications under the Monopoly and Restrictive Trade Practices (MRTP) Act and that is parliamentary legislation over which IRDA has no control.

CONCLUSION

In sum, the entry of private health insurance could have adverse implications for some of the goals of health policy, especially equity in the financial implications of ill health, and possibly costs of care. However, an informed consumer and a well-defined and implemented insurance regulation regime might be able to address some of the problems. There are areas where regulation with regard to health insurance would be clearly useful--in instituting benefit packages, restrictions on risk-selection procedures, and addressing aspects of consumer protection.

Addressing these issues, however, requires meeting at least the following challenges. The first is the issue of enforcement of regulation. Even Consumer Protection Act of 1986 (COPRA) that was meant to address the rights of consumers through the establishment of special consumer courts has suffered from delays of various kinds (Bhat 1996a, Hindu 1999).

There is, therefore, no reason a priori to expect that health insurance regulation enforcement would do any better. To be sure, as an independent regulator, the Insurance Regulatory and Development Authority (IRDA) would have much greater leeway in implementing its own guidelines-but the recent experience with a similar entity, the Telecommunications Regulatory Authority of India (TRAI), suggests that this is by no means certain.

Second, it is also the case that some of the regulatory changes envisaged in health insurance also appear to require, as a necessary condition, additional changes in the existing publicly financed and provided care. In particular, for uniform benefit packages to work and for competition to kick in among insurance companies, large buyer groups may have to be created on the pattern of the United States and various European countries.

For a start, such buyer groups may have to be formed out of existing publicly operated schemes, such as the Central Government Health Scheme (CGHS) and the Employees State Insurance Corporation (ESIC). Both, unfortunately, fall out of the regulatory ambit of the IRDA. Third, in so far as legislation on quality standards in health care provision is concerned, the IRDA faces an even greater challenge since many of the laws and their implementation are in the hands of individual states as a constitutional requirement. Moreover, all evidence indicates that these are incomplete in scope, poorly designed, and hardly ever implemented. This makes the design of insurance policy more difficult and suggests taking a comprehensive and long-term look at issues of health-insurance and care provision in India.

It may be some time before these regulatory challenges can be met. The actual magnitude of these effects may well depend on the size of the insurance market that emerges and we believe that to be small. We estimate this market size to be INR 24 to 40 billion in terms of annual premium income in 1995-96 (Mahal 2000b). Even at twentyfour to forty times the existing magnitude of GIC business at the time, it amounts to only about 6 per cent of the then prevailing national levels of health spending.

5

LESSONS FROM THE INTERNATIONAL EXPERIENCE WITH HEALTH SYSTEM REFORM

INTRODUCTION

The potential consequences of the entry of private health insurance for the Indian health system. The main conclusions findings were first that the entry of private health insurance sector may not necessarily have large cost-increasing effects in the health sector, especially if appropriate regulatory structures were in place and enforced.

The example of the United States notwithstanding, the international evidence on the association between costs of health care and private health insurance appears to be weak. A worrying factor, of course, was the generally poor state of the regulatory structure pertaining to the health sector in India. Second, it is unlikely that the entry of private health insurance would significantly worsen quality, although there is no reason to believe that it would lead to improved care. Needed is improved regulation and the implementation of regulation related to providers and medical technology-be it to fill in regulatory gaps related to medical infrastructure, continuing education, better implementation of regulation relating to accreditation, drug use or malpractice law.

Of course, private health insurance may reduce the quality of medical personnel available to people who continue to use public services, if returns to private practice increase which can lead to an exodus of experienced medical personnel from the public sector. Whether the equity worsening effects of the private insurance sector will be large, or small, depends very much on the size of the private health insurance sector and the continued presence of subsidized public facilities. If public expenditures continue to remain large, we would likely see large-scale selection by insurance companies in favor of healthier groups, as in Chile, followed by a reverting back of the sicker groups towards "universally" accessible public facilities. In this sense, the most visible short-term result of private health insurance entry would be little or no change in the public sector's burden of care, and pressures by the younger and healthier groups to reduce their contributions to public services.

Coupled with departures of medical personnel, this would signal both a decline in quality and given competing fiscal demands on the government, a reduced role for the government. If so, private health insurance would have a long-run effect towards worsening inequalities in the burden of health spending. If the response is increased government spending (to counteract the declining contribution of younger members of the population) to address the needs of the sick and the poor, then the impact of private health insurance would have been to increase the financial burden on the government. It is, therefore, not surprising to see that countries with national level insurance systems have imposed various restrictions on plans offered by private insurers (e.g., Canada and the United Kingdom), or on people who leave the public system (e.g., Germany).

If, as we assess, private health insurance is unable to promote the major goals of health policy, it may be worthwhile to consider other ways to address problems with high costs, equity and quality of care. In this section we consider four such possibilities (health systems) and examine their functioning for outcomes of interest to Indian policy makers. These four cases are presented in the form of country experiences. These are as follows: (1) The United Kingdom (National Health Service) (2) Netherlands/Israel/Germany (Social Insurance) (3) Canada ("National" Health Insurance) (4) Singapore (Compulsory Insurance/Fee for Service/Medical savings)

Reasons for Selecting these Country Experiences?

The main reason for considering these four cases is that they cover possibly the widest range of possibilities that can be analysed, given country experiences. Moreover, these examples serve to highlight different aspects of the Indian health system, which consists of a mix of private insurance supported care, tax-funded public services, wage-linked contribution schemes, and out-of-pocket payments to providers. The United Kingdom offers a model of a system that is primarily centrally funded by general revenues (along with some wage-linked payments) and one where, prior to the health reform of the 1990s), provision of care was an integral part of the functions of the government in the health sector. A major set of problems with the system in the United Kingdom, prior to the reform phase, was the existence of long waiting times for "non438 urgent" hospital treatment, substantial variation in performance across regions, and a perception of non-responsiveness towards patient's needs (Chernichovsky 1995; Ham 1997). The same, although perhaps to a much greater degree, can be said of public health services accessed by the Indian population. Canada has a framework similar to the United Kingdom in terms of financing, but differs in the way fees for health care are set and the choices that consumers are able to exercise among providers. In the net, it offers interesting insights into ways to contain health care costs without sacrificing patient satisfaction.

Netherlands, Israel and Germany offer examples of health care systems that are built around compulsory wage-linked contributions into a fund (or funds) to be used for purchasing health care, or more precisely, purchasing health care insurance from competing insurers. These compulsory wage-linked contributions and the idea of an "insurance fund" have much in common with the Employees' State Insurance Scheme (ESIS) that currently operates in India. One similarity is in terms of the population covered. According to the most recent estimates, there are about 35 million beneficiaries under ESIS, more than double the population of Netherlands, and about 40 per cent of the population of Germany (Garg 1999b, World Bank 1997). ESIS also shares a feature, common to Germany and Netherlands (but not to Israel), where only employees earning below a certain level of income are required to join (Schwartz and Busse 1997; van de Ven 1997; Government of Israel 1999.

The ESIS is distinguished from the systems in these countries in two significant ways. First, it comprises an extremely small segment of the Indian population (about 3 per cent), compared to coverage rates ranging from 65 per cent to 96 per cent of total population in Germany, Israel and the Netherlands (Schwartz and Busse 1997; Government of Israel 1999; Government of Netherlands 1998). Second, health care under the ESIS is provided in-house-either at its own hospitals and care centres, or at public facilities, which is generally not the case for Netherlands and Germany, and for three out of four Israeli sickness funds. Given that there is much dissatisfaction with ESIS funded health services (Wadhawan 1987), there is the possibility of learning from the experiences of these three countries in terms of efficiency improvements, patient satisfaction and quality of care. Singapore offers an example of how an "individually" oriented system that seeks to address the need for universal access, a high degree of choice with regard to providers, and a desire for cost containment might turn out.

The central element of the Singapore model is an individual medical savings account (along with a catastrophic insurance scheme) to which working individuals contribute, and can be used to pay for their own inpatient care and expensive outpatient services (The Harvard Team 2000). The Singapore model, with its compulsory medical savings accounts, is relevant for India primarily because it is a relatively unique idea, echoes of which can be seen in the report on Old Age Social and Income Security (OASIS) recently presented to the Indian Ministry of Social Justice and Empowerment (Expert Committee 2000). The OASIS report suggests that such a scheme can be quite effective in meeting the social security needs of segments of the population living in far-flung and rural areas of India, and those who do not have regular incomes.

COUNTRY EXPERIENCES

The next four sections provide case studies of the four sets of country health systems.

United Kingdom

The United Kingdom provides an example of a system which, until 1990, was centrally funded and had its own network of services. Nearly ninety per cent of the public health expenditure was supported by general revenues, and the remainder by social insurance contributions (The Harvard Team 2000). Hospital and community services were under the control of the government and a network of General Practitioners (GPs) provided basic care on a capitation fee system. Private insurance was available but could only insure services not covered by the National Health Service (NHS) (Kutzin 1998). The system provided care at a much lower cost, taken as the ratio of health expenditures to GDP, compared to other OECD countries, yielding health outcomes in terms of life expectancy and infant mortality rates that were among the best in the world (see, for example, World Bank 1993). But there were concerns about long waiting lists for non440 priority care, non-responsiveness to patients and variation in quality, that prompted a review of the system under the Thatcher government (Ham 1997). Following a review of the National Health Services (NHS) ordered by the Thatcher government in the late 1980s, reforms in the NHS were approved by the British parliament in 1991. These reforms (compared to the pre-existing system) consisted of the following key elements:

1. Financing (sources): The basic structure of the sources of financing was left untouched. That is, general revenues continued to be the main source of funding for health services in the United Kingdom.
2. Financing (allocation): The method by which funding was allocated by the government was, however, changed in two ways: First, overall funding was distributed among district level health authorities in relation to the population in their area, after adjusting for age, sex and other health relevant factors. This was different from the previous method, where the allocation was based on services provided, irrespective of the residence of patients. The best way in which this could be replicated in the Indian context could be, instead of the central government providing funds to the All India Institute of Medical Sciences on the basis of the number of patients served, the same amount of funding could be distributed across Indian states, based on the population. The same argument would, of course, hold good for state level funding of

hospitals in state capitals. Second, the district health authorities had to compete for funds, in a limited manner, with organizations of general practitioners (GP fund-holdings). GP fund-holdings are essentially groups of practitioners who take responsibility for providing a range of services for patients enrolled with them in return for command over a budgeted amount given in advance depending upon the number of patients enrolled. These services typically include both those services traditionally provided by GPs but also hospital-based inpatient care. Starting initially with a limited set of services, some GP groups have been provided the entire budget for the enrollees. Any amount left over at the end of the year in these funds could be kept by GPs. The setting up of GP fund-holdings was a voluntary exercise and a change from their previous function as a provider of GP services for a capitation payment.

3. Separation of financing and provision in the NHS: A third pillar of reform was the separation of the financing function of the NHS from that of providing services. Hospitals and community services that were previously under the control of the public health authorities were now spun off as semi-independent trusts, which now had to compete with each other and with private sector health institutions for government funds, whether allocated through district health authorities, or through GP fund-holders.

In theory, the reforms would have the following effects. By basing the allocation of central funds to districts on population-based measures, one impact would be the development of facilities and services closer to the people who need them. This should, all else the same, increase the efficiency of health spending and the level of patient satisfaction. Second, separating funding from provision by district health authorities, should ideally lead to a prioritization of scarce resources in line with the interests of the population in their districts, instead of being governed by provider interests. This tendency would also be promoted by the competition for funding from GP-associations. Third, giving GPs control over the budget for inpatient care of patients would have the effect of a better control over (rationalization of) referrals to higher order facilities, and presumably, increased provision of primary services by GPs.

There was the danger, of course, of GPs providing inadequate levels of care given the incentive of being able to keep the surpluses out of fund-holdings, or selecting better risks. This, however, was potentially addressed through regulating the purposes for which surplus funds could be used. Fourth, by promoting competition among providers, both NHS Trusts and private, the reforms would have the effect of increasing efficiency among the former public providers (reducing costs) and making them much more responsive to patients' needs. Finally, apart from the reasons mentioned above, patient satisfaction could be enhanced by the possibility of exercising choice with regard to inpatient care that might result from enhanced provider competition.

Given the short period that has elapsed since the introduction of reforms, it has proved difficult to provide anything more than qualitative evaluation of their effects. However, a few broad contours appear to be emerging. First, the changing rules for allocation of funds has affected the location of facilities in the expected direction-with declining numbers of facilities and consolidation in London and increased numbers in surrounding areas, presumably lowering the costs of service provision as well (Ham 1997). Second, there is some evidence of health authorities setting budgetary priorities and the types of health services needed, in consultation with GPs. Third, GPs have increasingly sought to provide a broader class of services, both primary and specialist care, at their clinics than they had previously done reflecting their concern for increased cost efficiency.

Thus far there is little evidence of risk selection by them, although recent reforms have sought to prevent this by greatly increasing the membership of fund-holdings (The Harvard Team 2000). The evidence on greater patient choice among providers as a result of the reform is mixed. GP fund-holdings appear to have been much more responsive to patient needs compared to NHS trusts that have benefited from block contracts with district health authorities. On the other hand, there is some concern that increased contractual requirements and multiple contracts that have to be negotiated between different buyers and sellers of care has increased administrative burdens and costs (Ham 1997).

Germany/Israel/Netherlands

Unlike the United Kingdom, these three countries have a health system explicitly built round contributions to different competing insurers/sickness funds. In all three countries, coverage by these insurance funds is "compulsory", although the extent of coverage varies. For example, all residents of Israel must, per force, be enrolled in the national insurance scheme. Currently, 96 per cent of the Israeli population is covered (Government of Israel 1999). In Germany, the scheme allows the self-employed, and people above a certain income level to opt out-currently about 88 per cent of the population is covered under this scheme-75 per cent compulsorily and 13 per cent voluntarily. The rest obtain private health insurance. The Dutch scheme is similar to the German in that it excludes the self-employed, people earning above a certain income level, and government officials. As a consequence, about 64 per cent of the population is covered, with the rest enrolled in private insurance or in government schemes. However, there is a compulsory element-catastrophic insurance is necessary for everyone, and contributions for this purpose are paid into a national fund (Government of Netherlands 1998; van de Ven 1997).

A key element of the health systems in three countries is the presence of multiple competing insurers. The precise format by which the contributions are paid to the insurers/ sickness funds varies across these countries. In the case of Netherlands and Israel, employees and employers contribute directly into a central fund (Government of Israel 1999; Government of Netherlands 1998).

Then, depending on which sickness fund an individual chooses to enroll in, an amount is transferred from the central fund to the insurer on a risk-adjusted basis. Unlike Israel, however, Netherlands allows insurers to charge a flat rate premium from enrollees, constrained to be the same for all enrollees, which they can vary at their discretion (van de Ven 1997). In Germany, contributions are paid directly by individuals (and their employers) to the sickness funds by the enrollees.

Until recently, there was little competition among the different insurers; of late, several national level sickness funds have begun competing with regional sickness funds (Schwartz and Busse 1997). The rate of contribution depends on projected expenditures and a balanced budget requirement, and varied between 9 per cent and 15 per cent in 1996 (Schwartz and Busse 1997; Chinitz, Preker and Wasem 1998).

In the Netherlands, there are limited co-payments for certain types of care and drug expenses, subject to an upper limit--in 1998, the co-payment was 20 per cent for certain classes of medical expenses, and subject to an annual limit of 200 NLG (dutch guilders). There was also a 20 per cent co-payment for drugs relative to a defined "reference price"

(Government of Netherlands 1998). In Germany too, there is a very limited co-payment for inpatient days of stay and a reference-pricing based cost-sharing arrangement for drugs (Kutzin 1998).

In all three countries, the basic package of services that the insurers have to provide to enrollees is pre-determined by the government. However, the field over which the insurers can compete for enrollees varies across the three countries. Competition among insurers in Israel is guided solely on the basis of quality, with little scope for price competition over the basic package. Moreover, the number of sickness funds is fixed at four with no prospect of entry for others into the compulsory scheme. In the Netherlands, both quality and price competition is possible, owing to the existence of the flat rate premium that companies can charge to enrollees with respect to the basic package. It is also relatively easy for new firms to enter the sickness fund industry in the Netherlands, including for existing firms to provide services in regions where they do not currently operate. In Germany, for a long time, there was limited competition among sickness funds/insurers, many of which had only a local reach. More recently, competition has heated up with the increasing spread of national level sickness funds. Competition can be over both price and quality since the contribution rates depend on expected expenditures and a balanced budget requirement. Moreover, in all these countries insurers (including private insurers) can offer supplementary packages, available for voluntary purchase to their enrollees, at prices determined by the insurer. This leads to a third possible arena over which insurers can compete.

Competition among insurers is only one element of these health care systems. A second key element, much in the mould of the reforms in National Health Services in the United Kingdom, is a focus on contractual relationships between providers and insurers, with an eye on provider competition. The objective of enhanced competition among physicians was explicitly pursued by the government of Netherlands, which in 1992 scrapped a law requiring insurers to compulsorily have contracts with all physicians in their region of operation. No such flexibility is currently available in the case of hospitals and rehabilitation centres, whose budgets insurers are obliged to fund. The size of the budget of these institutions is, however, fixed in consultation with insurer organisations. In Israel, the largest sickness fund owns its own provider facilities. By contrast, the other three sickness funds typically enter into contractual relationships with physicians and hospitals. Even this, however, ought to have an influence on the quality of services in the remaining sickness fund, if provider competition leads to better quality services by the other funds. Finally, in Germany the services are provided after a process of negotiation between provider associations and sickness funds. Till July 1998, the procedure was for sickness fund associations and physician associations to agree on a maximum budgeted amount, which was then allocated to individual physician members based on usage, and which could serve as a source of provider competition. Hospital budgets were similarly agreed upon with individual hospitals. However, after that period, these have been replaced by a fee schedule and a "target" volume of services (essentially a soft budget constraint). In each of these cases patients have a fairly substantial degree of choice across providers.

It is also worth noting that both the German and the Dutch governments have relied on various sorts of restrictions on prices charged by providers. During 1982-92 in the Netherlands, the governments specified a schedule of prices to be charged by providers, later dropped in the reforms (van de Ven 1997). Similarly, apart from directly specifying prices for specific types of hospital services, or the maximum budget size that could be negotiated for ambulatory care, the German government has, from time to time, stepped in if the provider organisations insisted on higher than "normal" amounts in their negotiations (Schwartz and Busse 1997).

As formulated, what are the likely implications of this structure for policy objectives of interest-such as cost of care, quality and equity? Competition among insurers for enrollees would suggest they would try to be responsive to consumers, in the sense of providing the best possible quality of service, both personal and technical, and at the least possible cost, given quality. Competition among insurers is promoted by five features of the system-multiple insurers, fixed package of basic services, people being able to choose which insurer to enrol with, funds following the enrollee in a capitation fee arrangement, and voluntary supplementary insurance. Moreover, having enrolled, the fact that there is also substantial choice for patients among providers, means that in a regime where insurers contract with providers, patient choice of provider can determine whether or not an insurer contracts with that particular provider. Thus one might expect better service provision by providers. Finally, provider-insurer contracts that are based either on capitation fees and/or on prospective budgets would address concerns on costcontainment, apart from the fact that large insurers can obtain better deals from providers.

In the Netherlands, with few exceptions, insurers are prohibited from providing health services directly (Government of Netherlands 1998, p.32). In sum, one might expect enhanced cost-containment, greater cost-effectiveness, and improved quality of care. A key concern in these systems has to do with the possibility of risk-selection by competing insurers/sickness funds, much as in a setting with only private insurers. This problem is not overcome simply by mandating an insurer to enroll everyone who applies, or to have a uniform basic benefits package for all applicants. Such measures fail as long as the insurers have some method of being able to select-by choice of the contents and prices of the voluntary package, for example. In principle, risk-adjusted payments ought to be able to address this problem.

However, the situation could be problematic in the Netherlands and Israel if the risk-adjusted payments by the central funds are somehow unable to capture reasonably well the variation in costs of care across patients. In Germany, this could happen by regional or national sickness funds focusing on healthy patients, and by offering lower contribution rates to such patients.

If risk-selection were common, this would have implications for the administrative costs of running the insurance schemes, and hence the overall costs of the health system. In each of these countries, the government has set up mechanisms to address this problem. In the Netherlands, the government uses two types of financial "adjustment" mechanisms to address this problem. First, at the end of each financial year, the budgeted amounts are adjusted across insurers so that those with higher costs in relation to budgets receive more-that is, resources move from funds with an "above-average budget balance to ...funds with a below-average budget balance." (Government of Netherlands 1998, p.30).

Second, differences between costs and budgeted amounts for insurance funds are made up directly through payments from the central fund operated by the government. The payments under these two methods currently account for as much as 97 per cent of the gap between expenditures and budgets of individual insurance funds, so that there is hardly any incentive for the gains from insurer competition envisaged earlier! (van de Ven 1997).

In Germany, there was considerable variation in contribution rates across sickness funds-and funds with wealthier and healthier enrollees with much lower contribution rates. Beginning in the mid-1990s, however, regulatory mechanisms have been set in place so that the funds' revenues are adjusted according to age, sex, income, or whether enrollees received an invalidity pension (Chinitz, Preker and Wasem 1998; Schwartz and Busse 1997). In Israel, it is unclear how this problem would be addressed beyond making enrolment by sickness funds compulsory, since the risk-adjustment mechanism only includes age. Chinitz seems to suggest that this would be done mainly through the government budget (Chintz 1995).

One might expect the compulsory nature of the schemes and the contribution into a common fund at constant proportion of income to promote greater equity in terms of the financial burden of care as well, although some caution is in order. First, there are upper bounds on the amount of contributions that are to be made under the central fund/individual insurance funds. In the case of the Netherlands and Germany, these take the form of opt-out clauses for people with income above a certain threshold (Government of Netherlands 1998; Schwartz and Busse 1997). In Israel, the highest payment is explicitly set-at the specified percentage contribution multiplied by four times the average wage in the country (Government of Israel 1999). The fact that contributions are non-decreasing in income is desirable from the point of view of equity, but the limits and opt-out clauses allow some scope for inequity.

In each of the three countries, the experiences with some of the features of health systems are much too recent to permit a comprehensive analysis of their effects. Some indicative evidence is available, however. According to one expert, following the partial Dutch health reforms in the early 1990s, there was substantial internal reform within sickness funds. These included longer hours of service by the funds (including mobile offices), electronic data systems, developing different systems for delivery of drugs (mail-order), and replacement of administrative oriented heads of institutions by more entrepreneurial ones. In their dealings with providers, sickness funds were able to break down some of the seller-cartels and thereby reduce provider charges by substantial amounts. Moreover, providers themselves seem to be focusing more on quality cost-effectiveness-one indictor being the increasing introduction and use of cost-accounting procedures in health care institutions. Indeed, better information about costs is probably the first step in such an exercise (van de Ven 1997, p.93). There is also some evidence that the Israeli system, particularly after 1995, has promoted greater equity in terms of the burden of health spending.

In addition to the qualitative evidence, we can also compare national level information in these three countries with other developed nations that do not primarily rely on a social insurance system. According to the most recent statistics available health expenditures in Germany, Israel and the Netherlands, taken as a share of GDP, were about 9.6 per cent, 7.7 per cent and 8.8 per cent, respectively. By contrast, Switzerland and the United States, which rely a lot more on private insurance, spent 9.6 per cent and 14.5 per cent of their GDP, respectively, on health.

Countries, such as Canada and the United Kingdom, which use general revenues to fund their health care spent about 9.5 per cent and 6.9 per cent of their GDP on health (Chinitz 1995; The Harvard Team 2000; World Bank 1997). Health achievement measures, such as life expectancy and infant mortality rates, is negligible across this same set of countries-ranging between 77 and 79 years for life expectancy at birth, and between 6 and 8 per 1,000 live births, respectively (World Bank 1997). It thus appears that in terms of cost-containment and cost-effectiveness, countries with social insurance lie somewhere in between those that rely on private insurance and those depending on general revenues to finance health care, but as demonstrated in Section 2, cross-national regressions do not lend strong support to this hypothesis.46 More crucial is the relative performance of these different country systems in terms of equity. One recent study of OECD member countries points out that social insurance has generally been regressive in Netherlands and Germany, but the overall effects pale in comparison to the regressive implications of private insurance and direct out-of-pocket payments. On the other hand, general revenues are much more progressive, so that the United Kingdom comes out to be progressive overall, and United States and Switzerland with relatively high regressive health financing systems (Wagstaff and Doorslaer et al. 1996). Thus, in terms of equity in financing, social insurance appears to lie in between systems that rely on private health insurance/out-of-pocket spending and those that rely on general revenues.

Canada

In the preamble to the Canada Health Act (1984), the Canadian Parliament recognized the importance of cooperation between "governments, health professionals, voluntary organisations, and individual Canadians.." and expressed a wish to "...encourage the development of health services...by assisting the provinces in meeting the costs thereof." (Government of Canada 1999, Chapter C-6).

Canada finances it national health insurance system through tax revenue with financial participation by both the provincial and federal governments. The insurance system itself is managed by provinces, with contribution of the national government typically taking the form of a lump-sum grant to each province (Harvard Team, The 2000).

However, the full contribution is conditional, and depends on whether the health care support regime satisfies certain criteria. The relevant list of criteria includes the requirement that the health plan be administered on a non-profit basis by a public authority, that the health insurance plan be: comprehensive, universal in terms of population covered, portable, and ensure accessibility.

The last requirement includes a statement that "must provide...services...on a basis that does not impede or preclude...whether by charges made to insured persons... reasonable access..." (Government of Canada 1999; Chapter C-6). Thus, patients are not required to give co-payments for medical services received, except in the case of purchasing drugs that do not belong to the class of "least cost alternatives". In the year 1997, the provinces covered about 60 per cent of their total health expenditures, and the federal government, the remainder.

The overall spending takes the form of expenditure caps set for hospital-based services and for physicians' services. Given these caps, rates are set for each unit of service (and specialty) by a process of bargaining within the medical associations of each province. Within this system, payment is by fee-for-service, which creates an incentive for doctors to oversupply services. This tendency is controlled by a centralized monitoring system-since all payments are routed through one provincial agency. As a consequence, doctors who appear to be violating the "norms" are brought to the notice of the medical association for appropriate disciplinary action.

The final key feature of the system is that patients have completely free choice of providers. There are some restrictions, in terms of certain services that are provided with delay (some forms of elective surgery) and others that are not covered (dental care). In general, however, there appears to be a high level of patient satisfaction with the Canadian health care system (Harvard Team, The 2000). It is also quite clear that given universal access and funding through general revenues, the system is also quite equitable. The one area of concern appears to be, and this was noted in the previous section, the high expenditure on health as a proportion of GDP-9.5 per cent (Harvard Team, The 2000).48 This is counter-balanced by two other factors. First, Canada is among the very few developed countries that have experienced a decline in their health spending as a proportion of GDP in the last few years (Harvard Team, The 2000, p.51). Second, it has done extraordinarily well in terms of indicators of life expectancy and infant mortality rates-78 years and 6 per 1,000 live births, respectively.

Singapore

Singapore's health care financing and provision system is organized around four main pillars. The first is a medical savings scheme (Medisave) which is compulsory for all employees and the self-employed. Contributions to the scheme take place through the intermediary of the Central Provident Fund (CPF). Of the 40 per cent payroll tax deposited into the CPF, between 6-8 per cent is allocated to the Medisave scheme. Half of the payroll tax is borne by employers, and the other half by employees. The contributions are tax deductible and earn interest (Nichols, Prescott and Phua 1997). There is a maximum limit to which the balance in the Medisave account can accumulate, after which additional amounts go into a retirement fund. Amounts can be withdrawn from the Medisave account to pay for hospitalization expenses for the individual and his family, subject to caps for charges per hospital/day and surgery expenses. Expenses for ambulatory care cannot be charged to Medisave, although there are exceptions for expensive forms of ambulatory care.

In general, patients are allowed to freely choose among the many private and public providers. Users of public services are required to make a co-payment at the time of consumption. The rate of co-payment varies by class of care, increasing as quality improves. At the lowest class, the co-payment rate is only 20 per cent. People who cannot afford care are subsidized from a common fund.

A second pillar is the so-called Medishield. The main problem with Medisave was that inter-temporal pooling (i.e. savings over the lifetime of an individual) is unlikely to ever be sufficient to pay for truly catastrophic illnesses. This role was best undertaken by cross-sectional pooling of resources. The Medishield scheme involves the payments of age-adjusted premiums for catastrophic insurance coverage up to the age of 75 years. The premiums and other charges related to Medishield can be paid out of Medisave accumulations. The scheme has a large (initial) deductible, a 20 per cent co-payment rate, and annual as well as lifetime limits. This scheme is compulsory for employees and the self-employed, but voluntary for their dependents and all others.

A third key element of the scheme is a provision for the very poor, people who cannot afford care, even at the most subsidized rates. This led to the creation of the Medifund. The government provides support for this fund on a fairly periodic basis, and those seeking relief under this category can simply apply to the management of a public hospital (a "Medifund Committee" exists at each hospital) for the requisite benefits. On the provision side, the government has sought to promote competition both by allowing patients a free choice among providers as well as by restructuring public hospitals. This has mainly involved their becoming more autonomous in terms of day-today management and control. However, there are restrictions on how much they can charge from their patients-that is, they are expected to continue to subsidize care users and are subject to revenue caps. The gap between their resources/revenues and costs is made up by government subsidies.

By allowing patients a free choice of providers, Singapore's system can be expected to promote patient satisfaction and quality care. However, as far as cost containment and cost-effectiveness are concerned, the picture is less clear. Medisave is likely to reduce the problem of moral hazard since the patients are effectively using up their own money and presumably likely, for that reason, to become more responsible, including using preventive care. This is further facilitated by the government of Singapore spending substantial amounts of resources on promoting low health risk behaviours, on free immunization services and the like. Costs are also likely to be curtailed by the "revenue caps" in public facilities since any increased provision of services would lead to enhanced revenues owing to co-payments.

On the other hand, if people do not view the amounts in Medisave as their own money and have a short-term horizon, they might end up consuming much more of hospital based care, even for relatively minor problems. Moreover, with little by way of intermediation between doctors and patients, there is a real danger of supplier-induced demand causing a sharp increase in overall health spending. Also, the level of integration between lower levels of care and hospital-based care are low, suggesting another cost-enhancing inefficiency by duplication of tests and medical services. Finally, the existence of Medishield-the catastrophic insurance coverage-can create expenditure enhancing income effects since the desire to keep a large balance in the Medisave account is counteracted by the ease with which one can reach the deductible level for the Medishield policy to kick in. In terms of equity, the Medifund provides substantial safeguards to the poorest people. It is possible, however, that for low-income (but not "least income") individuals the existence of substantial copayments may lead to a relatively large burden of health care spending.

The overall setting in Singapore seems to support the objectives of equity and quality of care. Indeed Singapore is known to attract patients from abroad to its facilities. However, its experience with costs in recent years is a little less impressive. At the moment it spends about 2.5 per cent of its GDP on health, which is quite low considering its achievements in terms of life expectancy at birth and the infant mortality rate-76 years and 4 per 1,000 live births, respectively. However, there is evidence that its expenditures are increasing at a rate faster than in the period before Medisave accounts were introduced, in the 1980s (Harvard Team, The, 2000).

LESSONS FOR INDIA

The experiences of these countries hold three key lessons for India, which is plagued by poor quality of health care, potentially high costs of care and increased burden of health spending on the poor. The first set of messages has to do with patient satisfaction and quality of care. It is quite clear that patient choice among providers and insurers is emerging as one of the single most valuable elements of health policy internationally. This is certainly the case for the private sector oriented United States, but also true of countries where the government has traditionally played an important role. The United Kingdom is the best example, but Netherlands, Germany, Israel and Canada all have provider choice as a key element of their public supported health systems. In some cases, people have choices over both insurers and providers and in others, only one.

A key issue is how to reconcile the need for choice among providers with costcontainment. The lesson here is the importance of various sorts of budgetary caps and supply side controls-as in Canada, the United Kingdom, Germany, the Netherlands and even Singapore, through its "revenue" caps on public hospitals. Indeed, countries that have focused on the demand side as a means to curtail costs have not done as well. The only demand side control that appears popular across countries has to do with copayments for pharmaceuticals. A classic example is the Republic of Korea which has experienced rapid increases in its health spending, despite co-payment rates as high as 50 per cent (World Bank 1989; Yang 1996). In our sample of countries, Singapore has experienced rapid increases in its health spending, even though its aggregate share of GDP is still quite small.

A third important message has to do with the reconciliation of consumer choice with equity. Private provision and private health insurance are one extreme, with high levels of consumer choice but low levels of equity. The work by Wagstaff and Doorslaer and others suggests that at least in terms of financing, countries that fund their compulsory health care by general revenues do better than those with social insurance, who in turn do better than private insurance, with out-of-pocket payments being the least equitable. In general some sort of cross-subsidy from the rich to the poor appears desirable and it is important that the richer groups participate financially in the scheme, directly or indirectly (through tax revenues).

We did not include in this discussion any significant reference to issues of technical quality, about laws on consumer protection, about government regulations on supply of medical personnel, infrastructure and equipment, and the quality and prices of drugs. Indeed, it is the case that government policy in these areas would have quite direct impacts on some of our objectives. For instance, it is often contended that an increase in the supply of doctors, instead of leading to reduced prices, may sometimes actually increase the average cost of care, through an increased number of specialties and supplier induced demand (Harvard Team, The 2000). Thus countries often put a range of restrictions on the number of doctors, proportion of specialists, number of immigrant doctors, and so on. Similar restrictions may arise on the introduction of new drugs and technology. Quality and cost of care is also crucially dependent (although not necessarily in the same direction) on laws for consumer protection and requirements for continuing education. All the countries that we discussed above have various forms of regulatory structures that deal with these issues. India too, does have such structures, but there are substantial gaps as in the case of medical infrastructure regulation and poor enforcement, especially in issues of consumer protection.

Also not discussed above was the fact that health reform is typically a long-term process, requiring close monitoring of outcomes. Most of the countries discussed in the previous section have been tinkering with their health sector for years to fine-tune and refine the system. For instance, Singapore introduced the Medishield scheme in 1990 nearly six years after it first introduced the Medisave scheme and two years later, added the Medifund scheme. Similarly, the Netherlands, Germany and the United Kingdom introduced several refinements in its health system during the course of the 1990s. In applying these ideas to India, policymakers are faced with a number of opportunities and challenges. For one, health care (but not health insurance) is primarily a state subject so any improvements in underlying regulations is a responsibility of the states and the not the federal government. Thus improvements in this area will require coordination among states.

Second, it may be useful to think of bringing together large funds such as the ESIS and parts of the health budgets of state governments, and use those to either buy private health insurance, or to negotiate contracts with private providers. This is one way in which patient choice among providers and quality can be enhanced. A potential problem is that with 75 per cent of the health spending already going to private sector, it may be difficult to imagine provider associations agreeing to anything like a fixed rate.

In a setting with limited budgets relative to health needs, however, there still remains the question about who will get to benefit from whatever subsidized scheme the government supports. It can be shown that substantial gains accrue to the poor if the government were to introduce some form of income/expenditure cut-off rules for beneficiaries (Mahal 2000b). But this faces the problem of sustained political support for schemes that undertake cross-subsidies from the richer groups to the poor. The question then as to where the cut-off would have to be to yield significantly large benefits to the poorer segments of the population becomes important.

6

HEALTH INSURANCE IN INDIA: PROGNOSIS AND PROSPECTUS

There is growing evidence that the level of health care spending in India-currently at over 6 per cent of its total GDP-is considerably higher than that in many other developing countries. This evidence also suggests that more than three-quarters of this spending includes private 'out-of-pocket expenses'.

Despite such a high share of expenditure by individuals, the provision of health care, that is adequate in terms of quality and access, is becoming more and more problematic. Particularly, public delivery of health care is poor in quality, presumably for reasons of inadequate financing. This highlights the need for alternative finances, including provision for medical insurance at a much wider level.

The paper attempts to review a variety of health insurance systems in India (defined here as any mechanism which covers the risks of payment for health care at the time of its requirement), their limitations and the role of the General Insurance Corporation as an important insurer agency. It also attempts to develop a prospectus of strategy for greater regulation and increased health insurance coverage by making suitable changes-particularly in claim settlements and the exclusion clause. Also highlighted is the need for a competitive environment (which is at present completely missing), and an opening up of the insurance sector.

INTRODUCTION

Since independence, the health care system in India has been expanded and modernised considerably, with dramatic improvements in life expectancy and the availability of modern health care facilities and better training of medical personnel. At the same time, however, much remains to be done. Several recent papers and reports have critically reviewed the Indian health delivery and financing system [Berman and Khan 1993; World Bank 1995; Ministry of Health and Family Welfare 1995; Planning Commission 1996, etc]. These studies have documented many serious problems with respect to the accessibility, efficiency and quality of the health delivery system. They have also made several policy recommendations to alleviate these problems.

One aspect of this ongoing has centred on health expenditure and health financing. As shown in the World Development Report 1993, health expenditure in India as a percentage of its GDP was 6 per cent in 1990 which is higher than the level in many other developing countries in the Asian region. Evidence indicates that this higher level of spending is not only due to price differences but also represents a real difference in health care spending [Berman 1996]. A very revealing calculation by Berman about sectoral shares in the total health spending indicates that in a break-up of this 6 per cent, as much as 4.7 per cent of the expenditure is accounted for by the private sector.

Moreover, of the 4.7 per cent, around 4.5 per cent comprises out-of-pocket expenditures of the households. The remaining 0.2 per cent includes contributions from private employers and other non-government organisations. Almost all of this private spending is on curative care: consultations, diagnostics and in-patient care. Most of the discussions on health care financing in India have centred on the financial constraints of the public sector-and the efficiency of resource allocation by the government. 'Health for all' has been seen as the central assumption of the health sector debate, thus making the government the central player. While we admit that the 'health for all' objectives are laudable, the overwhelming focus on a public health care delivery system appears somewhat unrealistic-particularly in view of the fact that health spending in India is mostly private.

This paper is devoted to one particular aspect of health care financing in India-namely, the enormous financial burden faced by individuals in the form of out-ofpocket expenses to pay for curative health care. These financial burdens are pervasive, and both contribute to many other problems which face India's health care delivery system and are reinforced by them. Evidence indicates that Indians tend to use health care services more frequently [Duggal and Amin 1989; Berman 1996].

Supply-side reasons include greater availability of health practitioners both because of the several branches of medicine unique to India and because of the easy and almost unregulated entry of a very large number of private practitioners in each of these branches every year. However, these reasons can at best be a small part of the explanation. Howsoever easily available health care is, no rational consumer is expected to spend large amounts of his or her income without very good reasons for it.

Excessive financial burdens on households arise for a variety of reasons. At one level, they can be blamed on India's public health care system, which is underfunded and suffers from quality and access problems, forcing consumers to visit the private and relatively more expensive treatments. However, as will be discussed below, recent household-level studies on utilisation of health care indicate that even public care is not all that 'free' after all: there are many incidental expenses that consumers have to bear on their own. If all the quality and access differentials between public and private health care were to be wiped out, there would still be some very heavy financial burdens on the consumers.

We contend that these financial burdens arise because the consumers are either not insured or are insured inadequately for their health care expenses. This is the focus of our paper as the title indicates. We examine health insurance in the broadest sense by which we mean any financing arrangement in which consumers can avoid or reduce their expenditures on health services at their time of use. Thus, not only private health insurance, but also the free public provisions and reimbursements-where health care is prepaid by consumers from their own salaries-can be seen as forms of insurance.

The findings in this paper are based on a variety of sources. In addition to reviewing a substantial mass of literature on health financing in India and elsewhere, we have benefited from extended discussions with a large number of researchers and individuals from government agencies, public enterprises, private firms, international agencies, insurance companies and hospitals. We also had conversations with numerous consumers of health services. The summary data provided by the General Insurance Corporation (GIC) about the health insurance cover and its components have been immensely useful. The remainder of the paper is organised as follows. Section II provides an overview of the existing pattern of health care financing in India, with an effort to reflect the full diversity of the financing methods currently in use. We do not attempt a comprehensive review of all the strengths and weaknesses of the system, but focus instead on the implications of the financial burden facing consumers in India. In Section III we develop a prognosis: an interpretation of the direction, strengths and weaknesses of the Indian health care system. This section focuses mostly on the health insurance policies, premiums and claims patterns of the GIC and its four subsidiaries. This focus is in view of the special role played by the GIC in insuring segments of the Indian population with the greatest ability to pay which forms a possible model for future forms of health insurance in the country. Finally, in Section IV we develop elements of a prospectus of strategy for increasing the coverage and extent of health insurance for the formal sector in India. In doing so, we apply principles from published theoretical and empirical literature on health insurance from other countries.

FINANCING OF CURATIVE HEALTH CARE IN INDIA

Recently, there have been many good reviews of India's health care financing [Berman and Khan 1993; Reddy and Selvaraju 1994; Upleker and George 1994; World Bank 1995; Alam 1998; Tulasidhar 1996]. It is beyond the scope of this paper to go into the details or summarise this literature, but we would like to highlight several recurring themes. One theme is that India's health care delivery system relies upon both public and private facilities to provide care. Another theme is that given the constraints on public resources that are available, it is desirable and appropriate for the public sector to increase its effort to subsidise, finance or provide primary health care services, and to seek other revenue sources for doing so. It has also been argued that the emphasis on preventive and promotive health services by the government has been at the expense of curative health care and that this has led to the unregulated growth of the private health care sector [Phadke 1994]. Finally, it has also been recognised that there are considerable variations across different Indian states and union territories in levels of health expenditure [Alam 1997], the respective shares of public and private health services, and the types of ailments.

The numbers in this table are derived from Sundar (1995), who based her analysis on data obtained from a health survey conducted by the National Council of Applied Economic Research (NCAER) in 1993. Similar findings are presented in studies by Bhat (1993), Berman and Khan (1993) and Kumar, Krishna and Kanbargi (1994). These analyses consistently show that a majority of people seek care during illness from private rather than public providers for out-patient care. A slight majority of ill people seek care from public providers for in-patient care. However, given that the out-patient episodes are much more common than the in-patient ones, a clear majority of all visits in India are to the private providers.

Another important feature of the health care system in India is that even visits to public facilities generally involve considerable out-of-pocket expenditures.

Numerous studies have shown that even consumers from the lowest income quintile often pay considerable amounts out of pocket for curative treatment by public providers [Upleker and George 1994; Sundar 1995; Planning Commission 1996].

These expenditures may take the form of payments for medicines, laboratory tests, dressings, linen and/or food or direct payments to providers. The right hand side of this table highlights that average spending per out-patient episode at the public facilities is about 40 per cent of the average expenditure on visits to the private sector, while the public in-patient treatment expenditures average about a quarter of the private in-patient treatment costs. Taken together, these two features of the Indian system imply that treatment from both categories of facilities imposes considerable financial burdens on individuals. Estimates vary and depend upon the definitions of 'public' and 'curative'.

But a consistent pattern emerges, suggesting that about three-fourths of all the expenditure for curative health services are private, and only one-quarter is public.

Given the extent of the burden, there is a need for greater protection-whether through public provision, conventional insurance, public subsidies or communitybased financing. The paper argues that such devices, of which India has a mix, are different types of 'insurance'. The reasoning is that any arrangement that enables the consumers to avoid, delay or reduce full payment is a form of insurance. Earlier literature on the Indian insurance system often ignored this full array of arrangements and confined itself to the formal system of insurance by companies like the GIC.

Table 3 indicates in summary form how curative services are paid for by various population groups. Each row in the table refers to different employment segments, while the first eight columns correspond to different mechanisms used to pay for the health care services. The 'X's are our best guesses of the approximate proportions of expenditures for each population segment on each type of payment system. The last column of the table estimates approximately the number of employees in that population group, while the last row at the end of table represents our estimate of the share of total expenditures arising from that payment system.

We would like to reiterate that the numbers shown in this table are our best guesses based on literature review and discussions with people. The point to note about this table is that no matter what kind of insurance a person has, there is always some out-of-pocket expense (see column marked 'out of pocket'); the extent of that expense depends on the type of insurance.

PUBLIC HEALTH FACILITIES

The best documented and largest system of health care delivery in India is the diverse network of hospitals, primary health centres, community health centres, dispensaries and speciality facilities financed and managed by the central and state local governments. These facilities are officially available to the entire population either free or for nominal charges.2 Along with some other networks of village health workers, maternal and child health programmes and speciality disease prevention programmes these public facilities carry out a central role in India's primary health care system. Numerous studies have indicated that these facilities are mostly underfunded, understaffed and short of drugs and essential supplies and that they sometimes suffer from low morale and inadequate work motivation [Upleker and George 1994; World Bank 1995]. Household surveys consistently report concern about the quality of these public facilities as one of the reasons why people seek treatment elsewhere [Duggal and Amin 1993; Sundar 1995; Shariff 1996]. Some observations also reveal that higher-income households and individuals with privileged access to other facilities avoid public health care services whenever possible. Households in the top 20 per cent of income distribution in Maharashtra make as much as 95 per cent of their visits for treatment to private facilities [Upleker and George 1994, based on Duggal and Amin 1989]. Discussion of the problems with referral hospitals is found in Sanyal and Tulasidhar (1995).

The health facilities made available to the public are managed and operated under the authority of central and state agencies. The state governments mostly own and manage the public sector delivery system and have to bear the costs of operation. But the central government plays a major role in the planning, financing and transfer of resources that determine new investment in health facilities and specialised programmes.

Much of the funding for health facilities originates from the union ministry of health and family welfare and is channelled to the state governments, which retain considerable authority for the spending decisions. Virtually all decisions are made by the central and state governments-including the staffing and supply decisions, with little autonomy for the providers of health care at the lower levels. Over the years, the central government has been the main source of funds for the primary health care facilities, whereas the states bear the major responsibility of recurrent costs, especially the costs of running hospitals. This system has added to the overall inefficiency of public health facilities.

CENTRAL GOVERNMENT HEALTH SCHEME

The Central Government Health Scheme (CGHS) was introduced in 1954 as a contributory health scheme to provide comprehensive medical care to the central government employees and their families. It was basically designed to replace the cumbersome and expensive system of reimbursements (ministry of health and family welfare, Annual Report 1993-94). Separate dispensaries are maintained for the exclusive use of the central government employees covered by the scheme. Over the years the coverage has grown substantially with provision for the nonallopathic systems of medicine as well as for allopathy. By 1993, there were a total of about 308 dispensaries-of which 230 were allopathic dispensaries. In addition, there were several polyclinics, laboratories and dental units under the scheme. The total number of beneficiaries was 4.5 million by 1993. In addition, the CGHS reimburses patients for part of their out of pocket costs on treatment at the government hospitals and some other facilities. The list of beneficiaries includes all categories of current as well as former government employees, members of parliament and so on. Since the large central bureaucracy in India definitely belongs to the middle-income and high-income categories, they are likely to make aboveaverage use of health services.

The CGHS is widely criticised from the point of view of quality and accessibility. A study by the NCAER (1993) on public hospitals in Delhi highlights many such problems. For instance, it suggests that people used hospitals disproportionately for access to specialist consultants and notes that individuals showed up without any referrals in 83 per cent of these cases. Other problems included long waiting periods, significant out of pocket costs of treatment (Rs 1,507 for first treatment in an episode), inadequate supplies of medicines and equipment, inadequate staff and conditions that are often unhygienic.

EMPLOYEES STATE INSURANCE SCHEME

Established in 1948, the Employees State Insurance Scheme (ESIS) is an insurance system which provides both the cash and the medical benefits. It is managed by the Employees State Insurance Corporation (ESIC), a wholly government-owned enterprise. It was conceived as a compulsory social security benefit for workers in the formal sector. The original legislation creating the scheme allowed it to cover only factories which have been 'using power' and employing 10 or more workers. However, since 1989 the scheme has been expanded, and it now includes all such factories which are 'not using power' and employing 20 or more persons. A useful overview of the ESIC programme is provided in Subrahmanya (1995). Mines and plantations are explicitly excluded from coverage under the ESIS Act. As of January 1995, the programme covered 1,62,191 employers employing 6.6 million people, or altogether 29 million employees and dependents. Only employees earning basic salaries of less than Rs 3,000 (recently enhanced to Rs 6,500) per month are eligible for ESIS cover. Any establishment offering benefits similar to or better than the ESIS is exempt. However, it is not clear how many persons are currently being exempted [Subrahmanya 1995].

The premiums for the ESIS are paid through a payroll tax of 4 per cent levied on the employer and a tax of 1.5 per cent levied on the employee (recently changed to 4.75 per cent and 1.75 per cent respectively).

As of 1993-94, medical benefits have comprised nearly 70 per cent of the total benefits provided under the scheme which also include cash payment for illness, maternity, temporary or permanent disablement, survivorship and funeral expenses. Health-benefit expenses grew 82 per cent from 1992-93 to 1993-94, as against a small decline in the number of employees covered [Subrahmanya 1995].

The primary way in which the medical benefits are provided under the ESIS is through the facilities dedicated to those on the rolls of this scheme. As of 1993-94, there were 1,427 dispensaries with 5,320 doctors, and 23,348 hospital beds (4.5 per cent of the national total) in 118 dedicated hospitals and 42 hospital annexes [Subrahmanya 1995]. Patients requiring treatment from specialists not available at the ESIS hospitals can receive them at the speciality facilities, with the ESIS programme bearing the expenses [Shariff 1995].

The programme has come under serious criticism from users, internal review committees and outside researchers. Subrahmanya (1995) quotes extensively from several such reviews and studies. A threepart article in the Times of India (Bombay, May 14-16, 1995) described the ESIS in Maharashtra as "falling to pieces in more ways than one". A committee for review of the scheme noted that "the criticism has been persistent and scathing" and that "the medical benefits provided have not kept up with the standard of facilities provided by the private clinics and diagnostic centres". A similar opinion was expressed by Ratnam (1995), who notes that "the operation of the ESI scheme and administration of hospitals and dispensaries under the scheme are also seriously faulted and scorned by both the employees and employers".

A report based on detailed patient surveys in Gujarat [Shariff 1994] found that more than half of those covered did not seek care from the ESIS facilities. The dominant reason given in the report was the "unsatisfactory nature of ESI services (which includes low quality drugs and long waiting periods)". This report has also revealed "impudent behaviour of ESIS personnel, lack of interest on the part of employers and low awareness of ESI procedures". The same study found instances in which employers deprive workers of their rights to coverage by not informing them of the necessary details, disallowing injury claims by changing eligibility conditions with retrospective effect, and manipulation of the work schedules of part-time employees so as to make them ineligible for ESIS coverage [Shariff 1994].

These reviews are consistent with our discussions with private and public firms in preparation of this note. One private firm dismissed the ESIS by saying that a person has to be "dead or unconscious before he will visit an ESIS facility". Other respondents indicate that their employees avoid ESIS coverage at all costs, even if it means reporting additional taxable income so as to become ineligible for the programme.

Mediclaim Policy of the GIC

The GIC was set up by the government in 1973 as a public sector organisation to market a range of insurance services, including hospitalisation cover. It introduced the standard 'Mediclaim' health insurance scheme in 1986, and became operational in 1987. This-policy was modified in 1996 to allow for differentials in premium for six age groups: 5-45, 46-55, 56-65, 66-70, 71-75 and 76 plus. This policy was framed by the GIC for both groups and individuals.

Before the GIC came into existence, a number of private insurance companies were engaged in offering group health insurance cover to most corporate bodies. With the formation of the GIC these companies were merged into four of its subsidiaries: the National Insurance Corporation (Calcutta), New India Assurance Company (Bombay), Oriental Insurance Company (New Delhi) and United Insurance Company (Madras). All the four companies operate nationally, although each has a regional concentration reflective of the location of its home office. They offer a full range of insurance types, with health accounting for a very small share of their total business.

One purpose of the merger of all the insurance companies was to standardise the coverage and various medical benefits. This was indeed accomplished. The standard Mediclaim policy covers only hospital care and domiciliary hospitalisation benefits. Although some insurance companies have earlier experimented with direct reimbursement to hospitals and other providers, at present all that is offered is reimbursement insurance. With this the 'enrollees' are reimbursed for their medical claims only after the payments have been made out of pocket to the provider.

The GIC so prescribes premiums, eligibility and benefit coverage for all the four subsidiaries that they do not compete along any of these dimensions. All four firms have significant delays in claims processing. We discuss these delays and other related issues below. Detailed overviews of the Mediclaim programme have been provided in studies by

Ratnam (1995) and the GIC (1995). These reviews present a more favourable user attitude to Mediclaim than to ESIS. This -is clearly reflected in enrolment trends. -Whereas enrolment in the ESIS programme has increased by only 10 per cent over the past five years, enrolment in Mediclaim insurance has increased by 174 per cent over the same period. The number of persons covered by the Mediclaim policies at the end of 1994 was 1.8 million. It is striking how premium revenues have grown more than twice as fast as the number of covered lives between 1989-90 and 1994-95 and how the number of claims settled has grown even faster than premium revenues. Thus far, the premium revenue of Mediclaim has managed to keep ahead of claim payments.

This, however may not hold good in future owing to the accelerating growth in amounts paid to the settled claims. It is also revealing that the claims per covered person have been growing 37.5 per cent annually between 1989-90 and 1994-95. One of the major weaknesses of Mediclaim is that it covers only hospitalisation and domiciliary expenses, leaving out routine out-patient care. Moreover, the coverage is subject to numerous exclusions, coverage limits and restrictions on eligibility. Many of the people that we spoke to mentioned incidents in which either the medical spending claim was disallowed or only partial reimbursement was received. A further criticism of Mediclaim is that the premiums are high in relation to the claim payments: as can be seen in Table 5, column 4, the average claim payments are only 58 per cent of average premiums.

Finally, there seems to be a mutually beneficial relationship between the Mediclaim programme and most of the corporate hospitals. These hospitals get regular business from the middle and upper income segments of the population [Phadke 1994] which are now increasingly covered by Mediclaim. These and other issues will be discussed further.

Specialised Insurance Scheme

The Life Insurance Corporation of India (LIC) introduced a speciality insurance programme in 1993 which covered medical expenses for only four dreaded diseases. This programme was withdrawn subsequently, but reintroduced in 1995. By definition, it is very limited in scope. It does not, therefore, serve to reduce the risk of financial burdens to any significant extent. It also remains to be seen whether or not this programme will be a popular method of insurance.

The GIC's Jan Arogya Bima Policy is yet another scheme of medical reimbursement being offered to people on an individual basis. The annual premium for the youngest people age group is only Rs 70, as against the coverage limit of Rs 5,000 per year. Higher premiums are charged for older persons or those with spouses or dependents. Yet the premiums remain low in relation to the maximum coverage. Even this low-maximum coverage level will provide considerable coverage against low cost hospitalisations. Another significant difference is that it also covers maternity expenses. Apart from these few differences, this policy retains most of the Mediclaim features. It remains to be seen how successful is in comparison to Mediclaim.

EMPLOYER-MANAGED FACILITIES

Most discussions of health insurance in India end after the ESIS and Mediclaim are dealt with. Yet these are not the only forms of health insurance in India. "Employer-managed health facilities", and the "reimbursements of health expenses by employers" are also ways to insure people against the risk of illness. These facilities are common for large public and private enterprises. Expenses incurred on these facilities are generally not tabulated in official records. Certain observations by Ratnam (1995) on this issue are very revealing, as is this one:

Nearly half of the public sector companies did not specify financial limits because almost all public sector manufacturing enterprises covered, being large in terms of size of employment, invariably have their own dispensary and hospitals and provide medicines, etc, across the counter, usually within the company premises/township. The same applies to large private sector companies, which too have similar facilities and practices (1995:4).

Ratnam also describes the medical benefits provided by 18 public and 99 large private establishments. In Table 3 we speculate that perhaps about 30 per cent of the expenditure incurred on curative health by the public sector employees and their dependents is provided directly by the employers. This may be about 10 per cent for the large-scale private establishments. Krishnamurthy (1995) documents another segment of the Indian population that is covered by employer-managed facilities: the plantation sector. This sector employs about 1.6 million workers, and health services are regulated by the Plantation Labour Act of 1951. This Act (and subsequent legislation) specifies minimum standards for dispensaries and hospitals. Krishnamurthy also tries to show that some plantations more than comply with the hospital standards, while others do not (1995:34).

Like the plantations, the railways also maintain an extensive set of clinics and hospitals for their employees and their dependents. The mining sector provides medical and other facilities to its employees-particularly the mica mines and the iron ore, manganese ore, chrome ore, limestone and dolomite mines (Ministry of Health and F W 1992).

Another segment of the public sector which maintains its own medical services is the defence set-up which along with other security forces (police, paramilitary forces) employs about two to three million persons. Yet another segment which provides some of these facilities to its employees comprises certain educational institutions, particularly universities. These facilities no doubt compete with other public facilities for staff and financial resources.

Although precise estimates are not possible in the absence of data, it appears that around 50 million persons would have been covered either wholly or partially by employer-managed facilities, and the expenditures on these facilities may be much larger in magnitude than that on the ESIS.

EMPLOYER REIMBURSEMENT OF HEALTH EXPENSES

A common but frequently-ignored segment of the health insurance system in India comprises numerous reimbursement plans offered by the employers for private medical expenses in the private sector, as well as in autonomous institutions and organisations-including commercial banks.

For many workers this is the only form of insurance other than public facilities. All the seven large firms we spoke to in Delhi said they offered reimbursement schemes in addition to GIC or ESIS cover. Two kinds of reimbursement systems are predominant. In about half the cases, the system requires employees to set apart a share of their own income to save towards medical expenses. In all such plans, employees are able to spend up to the annual level of their own contribution. Typically, limits are set which depend upon a given employee's salary. In some cases contributions are voluntary, but in most cases they are not. Coverage for outpatient expenditures is more common than coverage for hospitalisation expenses.

The other common system of reimbursement is an employer self-insurance system, generally known as the medical benefit or medical allowance scheme. Under this arrangement, employees incurring medical expenses are required to submit claims to their employers for reimbursement, and reimbursements are not linked to the individual's contribution. In general, such programmes have coverage limits which vary according to the employee's salary or job category.

Using data collected through a survey of 99 private and 18 public enterprises, Ratnam (1995) provides a very useful overview of the reimbursement systems now in vogue. He notes that employees in most private enterprises are provided with some form of medical reimbursement or medical allowance facilities and that limits and coverage features are quite variable. A few companies like Bajaj Auto Limited offer special assistance to their employees such as a programme for insuring those whose annual health care expenditures exceed Rs 20,000. In such cases, the company pays 75 per cent of the health care expenditure amounting up to Rs 1,00,000 not covered by other insurance programmes.

The NGO Sector

An important part of private health finance in India is the services provided by voluntary and charitable organisations. As noted by Berman (November 1996), while such groups do not account for a large share of health care, they are often the only source of health services, or the only trusted one, for the population they serve. While it is very difficult to estimate even approximately the exact coverage of these varied services, Berman speculates that they cover more than 5 per cent of the population. A review of non-governmental approaches to community health has been provided by the Ford Foundation under its Anubhav project.

This project has looked into all aspects of NGO involvement in the provision of health services, and may therefore be used as an important source of information about the NGOs and their activities. Some of the important NGOs offering health services are Child in Need Institute (CINI), Self-Employed Women's Association (SEWA), Streehitkarni and Parivar Seva Sanstha. Most of these NGOs offer comprehensive assistance packages with the underlying assumption that health is only one aspect of development and should therefore be tackled along with other social problems in a holistic fashion. The government has realised quite early that NGOs could complement-the services they offer. One encouraging feature of this realisation has been the co-operation and help extended to many NGOs by the government. Each five-year plan has a stated amount for allocation to the NGO sector. For example, the Seventh Plan earmarked Rs 150 crore for them. The government has used the health sector NGOs for two main purposes: to train its functionaries and to implement its health care delivery programmes [Sundar 1995]. CINI and SEWA are good examples of such co-operation.

To sum up, NGOs are providing valuable health services in many parts of India, especially in the rural areas and to disadvantaged people. It remains clear, however, that despite its growing role this sector has not yet reached a level where it can make a significant dent in private expenditure on curative care in India.

Private Out-of-Pocket Expenses

Almost all segments of the Indian population bear some direct out-of-pocket expenses for the utilisation of the health care services, the lightest burden being borne by workers in the public sector or those employed in large private firms. The heaviest burden is borne by the people engaged in non-formal rural and urban activities. Even government employees with other forms of coverage bear considerable out-of-pocket expenses because they use private facilities and pay for drugs and services which would otherwise be cost free. Though firm evidence does not exist, we estimate that approximately 65 per cent of all spending on curative and diagnostic care in India consists of direct out-of-pocket expenses which are not reimbursed and which therefore impose a significant burden on consumers.

PROGNOSIS

The existing structure of paying for health care in India has important implications for effective government policy and the direction of health insurance. In this section we interpret the above description of the Indian system. We call this a prognosis because it attempts to understand the causes and consequences of the problems facing our curative health care system. We defer till the next section a prospectus which seeks to suggest certain directions in which the health system in India might move.

Financial Burdens for Curative Health Care

The financial burdens of health care in India are enormous and growing. Given the constraints and difficulties in raising additional public resources and the rapid growth in spending on health care, if will be very difficult for the public health system to keep pace. We argue that even if the government decides to increase the level of public spending on health services dramatically, a substantial financial burden would still remain for users of health services. To be more precise, if direct public spending on health facilities is increased by 50 per cent-which would indeed be a remarkable achievement-it would at the most reduce the share of private expenditure on health from 75 to 62.5 per cent. It is also very likely that the additional public spending would augment private expenditures rather than replace them.

Public spending should be focused more on primary health care and treatment for those with very limited ability to pay. Already, the demand which for such services exceeds the supply [World Development Report, 1993]. There is enormous scope, therefore for increasing public spending on health without reducing the demand for private health services. The public health sector is rapidly becoming the "provider of the last resort". Higher income individuals and those without chronic disabilities rely increasingly on private providers with some degree of insurance or reimbursement. As this progresses, it may result in further deterioration in the quality of public health facilities and the public support for them.

Limitations of Insurance Sector

An important conclusion emerging from the preceding discussion is that a large proportion of the population in India does not have the choice of facilities available to the workforce of the formal sector. The large number of separate networks of providers tends to make for reduce inefficiency and the choice among providers: only a limited set of providers is offered to a given employee.

A majority of the large public and private establishments are either self-insuring or provide reimbursement plans to their employees. These employers may be more than willing to switch over to private third party insurance, should it become available. This is particularly true for the largescale enterprises which provide their own clinics and personnel. Given that the employee demand for quality treatment and specialists' care is increasing rapidly, these enterprises would find it worth their while to switch to an insurance structure.

Reforming ESIS and CGHS

Although the number of beneficiaries of the ESIS has grown modestly over time, enrolment has not kept pace with growth in the GIC, the organised sector or even the number of low-wage workers that the ESIS is supposed to cover. For reasons discussed above, employees have been reluctant to avail themselves of the ESIS facilities. Here again, the argument of improving quality of services offered under the ESIS holds. Numerous studies have shown that the providers of treatment at ESIS and CGHS facilities do not have adequate incentive to exert themselves. These facilities generally suffer from low provider morale, understaffing and equipment shortages. Improvements in the quality of services offered by these facilities can be effected by decentralising the decision-making process and introducing reforms in financing norms. An incentive may be provided by allowing the facilities to charge user fees-even if the fees are paid by the government on the basis of the patient-load factor. An alternative strategy might be to merge the two systems of facilities with the rest of the public health system.

Lack of Incentive for Cost Optimisation

There are important signs that health insurance in India is causing a 'moral hazard' problem. In a health insurance setting, the hazard can be of two types: insurance may induce individuals either to take fewer precautions to avoid the need for treatment or to use more health services when they fall ill. Both actions tend to increase health expenditures. Increased spending when illness is the main phenomenon observed in health markets: patients and health care providers both respond to the presence of insurance by increasing the level of spending on health care. In some cases this increased spending may be socially desirable, such as spending on essential primary care or underutilised, expensive in-patient treatment. In other cases it may lead to increasing levels of inappropriate care, unnecessary treatment, excessive laboratory tests or overcharging. This moral hazard may be reduced by changing incentives either on the demand side or on the supply side.

The current structure of insurance offered in India generally steers clear of cost-sharing. While substantial cost-sharing may reduce access to medicare, low levels of cost-sharing may deter unnecessary treatment.

Furthermore, if consumers do not face at least some out of pocket expenditure on health care, they may not have sufficient incentive to avoid the most expensive facilities, or the most extensive set of diagnostic tests. Results from other countries (e g, the Rand Health Experiment in the US) suggest that even nominal fees would discourage a significant amount of use.

Charging higher fees or higher co-payment for more expensive facilities will encourage consumers to get referrals and become better informed about the necessity of treatment. The lack of a governmental focus on curative care has led to almost unregulated growth in the private medical system. Phadke (1994) describes some of these problems: substandard but expensive private medical education, lack of continuing medical education and training for doctors in the private sector, irrational drug use, unnecessary medical interventions, lack of regulation and standardisation of nursing homes, etc. These features often inflate costs for the health system as well as for consumers.

Nor are supply side incentives being used to constrain expenditures. As a matter of fact, the GIC subsidiaries indirectly encourage expensive corporate hospital treatment by not devoting enough attention to the appropriateness of claims. Our reading is that it may be easier to get reimbursement if one is treated in one of these expensive and well known facilities rather than in a lesser one.

So far as the monitoring of claims is concerned the GIC subsidiaries appear to be more preoccupied with whether services are being provided with pre-existing conditions than to whether or not the fees paid are justifiable or the facility used by the claimant is qualified and the treatment appropriate. As more expensive and more complex procedures are increasingly being resorted to, it will-be important for the insurers to play a more active role in claims monitoring and fraud detection. Computerising the entire claims processing system would facilitate this.

Need to Reform the GIC

There is a lot of debate on the scope for 'privatisation' of health insurance. The Mediclaim system comes closest to this concept. The system of having four dominant insurers-who generally compete on service quality but have regulated prices, eligibility and benefit features-does avoid some of the more severe problems of adverse selection and undesirable forms of benefitfeature competition. Other problems with the GIC system, however, remain.

Evidence suggests that over the past five years the GIC's claims have been growing at more than 30 per cent a year-which substantially exceeds the growth of public health-care spending or individual spending. It seems plausible that this growth is in part the moral hazard response to insurance. However, such high rates of increase imply that there is enormous potential for increased spending by other segments of the poulation, should the insurance coverage be extended to new groups.

The manner in which the GIC premiums are changed from one year to the next is clever in that it ensures that the corporation does not have to take in premiums that are persistently below claims. A further clarification on this is as under.

Even the high margin of GIC premiums over claims understates the true margins. Subsequent-year premiums are calculated on the basis of incurred claims, not on paid claims. If the claims are eventually denied the difference would apparently go unreconciled while adjusting future premiums. Besides increasing profit margins this feature builds in an incentive for the insurers to delay payment on claims. This is one of the major complaints against the GIC's Mediclaim policy.

The existing GIC programme covers only in-patient and hospital domiciliary expenses. This leaves consumers to shoulder financial burdens arising from out-patient expenses. Finally, there is a lot of uncertainty about the amount an insurer will reimburse and the time within which it will do the needful. This discourages resort to insurance.

Unregulated Limitation of Coverage There is considerable resentment of the current practice of permitting GIC subsidiaries to exclude from coverage a long list of specified conditions and selected chronic conditions which are pre-existing at the time of enrolment. The existing Mediclaim plan excludes all treatment costs for HIV or other sexually transmitted diseases (STDs). Such exclusions in most developed countries are regulated and not left to the decision of the insurance companies. A desirable policy might be to allow exclusions for a fixed period (say one or two years), after which the health plan enrollees may become eligible for coverage.

The insurance companies and some researchers might argue that disorders existing at the time of enrolment are known health risks and, therefore, not insurable events. It is true that these expenses will be predictably higher, and insurance companies will tend to lose money on these enrollees. However, if all health plans are required to cover chronic conditions on the same basis, such coverage need not create unfair losses. Also, it would be unfair on equity grounds to force those who face chronic (or selected excluded) diseases to pay for the full cost of treatment out of pocket or to shift the burden of treatment for such diseases to the public health care providers.

Regulation is also needed to ensure that the health plans do not enter into competition for attracting only profitable, low cost patients. There is danger that biased selection will undermine GIC's recent efforts to expand coverage limits. In 1996, a new benefit plan was introduced which offers substantially higher caps on coverage (up to Rs 3,00,000 versus an upper limit of Rs 33,000 under the previous system).

Although there is some evidence of biased selechon, this has so far not been a serious issue in India. The fact that group coverage predominates over individual coverage is a possible explanation. It clearly suggests that the average claim expenses increase with age. The third column shows that premiums do not increase appreciably with age. This indicates adverse selection: if there were no biased selection there would be the same proportion of enrollees in each category. However, the problem has yet to assume a serious dimension.

Relative Neglect of Unorganised Sector Employees

The existing Mediclaim structure does not properly serve the large segment of population engaged in low-paid informal activities. There are several reasons. First, the procedure used to fix the Mediclaim premium strongly favours the large-scale public and private establishments. It is clear from Table 6 that the premiums on individual policies are substantially higher than those on group policies. This table also shows that the discount on premium for group insurance ranges from 15 per cent for a 101-500 group to 66.7 per cent for a group more than 50,000 strong. In our view, such discounting policies fail to conform to the equity criterion and appear somewhat regressive. As an outcome of this policy, we notice that individual coverage remains completely subdued in the entire scheme. Since the bulk of the group coverage emanates from the formal sector, the discounting norms strongly favour formal sector enterprises and leave more than 90 per cent of those engaged in informal economic activities to fend for themselves.

PROSPECTUS: DIRECTIONS FOR THE FUTURE

In most policy debates in India, the issue of equity in the delivery of health care has been given precedence over that of efficiency. It may, however, be argued that the current system, which is a mix of different forms of insurance, has not been able to achieve even this objective to a significant extent. Nor has the system been able to utilise available public resources most efficiently. As the health system in India is complex, simple prescriptions for its improvement may not suffice. We, however, attempt to suggest some critical areas where some changes can be made at appropriate times. These recommendations are not mutually exclusive and often overlap in their policy implications.

Consolidation and Improvement in Cost-Effectiveness

At this stage, it is important to strengthen and improve the existing public-funded facilities to improve efficiency, quality and equity. We suggest the following three areas specifically related to insurance for the consideration of policy planners: (i) Focus on public spending on primary care and public health activities: We mention this approach first because it remains the core of public health care spending. Reducing the burdens of disease is an important mechanism for simultaneously reducing the financial burden of treatment. It also affects the health of population directly. (ii) Reform ESIS and CGHS: To go by a growing body of evidence, the CGHS and ESIS facilities are performing poorly in terms of both coverage and quality of care. It may make for greater efficiency to merge them into a single public health network or even convert them into private facilities. One strategy may be to convert coverage-for those currently covered by the ESIS and the CGHS to policies similar to Mediclaim. (iii) Withdraw or reduce public subsidisation of services for those with ample ability to pay: At present there are many public subsidies to health services which may be dispensed with. For example, expensive tertiary level public hospitals are subsidised to the same extent as the inexpensive primary care public facilities. Facilities such as the Apollo Hospital in New Delhi receive public loans and equipment; and corporate health insurance receives a tax subsidy even when it is so costly that only the better off can afford it. Given the paucity of public resources, there is little justification for subsidising such costly services.

One way of reducing these subsidies may be to initiate a uniform system of user fees in most of the public hospitals in the country. There should be careful studies of demand and supply conditions before a schedule for the user fees is drawn up. Such studies can be launched in West Bengal, Karnataka, Andhra Pradesh and Punjab-assisted by the World Bank recently to improve and upgrade their secondary hospitals.

Public facilities should also be permitted to recover additional fees from the privately insured patients that they treat. There is no reason for the public sector to fully subsidise those with ample ability to pay.

Regulate Private Health Care

The private health sector will continue to be a major player in providing health services, especially curative health care. The growth of health insurance increases the need for licensing and regulating private health providers since firm and specific criteria would be needed to decide upon appropriate services and fees.

Given that private sector health care is predominant in India, that it has grown rapidly, and that it is likely to grow even more under the liberalised environment there is an urgent need for recognition of its far-reaching impact on the health of the people. Many aspects of regulation (for example, those related to drugs) have already been discussed by others [Tulsidhar 1996]. We will not go into them here except to mention the ones that have a direct impact on the out-of-pocket expenses of individuals and health insurance.

(i) Licensing: Implement a programme of strict licensing of all hospitals, nursing homes and medical practitioners. There are at present virtually no laws to regulate the establishment of hospitals and nursing homes in India. This not only means that there are no minimum standards, but also that insurance companies are unable to establish criteria for appropriate reimbursements for treatment at different levels of facilities.

(ii) Fees: Fees structure at private facilities should be formalised and monitored, mainly to avoid exploitation of uneducated patients but also to facilitate the establishment of appropriate reimbursements for specified procedures by insurers. Written itemised receipts should be made compulsory, and published rate lists should be either displayed or supplied on demand.

(iii) Subsidies: Reduce public subsidies of private corporate facilities. As already mentioned, subsidies to corporate facilities are not really justified, and these should be allowed to compete for funds and other resources in the market like any other commercial enterprise.

Review and Revise Mediclaim

If the objective of providing some kind of insurance to the general population is a priority area for health policy planners, a beginning can be made by carefully reviewing the mediclaim system. Some areas which need particular attention are as follows.

(i) Premium structure: The current premiums are too high in relation to claims payments. The current bonus and 'malus' system for adjusting claims is such that the insurer is always guaranteed at least a 20 per cent margin over the previous year's level of incurred claims. Also there does not appear to be a mechanism through which premiums are reconciled according to settled claims rather than proffered claims. Finally, the discount on group insurance for large employers is unrealistically large. Revising the premium schedules will make health insurance more accessible to individuals from lower socio-economic categories.

(ii) Out-patient coverage: There is a need for insurance cover to meet the growing cost of out-patient treatment. The reasons why some people pay a great deal out of pocket even when they are already covered by the GIC or the ESIS should be identified so that corrective measures could be devised.

The obtaining of referrals before going to expensive secondary and tertiary facilities can be encouraged by providing for the GIC to give lower reimbursement when higher-level care is sought without a referral.

(iii) Limit exclusions for pre-existing conditions: At present Mediclaim does not cover most of the chronic or preexisting conditions. This leaves out large segments of the population who suffer from diseases like diabetes, hearing disorders and STDs. Such exclusions should be carefully reviewed and amended, for example, exclusions for pre-existing conditions can be made valid for not more than a year.

(iv) Require greater efficiency in processing of claims: Consumers should be given a time schedule so that there is no uncertainty about the amount of reimbursement and the time within which they can hope for reimbursed. Delays in prepayment and arbitrary denial of claims need to be minimised.

(v) Increase visibility: In our assessment Mediclaim is not an exceptionally popular scheme. Most prospective consumers know little or nothing about it. This should be rectified through publicity.

(vi) Require greater monitoring of fraud and excessive fees: The government should make it mandatory for all insurance companies to devote more resources to monitoring fraudulent claims and establishing schedules of appropriate fees for specified procedures.

Regulation of Health Insurance

The foregone points regarding a complete review of the health insurance sector are related to its regulation as well. This suggestion is applicable to all the health insurance agencies, be it the GIC or any other corporation or company. In addition to regulation of premium structure, exclusion clauses, extent of coverage, etc, the following measures may also be necessary.

(i) Discourage 'dreaded disease' or other specialised policies: The government should discourage schemes like the one currently offered by LIC which covers only four selected diseases. Such specialisation further segments the coverage rather than broaden it.

(ii) Encourage health insurance for the specially vulnerable: Health insurance cover for the elderly, unemployed, permanently disabled, etc, deserves special attention. Subsidised insurance plans for these categories of people are worth exploring. Mediclaim benefits, now available only to employees, their spouses and children, may be extended to dependent adults (perhaps just grandparents initially) for a supplementary premium. This is just one example of which can be done.

Encouraging Community-Based Health Programmes

Community-based health insurance programmes offer the best hope for reducing the financial burdens caused by sickness to a large segment of the low-income population. They would benefit from systematic review and government subsidies. Conventional reimbursement-type insurance systems are unlikely to be effective in rural areas, where consumers have limited ability to pay. Community-based programmes need to be fostered.

The SEWA insurance system, and those of other NGOs as described in Uplekar and George (1994) should be strongly promoted. These NGOs have been innovative in both raising finance and initiating community financing. For example, there are instances of user fees for selected services, pre-payment insurance schemes for curative care, and community income-generating programmes. Although, the government is already collaborating with the NGOs, there is a need to recognise the significance of their role more explicitly and give them financial, administrative and other support.

A related point to be made is that not only reimbursement type policies but also insurance plans which integrate financing and delivery of care should be encouraged. To be found in developed countries, such integrated insurers and providers are mostly able to manage care and monitor expenses.

Need for an Information Bank

This and several other studies have identified a variety of insurance issues that have not been fully documented or understood. There is an immediate need for more information on various aspects of demand for medical care (in the context of health insurance) to enable us to understand:

(a) the distribution of medical expenditures, and

(b) the question of who ultimately pays for them.

Greater information is required for assessing the prices, quality and access of providers and their patterns of operation. Insurance companies may be encouraged to keep data in a format that is user-friendly and accessible to researchers and regulators.

CONCLUDING REMARKS

Central to the preceding discussion have been two important limitations of the present health care system and its financing in India. The first limitation is exceptionally high health care expenditure over threefourths of which is private out-of-pocket expenditure.

The other one relates to unsatisfactory outcomes of these expenses. Most of the out-of-pocket expenses are borne by households engaged in lowincome informal economic activities. Those in the organised sector are covered by health plans.

But the majority of the low-income people are left to suffer either from poor health-care delivery or to incur high out-of-pocket expenses, or both. Even those covered by health plans experience growing inefficiencies and low quality of services. A revamp of the health system with expanded and improved health insurance facilities, is therefore essential.

The paper comes up with a series of recommendations including improvements in delivery of health care and its financing, efficient functioning of the ESIS and the CGHS, ammending the Mediclaim system to tap the huge market potential, modification of the benefits and claims system of Mediclaim policies, alterations in the exclusion clause, enhanced competition and the possible privatisation of health insurance within a strict regulatory regime.

TIME FOR CONSCIOUS REVOLUTION

Healthcare, with global revenue of over Rs.2.75 trillion is the largest industry in the world. Where does India stand against the new disease management practice in health insurance in developed countries?

The nation of India with a population of 1000 million experiences a vast inequity that exists in the healthcare industry with barely 3 per cent of the population covered by some form of health insurance, either social or private. The guiding principle of Bhore Committee in 1946 that 'no individual should fail to secure adequate medical care because of inability to pay for it' looks unreachable still, after 50 years of Indian independence.

In India, presently the health insurance exists in the form of Mediclaim policy offered to the individual or to any group, association or corporate bodies. Although, total expenditure on health in India is nearly 6 per cent of the entire GDP, the government spending is less than 25 per cent against the average spending of 30-40 per cent in other developing countries. Penetration of Mediclaim is currently done by state-owned insurance companies, covering only about 2.5 million people i.e. less than 0.50 per cent of the country's population.

In Alma Ata (in old USSR), a global initiative towards health-related research and action was held in 1978. All the participants, including India, affirmed to ensure health for all by the year 2000, with primary health care as their top priority. But India perhaps understood it in a different manner what Plato said "Attention to health is the greatest hindrance in life". Indian health insurance sector is still an immature baby, victim of 'no common sense' of government.

The primary health care system in India is managed mainly by the shallow structure of government health-care facilities and other public-health care systems in a traditional model of health funding and provision. But, it is unable to justify the demand for health security for 200 million Indian health insurable population mainly due to service costs being out of the reach of many people, absence of good and effective number of physicians, low rate of education programs, less number of hospitals, poor medical equipment and over all, the poor budget of government towards the health program.

Even Social insurance schemes available in India, such as the Employee State insurance Scheme (ESIS) and Central Government Health Scheme (CGHS) have restricted coverage to a very small segment of the population, around 3 per cent.

Therefore, the health insurance policy in India is nothing but a burden of inefficiency of a government run system. Moreover, the uncontrolled and no-innovative attitude of Indian bureaucracy always argued against the private players in the health insurance sector in India. Albert Einstein surly sleeps happily in the grave after seeing the Indian government's practice of health management credo based on what he said fifty years back, "Common sense is the collection of prejudices acquired by the age of eighteen". Unnecessary prejudice never allows our government to open the doors of health insurance to others.

Indian government has never been sensible to understand that the opening of insurance sector in India will move individual health spending to a collective spending backed by a huge capital inflows into the health industry. The existing limited medical coverage and inefficient administration is likely to be demolished by the increasing service efficiency.

Furthermore, the intermediaries like service providers, health management organizations, preferred provider organizations and third party administrators would not only assist in increasing the coverage, but would also improve the quality of the system-the transition of health care from curative to managed care-the disease management as practiced by developed countries.

At its best, disease management is neither a turf protector for specialists nor a marketing vehicle for drug companies. It's a common-sense approach to unifying care for a condition, and it depends on primary care physicians. In other words, disease management is a way to reduce the cost of Health Maintenance Organization (HMOs) and Preferred Provider Organizations (PPOs) in developed countries, more specifically in United States that sharpens the Managed Care plans of health insurance sector. Managed Care plans are so popular in the US that they now employ more than 70 per cent of all the physicians in the country.

Notably, when Disease management decides the profit of insurers by constructing a system of care for a particular condition such as asthma, diabetes or cholesterol, that is intended to reduce costs and improve outcomes, Managed Care is a step ahead of traditional insurance system assuring quality into the system. Disease management means more teamwork between primary care physicians, sub-specialists and non-physician providers. Thus in a disease management program, health plans and physicians attempt to identify patients who would benefit most from intense prevention and treatment protocols. Managed Care, in-turn ensures out-of-pocket costs, are generally lower, and there is far less (if any) paperwork for plan members to contend with.

After comparing this systematic, quality packed, value-added health system with Indian health insurance sector, it is clearly understood, we have a far way to go to touch the global health insurance wave. Replacement of the existing system will hardly do anything, unless a conscious revolution comes with private players in this sector. And "The first duty of a revolutionary is to get away with it". What do you say-time for our government to play revolutionary?

7

HEALTH INSURANCE FOR THE POOR IN INDIA

Community based health insurance (CBHI) is more suited than alternate arrangements to providing health insurance to the low-income people living in developing countries. The universal health insurance scheme, launched recently by the Prime Minister of India, is only one of the forms that CBHI can take. While analysing the proposed scheme, we examine alternate forms of CBHI schemes prevalent in the country.

The development of private health insurance market in the country will not leave the poor unaffected. Insurance sector reform can affect the poor through its effect on the provision of health services (i.e., cost, quality and access) used by the low-income people as well as through its access to financing of health care. In this paper we also explore how insurance sector reforms alter health insurance prospects facing the poor in India, and what changes on the health front affecting the poor have happened or are likely to happen as a result of insurance sector reforms. We conclude that in diverse settings of India all forms of CBHI have a role to play and therefore need to be encouraged by the government through appropriate interventions. Formal insurance providers can also be reigned to serve lowincome population. At the same time, developments in formal health insurance market need to be guided so as to minimise cost escalation of health care provision.

INTRODUCTION

Health care financing in India can be considered almost unique in several respects. One, the share of public financing in total health care financing in the country is considerably low--just around 1% of GDP compared to the average share of 2.8% in lowand middle-income countries or even relative to India's share in disease burden. Two, the beneficiaries of this limited public health financing are not only the poor as one would expect in a limited public spending to be, but also the well-off section of the society. Third, over 80% of the total health financing is private financing, much of which takes the form of out-of-pocket payments (i.e., user charges) and not any prepayment schemes.

Reliance on out-of-pocket payments is not only inefficient and less accountable than other methods of financing, it is also iniquitous to the poor on whom the disease burden falls disproportionately more, who are more susceptible to disease and who are much likely to be pushed into poverty trap (Gumber 1997, Visaria & Gumber 1994). The World Bank (2002) estimates that one-quarter of all Indians fall into poverty as a direct result of medical expenses in the event of hospitalisation. One of the important challenges facing the Indian health policy experts is: how to convert predominantly private out-of-pocket spending into health insurance premium whereby this amount is collected from a much larger group of insured individuals rather than from the limited number households affected by illness.

Another important challenge is: how to provide health insurance to the people who cannot afford to pay (full) premium. Before digging deep into the issues involved let's look at the broad health care financing options.

In financing of health services a country may, in principle, choose between public financing through general taxation or private financing through health insurance. Public financing is justified where equity concern overrides efficiency objective. Where the opposite is true, reliance is often placed on the private insurance market. Equity considerations in private insurance market can generate inefficiency and market failure as it involves tradeoff between desired distribution and the distorted incentives that accompany such redistribution. Therefore, where equity is the prime consideration it can best be achieved under public financing. In practice no health financing system is either purely public or private. Countries where private health insurance dominates, some public financing can still be observed. Similarly, some private insurance can be seen even in a public funded health system. All insurance systems, public or private, must strike a balance between economic efficiency and equity.

The choice between public health financing or private insurance is hardly available to countries like India because of their governments' limited ability to marshal sufficient resources to finance health spending, and also because the nature of employment (where majority of workers are self-employed, or do not have a formal employer or steady employment) is such as to provide little scope for payroll taxes. Given this, heavy reliance on private spending is necessary for financial reasons, notwithstanding the declared policy of the state to provide universal, comprehensive primary health services to the entire population. Private spending may also be desirable on efficiency grounds. But the form that bulk of private spending takes need to change from out-of-pocket payments to private insurance.

Insurance or pooling of risks through prepaid schemes has a number of advantages. Besides being more equitable, it is one of the significant drivers of improvement in the healthcare provision by encouraging investment and innovation. Also, it helps improve the quality and efficiency of public health care system by continually benchmarking it. Private insurance has certain pitfalls too such as leaving out the low-income individuals who may not be able to afford premium, denying coverage to people who are sick, and limiting the coverage for high-cost conditions or services. In a country like India where public health care suffers from poor management, low service quality, weak finances, and lack of responsiveness to patients' needs and demands, development of health insurance is likely to bring improvement in public health care system.

Even the private health sector in India that has grown in an undirected fashion, with virtually no effective guidance on the location and scope of practice, and without effective standards for quality of care or public disclosure on practices and pricing (World Bank 2002). Development of health insurance will necessitate improvement in private sector as well. The pitfalls associated with private health insurance can be reduced through appropriate regulation. To the extent that certain per cent of population can be covered through private health insurance, development of health insurance will tend to reduce the need for government financing of secondary and tertiary care. This would help government to develop and maintain smaller and well targeted system of health care financing to serve people who would not have access to private insurance, and to address public health priorities such as immunisations that are quasi-public goods (Srinivasan 2001).

Before launching any major health initiative, there ought to be a well articulated vision of health care system for the country, and public health policy must be devised to realise that vision. Ideally, certain basic health services, including inpatient care, must be made available to every member of the society. These services must be paid through insurance, which means that every member must have health insurance cover or at least have access to health insurance, with government subsidising insurance premium, in full or in part, for those who cannot afford it. For the upper-and middle-income people, private health insurance market with effective and sound regulation can take care of health financing. However, with the development of private insurance market, only half the country's population can at best be reached.

The other half, which consists of lowincome population (30% of the population below the poverty line and add to it another 20% living dangerously close to this line) is likely to remain outside the ambit of private health insurance unless there is an explicit social obligation in this respect which can come only from insurance regulator. For the low-income people, who are the main focus of this paper, neither government provided nor market mediated arrangement is appropriate. Community based health insurance (CBHI) because of its certain features such as, the voluntary participation of the people, not-for-profit objective in organising the scheme, scheme management by the community itself, and some degree of risk pooling, is more suited to insuring the poor. The CBHI schemes themselves can take different forms. The forms that are prevalent in India are discussed in the paper.

The paper is structured as follows: in the next section (section 2) we discuss different forms of Community Based Health Insurance (CBHI) schemes prevalent in India, and critically examine "universal health insurance scheme" launched in the country recently. Development of private health insurance in the country too will have a bearing on the access to health care services by the poor. Health Insurance for the poor For the low-income people, insurance was never considered to be an option in the past. They were assumed to be too poor to save and pay premium. Hence, the government assumed the responsibility of meeting health care needs of the poor. One could argue that if government pays for the poor anyway, why think of insurance at-all? Instead, why does government not continue providing free health services to the poor, as in the past? Well, the strategy of free public health provision has not worked well in most states. Shrinking budgetary support to the public health services, inefficiency in provision, and unacceptably low quality of these services is reflective of this. Even in states like Tamil Nadu where public health care provision is reasonably developed, and may even get better as the decentralisation process deepens, there are reasons for introducing health insurance.

First, it is being increasingly realised that even low-income people can make small periodic contributions, which can add up to a significant amount, thereby taking some financial burden off from the already strained state revenues. Second, the insured individuals would have an option of going to either public or private service provider, which in turn would generate competition among providers for better services. Finally, health insurance can be used to promote certain desirable behaviour. For example, the Aarogya Raksha scheme of Andhra Pradesh links family planning to health insurance. Conceptually, a society can be thought of as consisting of two groups of individuals, those who can afford to buy health insurance that promises certain "minimum" level of benefit, and those who cannot afford to buy the "minimum" benefit on their own and need some public subsidy. As mentioned above, development of private health insurance may take care of those who can afford to buy insurance.

For those who cannot afford, alternate approaches with some public subsidy are suggested. However, while operationalising the idea, this conceptual distinction gets blurred. Government's attention gets confined only to those who are below the poverty line. While those below the poverty line definitely need to be covered with government support, the non-BPL population with low-income also need to be covered, with our without government support, since market insurance is likely to bypass this section as well. An important policy question here is: how best to target and reach this section of the population? One way is to redefine the BPL population so as to include low-income people as well. Another approach is to include non-BPL population also in the scheme meant for BPL population with lower level of subsidy.

Even though the government's approach is to support voluntary insurance rather than to expand the existing social insurance schemes, the following approaches may be suitable for the different sections of the society. For the upper and the middle income people social insurance and voluntary insurance are suggested to be the two dominant forms of financing health care. State's role is primarily to develop an appropriate legislative framework, to appoint independent regulator, and to formulate procedures and regulations to avoid well documented market failures (Misra et al. 2003). Even for lowincome people who are employed in the formal sector, social insurance may be a better way of providing health protection.

However, it is for the low-income people working in the unorganised sector and those below the poverty line that alternate approaches are needed. One approach suggested in the literature, which is relatively straight forward, is to create a sickness fund for this section of society. The fund could be used to cover all hospitalisation expenses of such families in public facilities as well as designated private facilities. T N Krishna estimates the size of fund required to cover hospitalisation costs of 300 million BPL population. Assuming 4% of BPL population require hospitalisation every year and the cost per episode (at 1995-96 prices) is

Rs. 2,100, the size of fund comes to Rs. 25,000 million per annum. Misra et al. (2003) revised this cost figure and arrived at Rs. 40,000 million required for covering hospitalisation cost per annum of the BPL population. If, instead of directly bearing the cost, government provides them health insurance the demand on government funds may come down significantly as insurance helps in some resource mobilisation from the people themselves.

Health insurance for the poor can take different forms. It could be community based (examples to follow) or non-community based (like Jan Arogya policy of the government). Community Based Health Insurance (CBHI) can itself take several forms. Two types of CBHI schemes that are observed in India are: where an NGO acts as an intermediary between a formal insurance provider and the insured community (for example, SEWA in Ahmedabad, ACCORD in Nilgiris) and where the NGO itself provides insurance to the target community. In the latter case, where an NGO itself insures the target population, the NGO may itself be the health service provider (for example, Sewagram Hospital) or may have an arrangement with the health service provider (for example Tribhuvandas Foundation). All these forms currently exist in the country but only in small pockets. These forms need to be explored. Each of these forms may be relevant depending on the local conditions that vary considerably across regions. For as diverse a country as India there can be no Pan India model. Indeed, CBHI schemes could be designed in a number of ways, depending on the socio-economic characteristics of the target population, health profile of the population, and the health risks prevalent in the region. Even within states different schemes could be designed for different districts. This calls for scientific approach with begins with good experimentation, and fine-tuned subsequently as experience accumulates. The decentralisation process initiated in the country with the 73rd and 74th Constitutional Amendment aimed at promoting local bodies (Panchayati Raj Institutions (PRIs) in the rural areas and Nagar Palikas in the urban areas) has raised hopes of being able to reach the poor through community based initiatives with some subsidy to those who cannot afford the costs (Gumber & Kulkarni 2001).

The real benefit of CBHI lies in keeping the transaction costs low, in the design of scheme suited to the community needs, in influencing health behaviour through health education, and in influencing the supply of health care. Popularising insurance among low-income people requires conveying the idea, canvassing for it, collecting premium, and verifying claims and then reimbursing these claims. In case of formal providers, all these functions typically take up significant part (at least 20 per cent) of the premium amount. In CBHI schemes such costs can be kept low, say to 5-6 per cent. This is because many of these tasks can be performed by the community members themselves. Besides, in poor communities financial barrier is only one of the barriers to accessing health care. Often, there are many non-financial barriers that must also be overcome through the design of schemes which ought to take into account characteristics of the community. All these aspects can best be handled if the scheme is community based.

Additionally, the problems of adverse selection and moral hazard that arise due to informational asymmetries too can be reduced by making use of local knowledge that is readily available among people living in close communities. CBHI scheme is more appropriate in reducing informational asymmetries. CBHI schemes also help in influencing provision of health services. By its very nature, CBHI scheme can be designed to meet health care needs that are specific to a community. By this reckoning, Jan Arogya type of policy, which is not tailored to the needs of the target community, cannot be hoped to be very successful.

There is no community participation in the scheme, and this type of policy is also more prone to abuse. Generally, CBHI scheme is organised through an NGO that is conversant with the target community. A CBHI scheme where an NGO mediates between community members and the formal insurance provider seems to combine the participatory feature with the efficiency aspect characteristic of the formal insurance provider. However, some forms of CBHI also have important limitations. For example, where an NGO itself provides insurance (acts like an insurer) the ability of the NGO to have a pool of well diversify risk is limited. This in turn restricts the ability of NGO to cover or insure variety of risks facing the target population. Moreover, where CBHI schemes are critically dependent on external funding, extending the reach of these schemes then depends on the amount of such funding available. Furthermore, the insurance schemes launched either by national or state-level governments when elections are in sight tend to be populist or vote-catching ploy. Since such schemes have to be renewed every year, these tend to be dropped once the elections are over. It is to be seen if universal health insurance scheme belongs to this category.

Insurance Reforms and Health Insurance Prospects for the Poor

Where an NGO itself provides insurance to the target community, insurance sector reforms do not directly affect formation of such schemes, though appropriate regulatory changes designed to encourage such grouping may positively affect their formation. The scope for introducing such changes is greater now than prior to liberalisation. Where insurance reforms do affect is in non-community based scheme (where the government directs public insurance companies to offer a product to the poor with or without some subsidy from the government) as well as in NGO mediated CBHI scheme (where an NGO ties-up with the formal insurance provider in ensuring certain benefit package to the targeted poor, e.g. SEWA type arrangement). Both these types of schemes were more likely when insurance was a public monopoly. Now with the introduction of competition, for-profit companies will voluntarily serve only those segments and introduce those products that are profitable in descending order of magnitude to the company. Typically, providing insurance to the poor is not profitable and insurance companies are unlikely to take up this moral obligation on their own volition. Furthermore, even public insurers that have mostly entered into such commitments may no longer be willing to do so as competition in the market intensifies. The regulator imposed uniform obligation across all formal insurers can then improve the prospects of NGO-mediated CBHI or non-community based scheme for the low-income people. The current social and rural sector obligation imposed by the Insurance Regulatory and Development Authority (IRDA) is on the insurance business in general and does not specifically apply to health insurance. Furthermore, this obligation does not require insurance companies to subsidise premium. This obligation is just to ensure that some amount of insurance activity also moves to rural areas and doesn't remain confined to big cities and towns.

In the past, public insurer cross-subsidised the policies meant for the disadvantage sections of the society. Now, for cross-subsidy to work properly, a uniform social obligation needs to be imposed on all insurance companies and not only on public insurers. Such an obligation would then come from the regulator and not from the government. The regulator, for example, could mandate all insurance companies to offer "basic" benefit package covering maternal, preventive, catastrophic and chronic care at standard prices to the poor, especially in rural areas with some subsidy from the government. In this case, the regulator may limit exclusions, mandate guaranteed renewal, and make accreditation of service provider public. Here too NGOs can play a crucial role as an intermediary between the private insurers and the community. Whether having a cross-subsidy obligation uniformly on all insurance companies is the best (most efficient) way of reaching the poor is an open question. Generally, subsidy that comes from general revenue of government is the most progressive.

Moreover, if prepayment schemes run by charity hospitals are also brought under the insurance regulator's supervision, this can give a boost to such managed care arrangements. If the legal constraint becomes a real obstacle for the expansion of managed care oriented health insurance the indemnity model may de facto get encouragement, resulting in cost escalation and reduction in the potential market for private insurance (Ferreiro 2000).

Community Based Universal Health Insurance Scheme

Prior to the announcement of the proposed community based universal health insurance scheme by the finance minister of India, various states governments were contemplating to launch a health insurance scheme for its poor population. State governments intensified their efforts when a similar announcement by the central government a year ago (in the budget 2002-03), didn't take off. Without sufficient knowledge base, the state governments were trying to enter into an arrangement with the providers of medical services, public insurance companies and the target community whereby insurance companies would reimburse treatment costs of the target community and the governments would subsidise the premium to the insurance company for the insurance sold to the target community. Some state governments had thought of paying the premium through their general revenues while others had planned to cross-subsidise premium by bringing state government employees also under Mediclaim policy (Punjab and West Bengal governments were thinking alone these lines). With the recent announcement (in the budget 2003-04) made by the finance minister to launch "community based universal health insurance" scheme for the low-income people, state governments have put off their plans.

Before analysing the scheme launched recently, let's first look at some of its important features. The scheme comes in three different flavours: (i) Re 1 per day per year for an individual (ii) Rs. 1.5 per day per year for a family of up to five members, and (iii) Rs. 2 per day per year for a family of upto seven members. Given this, the bias towards family enrolment, as opposed to individual enrolment, is obvious. What are the benefits provided? Well, in case of hospitalisation the scheme provides medical expenses upto Rs. 30,000 per family,[13] and if an earning member falls sick the scheme also provides for the loss of livelihood at the rate of Rs. 50 per day upto maximum of 15 days, and in case of death of the earning head of the family due to personal accident Rs. 25,000 is to be given to the nominee.

In all these flavours the government provides a subsidy of Rs. 100 which remains fixed whether it is an individual who buys insurance or a family of five or of seven. While the scheme is open to anybody who wants to participate in it, the subsidy is given only to the BPL families. Moreover, the scheme is designed to cover not a poor individual/family on Indian streets but those who are members of some group or the other such as cooperative societies, bidi workers, handloom weavers etc. In other words, the proposed scheme is a group insurance scheme with membership of at least 100 families. The scheme is not designed to cover the entire BPL population, at least not in the initial phase. If the scheme survives and does not get extended to include other BPL families, state governments would then need to think of reaching those poor who are not a part of any occupation-based or any self-help group for which the scheme is currently intended. Some other salient features of the scheme are (i) individuals between the age of 3 months and 65 years can join the scheme (ii) total hospital expense that can be reimbursed under the scheme for any one illness can be up to Rs, 15, 000, with a cap on the amount payable for different types of hospital expenses (iii) a number of illnesses/situations are excluded, for example maternity insurance is not included, and (iv) claims will be settled either by an intermediary called third party administrators (TPAs) or by the insurance companies themselves.

The way in which the scheme is designed, it cannot be termed as a community based scheme. The scheme is so designed as to keep the transaction costs low. But here too the presence of TPAs limits the scope of reduction in transaction costs. Because the scheme lacks "community character" the other potential benefits of community based scheme cannot be reaped. Furthermore, a universal standard package of costs and benefits, takes away the needed flexibility in designing a scheme appropriate to local conditions.

The scheme is expected to cover 10 million families that are below the poverty line in the first year. The government subsidy is capped at Rs. 1000 million. Assuming all 10 million families get covered, the resource mobilisation that can be effected is in the range of Rs. 3650 million to Rs. 7300 million, with considerable variation in the claims liability. An important point to note is that the scheme is designed on the assumption that even the poor can contribute some payment towards their health security and the amount that is sought to be mobilised is significant.

If this scheme is to be made available for the entire BPL population of about 300 million, the extent of resource mobilisation that could be effected is quite significant indeed. Assuming average family size to be 5. There would be 60 million poor families (assuming 300 BPL population). If each family pays premium of Rs. 540 (i.e., Rs. 1.5 X 365) per year, the total premium amount would be Rs. (540 X 60) 32,400 million. Of this amount the government contribution by way of subsidy (of Rs. 100 per family) would be Rs. 6000 million. So, the amount that could be mobilised from the BPL population would be around (Rs. 32,400 million-Rs, 6,000 million) Rs. 26,400 million. If we compare this figure with the amount estimated by Rajiv et al. of Rs. 40,000 million, around 65 per cent of the funds can be mobilised from the people themselves! However, there is a catch here. These estimates only pertain to hospitalisation costs whereas the costs involved in case of health insurance are higher as it also provides for wage loss.

In principle, both public and private insurance companies can participate in the scheme. In reality, participation of private insurance companies seems unlikely, especially when there are other more lucrative areas still to be tapped. Prior to liberalisation, when insurance was a public monopoly, launch of such a scheme would have made perfect sense. Indeed, two health insurance products-Mediclaim and Jan Arogya-were launched at that time, and we are all too aware of the dismal record of these products. Now with competition at the market place, wouldn't encumbering public insurers put them at a disadvantage? Even though the subsidy is being paid by the government to cover for any possible shortfall, it is unlikely to attract even the public insurance companies. One, claims liability under the scheme is open ended whereas the government subsidy is capped. Two, the public insurers showed total disinterest, even scorn, when similar scheme " Janraksha" was announced in the budget 2002-03. Little surprise why the scheme failed to take off the ground!

Health insurance scheme for the poor should take care of not just the inpatient or hospital care, as designed in the proposed scheme, but also of the outpatient care. It is often suggested that insurance be provided only for inpatient care and that outpatient care be left outside the ambit of insurance. The reasons given are: that people can, by and large, afford out-patient care because it is relatively inexpensive; it is the inpatient care that pushes them into poverty trap; that administratively it is difficulty to include outpatient care; and, that out-patient care would lead to cost escalation. Ideally, both inpatient care and outpatient care be covered, and the decision of whether or not a patient needs hospitalisation be professionally made and should not be a function of whether or not the patient has health insurance cover.

For this reason the UNDP sponsored experiments on community based health insurance, launched recently, have addressed the issue of outpatient care as well. Community character of CBHI schemes is used to tackle the problem of outpatient care as well. (For other issues in design of CBHI schemes see Ranson and Jowett 2003). However, with the launch of universal health insurance scheme, it is not clear how this would affect the prospects of an NGO negotiating a health insurance package for and on behalf of a target community with the public insurance companies.

In the current debate on health security for the poor, health insurance is made out to be panacea for all the ills facing the poor. Health insurance, no doubt, has emerged as an important financing tool as it promises to mobilise some resources from the people themselves i.e., those who buy insurance. But health insurance, which strengthens demand side, makes sense only when the supply of health care is reasonably well developed. Where this is not so, health insurance is meaningless. The supply of health care in the rural and remote areas of country is far from satisfactory. Although public health care centers are pervasive, these centers have degraded overtime in most states due to lack of funds,-accountability and so forth.

Any attempt at introducing health insurance for the poor must also be accompanied by revival of health care facilities at these centers. The need for stepping up public health spending is endorsed by many expert studies. Unfortunately, the launch of the scheme is not accompanied by either an increase in public health expenditure or any commitment to reorient the public health system, and this seems to suggest lack of seriousness in providing health security to the poor (Sankar and Kathuria 2003). Finally, both the provision and access to health care services should be a part of a bigger health strategy which includes other public health programs such as safe drinking water, sanitation, family planning etc. as each of these are important determinants of health outcomes. In other words a comprehensive approach is needed. With the view to understand how the development of private health insurance in the country is likely to impact the poor, we now turn to the factors that are currently affecting its development.

PRIVATE HEALTH INSURANCE IN INDIA

Unlike most OECD countries where private/social health insurance is the main source of health care financing, in India, and more generally in developing countries, most private insurance is a supplementary service. Health insurance, whether social and private, whether formal or informal, is extremely limited in India. Existing health insurance schemes in India are mandatory schemes, private (voluntary) schemes, employer based insurance, and the schemes in the NGO/voluntary sector. All these schemes put together cover about 110 million people or about 11 percent of the population (Garg 2000). This number falls far short of the private health insurance potential that is estimated anywhere between 400 and 500 million people. What is holding back the realisation of this potential?

Although a number of private insurance companies have entered after the liberalisation of the insurance market in 2000, no significant change in health insurance has been observed either in terms of new health insurance products or in terms of the volume of business. The two health insurance products namely Mediclaim for the general public and Jan Arogya for the poor, launched prior to the liberalisation, have not shown any significant growth either in terms of volume of business or in the number of policies sold post liberalisation.

The new general insurers have introduced slight variations of the existing Mediclaim and the new life insurers have introduced some health riders to their life policies. However, their volume of business is negligible (GOI 2002). Why has the scope of existing health insurance schemes remained limited? Two important reasons cited are: (i) poor product design, and (ii) lack of vigorous marketing of the products to sensitise the public of the need for health insurance. The existing health insurance schemes are indemnity based products wherein the payment to the health provider is first made by the sick individual and this amount is later reimburse (partly or fully) by the insurance company to the insured individual. A large section of population who cannot afford such large payments at the time of illness, even if these payments are reimbursed later, does not feel attracted to this type of insurance. Furthermore, the scheme provides for reimbursement only in case of hospitalisation, and not for out-patient care, and for allopathic treatment and not for treatment as per alternate system of medicine.

Reimbursement of hospital expenses exposes the policyholders to the "service" of insurers which is far from satisfactory. Coming to the second reason, when the public is not much aware of the need for health insurance, vigorous marketing of schemes becomes essential for popularising the scheme. Finally, health insurance is not demanded for its own sake but for reducing financial barrier to health services. In rural and remote areas where supply of health services particularly inpatient facilities is weak, demand for insurance naturally gets constrained.

More generally, why has health insurance business remained underdeveloped in India? Why no reputed global health insurance company has entered the market? Impediments to the establishment and development of private health insurance stem directly or indirectly from government policies regarding insurance, and health care sector (GOI 2002). The most important impediments arise from the supply side i.e., from the side of health care providers. Lack of standards for diseases and treatment procedures (and where these standards and procedures exists, their adoption is lacking); absence of rating and credentialling of the providers; non-existence of centralised database, standardisation of billing, claims and proposal forms are some of the problems facing the health care industry.

On the insurance regulation side too there are some issues affecting the development of the market. For example, the minimum capital norm for exclusive health insurers is deemed to be lower than what is currently prescribed. Similarly, solvency margins and reinsurance requirement appropriate to health insurance which is less volatile than property and casualty insurance are deemed to be different from those applicable to other lines of general insurance business. Currently, such requirements that apply to general insurance business apply to health insurance as well. Similarly, there are no minimum capital requirement and solvency norms for health care providers interested in establishing and running managed care schemes.25 Besides, current Mediclaim policy that distorts the balance between price adequacy and coverage, restricts the ability of competitors to come up with more balanced products.

Once the entry barriers are removed, additional regulations need to be put in place for the smooth functioning of health insurance business. Even though, insurance regulations meant to ensure fairness, efficiency, and financial accountability in health insurance are similar to those applicable to general insurance business, health insurance business always involves additional regulations. These relate to meeting social objectives of access, adequate benefits, and consumer responsiveness.

Typically insurers tend to develop a number of underwriting and pricing practices to avoid accepting high risk people. This kind of market segmentation is economically efficient but may be considered socially unacceptable. Often regulators ensure that equal access is available to the payers of health care, that companies cannot exclude high-risk individuals or costly preexisting conditions. Moreover, health insurance contracts are typically more complex than other insurance contracts. Regulators need to ensure that consumers understand the provisions of the contracts and that contracts are written in a manner understood by the buyers.

Since health insurance is closely linked to health care provision, interventions required to correct these problems call for a coordination with other arms of the government such as the Ministry of Health and Family Welfare, and bodies like Medical Council of India, the regulators. Finally, government's role in promoting or impeding private health-related investment is a key element in the growth of private health financing and delivery. Unless these issues are dealt with one cannot expect any significant development to take place in health insurance business in the country.

IMPACT ON THE POOR

Developments on the health insurance front will not leave the poor unaffected. Even though private for-profit insurance companies are not expected to voluntarily provide health insurance cover to the poor, the poor may still be affected on account of the influence that development of health insurance will have on the supply of such services. Furthermore, the poor may also directly benefit if insurance regulations are specifically designed to achieve redistribution and equity objectives. At the minimum the government must ensure that (i) the liberalisation of insurance market provides value for money for the direct beneficiaries (ii) the poor are not adversely affected by the liberalisation (Peters et al. 2000). However, the government can definitely aim higher by ensuring that the poor too benefit from the developments in health insurance. The likely impact of developing voluntary insurance on the poor is far from clear. There are both potential benefits and risks associated with it. Development of health insurance would influence supply of health services both in terms of its quality and price. It would also influence the extent of public funds available for subsidising the poor. The potential benefits and risks are formally listed below:

Potential Benefits:

- If the introduction of evidence-based medicine trickles down to other providers that are used more often by the poor, the poor could benefit from the improvement in quality in the private sector;
- If public subsidy to the non-poor who join health insurance decreases, greater public resources may be available for providing subsidy to the poor Potential Risks:
- The gap between the poor access at present and the required access may increase with cost escalation;

- As the non-poor make a switchover from public to private hospitals there is a risk of political support for public financing getting reduced which would impact the poor by excluding them quality care from private market or by deteriorating quality and weakening support for public services (Peters et al. 2002)

The poor might benefit from the expansion of private providers if the supply of health care expands due to increase in affordability resulting from health insurance. However, if prices grow faster than delivery capacity, cost escalation may even expand the existing gap between the poor and the required access to health care. All this is unpredictable, since it depends on the supply response of health care and the model of health insurance implemented in the country.

Regarding the latter, it is clear that an indemnity/fee-for-service system will unavoidably result in a severe cost escalation whereas a managed care which coordinates financing and delivery of healthcare would probably be capable of maintaining costs under control.

Managed care by containing of unnecessary treatment helps in containment of costs and thereby makes health insurance more affordable to larger number of people; provides incentives for improving healthcare delivery; promotes preventive care such as medical check ups, immunisation and so on. Since fee-for-service approach to payment of health providers tends to escalate costs the government should encourage managed care models.

The pro-poor recommendations made in the World Bank organised national seminar on the topic are:

(i) reduce the public subsidy to the wealthy by charging full cost recovery to the insured who use private insurance

(ii) define minimum package of services cover that include preventive, maternity, and catastrophic cases

(iii) encourage informal community financing schemes, for example, managed care schemes through NGOs with less regulation and lower capital deposit requirements.

CONCLUSIONS

Health insurance is emerging to be an important financing tool in meeting health care needs of the poor. Neither market mediated nor government provided insurance is an appropriate way of reaching the poor. Community Based Health Insurance (CBHI) is more suitable arrangement for providing insurance to the poor. Development of private health insurance in the country has both potential risks and benefits in improving the access of the poor to health services.

Appropriate regulatory changes can minimise the risks and turn potential benefits into concrete gains for the poor. However, currently even the private health insurance market lacks development for the want of proper regulatory decisions both on the supply of health services and on the demand for health insurance.

CBHI, which is more appropriate insurance arrangement for the poor, could take different forms and each of this form may be suitable depending on the characteristics of the target population, their health profile, and health risks to which the community is exposed. Indeed, for a country as diverse as India there can be no Pan India model and all different forms need to be explored.

The scheme announced in the last budget and recently launched by the Prime Minister of India seems promising provided the insurers find it attractive enough to partake in the scheme. The liberalisation of insurance market has made this less likely, as competition in the market place will turn the focus of companies in most profitable lines of business. However, a regulatory requirement to this effect may then be a possible way out.

The proposed scheme being a group insurance scheme is not meant to cover the entire BPL population. Also, it excludes outpatient care. As experience accumulates, the scheme can be fine-tuned and expanded to cover all low income people. But increased public health spending and reforming of public health facilities is a must for the success of these community based health initiatives.

8

THE OPPORTUNITIES, CHALLENGES AND CONCERNS

INTRODUCTION

Over the last 50 years India has achieved a lot in terms of health improvement. But still India is way behind many fast developing countries such as China, Vietnam and Sri Lanka in health indicators (Satia et al 1999). In case of government funded health care system, the quality and access of services has always remained major concern. A very rapidly growing private health market has developed in India. This private sector bridges most of the gaps between what government offers and what people need. However, with proliferation of various health care technologies and general price rise, the cost of care has also become very expensive and unaffordable to large segment of population. The government and people have started exploring various health financing options to manage problems arising out of growing set of complexities of private sector growth, increasing cost of care and changing epidemiological pattern of diseases.

The new economic policy and liberalization process followed by the Government of India since 1991 paved the way for privatization of insurance sector in the country. Health insurance, which remained highly underdeveloped and a less significant segment of the product portfolios of the nationalized insurance companies in India, is now poised for a fundamental change in its approach and management. The Insurance Regulatory and Development Authority (IRDA) Bill, recently passed in the Indian Parliament, is important beginning of changes having significant implications for the health sector.

The privatization of insurance and constitution IRDA envisage to improve the performance of the state insurance sector in the country by increasing benefits from competition in terms of lowered costs and increased level of consumer satisfaction. However, the implications of the entry of private insurance companies in health sector are not very clear. The recent policy changes will have been far reaching and would have major implications for the growth and development of the health sector. There are several contentious issues pertaining to development in this sector and these need critical examination. These also highlight the critical need for policy formulation and assessment. Unless privatization and development of health insurance is managed well it may have negative impact of health care especially to a large segment of population in the country. If it is well managed then it can improve access to care and health status in the country very rapidly.

Health insurance as it is different from other segments of insurance business is more complex because of serious conflicts arising out of adverse selection, moral hazard, and information gap problems. For example, experiences from other countries suggest that the entry of private firms into the health insurance sector, if not properly regulated, does have adverse consequences for the costs of care, equity, consumer satisfaction, fraud and ethical standards. The IRDA would have a significant role in the regulation of this sector and responsibility to minimise the unintended consequences of this change.

Health sector policy formulation, assessment and implementation is an extremely complex task especially in a changing epidemiological, institutional, technological, and political scenario. Further, given the institutional complexity of our health sector programmes and the pluralistic character of health care providers, health sector reform strategies in the context of health insurance that have evolved elsewhere may have very little suitability to our country situation. Proper understanding of the Indian health situation and application of the principles of insurance keeping in view the social realities and national objective are important.

This paper presents review of health insurance situation in India-the opportunities it provides, the challenges it faces and the concerns it raises. A discussion of the implications of privatization of insurance on health sector from various perspectives and how it will shape the character of our health care system is also attempted. The paper following areas:

- Economic policy context
- Health financing in India
- Health insurance scenario in India
- Health insurance for the poor
- Consumer perspective on health insurance
- Models of health insurance in other countries

This paper is partly based on a deliberations of a one day workshop (IIMA 1999) and a conference held at 11M Ahmedabad (IIMA 2000) in 1999-2000 on health insurance involving practicing doctors, representatives from government insurance companies, medical associations, training institutes, member-based organizations and health policy researchers. Workshop and conference were part of the activities of Health Policy Development Network (HELPONET) and is supported by the International Health

Policy Program. The paper also draws on several published and unpublished papers and documents in the area of health insurance.

ECONOMIC POLICY CONTEXT AND IMPERATIVES OF LIBERALIZATION OF INSURANCE SECTOR

There are several imperatives for opening of the insurance and health insurance sector in India for private investment. Here we review some of these imperatives. Economic policy reforms started during late eighties and speeded up in nineties are the context in which liberalization of insurance sector happened in India. It was very obvious that the liberalization of the real (productive) and financial sector of the economy has to go hand in hand. It is imperative that these sectors are consistent with policies of each other and unless both function efficiently and are in equilibrium, it would be difficult to ensure appropriate economic growth. Given these facts liberalization of both sectors has to proceed simultaneously.

Indian economic system has been developed on paradigm of mixed economy in which public and private enterprises co-exist. The past strategies of development based on socialistic thinking were focusing on the premise of restrictions, regulations and control and less on incentives and market driven forces. This affected the development process in the country in serious way. After the economic liberalization the paradigm changed from central planning, command and control to market driven development. Deregulation, decontrol, privatization, delicensing, globalization became the key strategies to implement the new framework and encourage competition. The social sectors did not remain unaffected by this change.

The control of government expenditure, which became a key tool to manage fiscal deficits in early 1990s, affected the social sector spending in major way. The unintended consequences of controlling the fiscal deficits have been reduction in capital expenditure and non-salary component of many social sector programmes. This has led-to severe resource constraints in the health sector in respect of non-salary expenditure and this has affected the capacity and credibility of the government health care system to deliver good quality care over the years. Given the increasing salaries, lack of effective monitoring and lack of incentives to provide good quality services the provides in the government sector became indifferent to the clients. Clients also did not demand good quality and better access, as government services were free of cost. Under this situation more and more clients turned to the private sector health providers and thus the private sector healthcare has expanded. Given the socialistic political thinking and populist policy it has been generally difficult for any government to introduce cost recovery in public health sector. Given that government is unable to provide more resources for health care, and institute cost recovery, one of the ways to reduce the under-funding and augment the resources in the health sector was to encourage the development health insurance.

Another imperative for liberalization of the insurance sector was the need for long-term financial resources on sustainable basis for the development of infrastructure sector such as roads, transports etc. It was realized that during the course of economic liberalization, the funds to development the infrastructure also became a major constraint. Country certainly needed infrastructure development. For this the finances are major constraint. In these investments the benefits are more social than private. The major concern was how these finances can be made available at low costs. In past the development of social sector were financed using government channeled funds through various semi-government financial institutions.

Under the liberalized economy this may not be possible. One hope is that if the insurance sector develops rapidly under privatization then it can provide long-term finance to the infrastructure sector.

The financial sector, which consists of banks, financial institutions, insurance companies, provident funds schemes, mutual funds were all under government control. There was less competition across these units. As a result these institutions remained significantly less developed in their approach and management. Insurance sector has been most affected by the government controls. Government had significant control on the policies these insurance companies could offer and utilization of the resources mobilized by insurance companies. One can see that most of the insurance products (e.g., life insurance products) were promoted as mechanisms to improve the savings and tax shelters rather as risk coverage instruments. Other segments of the insurance products grew because of the statutory obligations (e.g., Motor Vehicle, Marine and Fire) under various acts. The management and organization of insurance sector companies remained less developed and they neglected new product development and marketing. Thus one of the hopes in opening of the insurance sector was that the private and foreign companies would rapidly develop the sector and improve coverage of the population with insurance using new products and better management. Last imperative for opening of the insurance sector was signing the WTO India. After this there was little choice but to open the entire financial sector-including insurance sector to private and foreign investors. (Dholakia 1999).

HEALTH SECTOR AND ITS FINANCING: PRESENT SCENE AND ISSUES FOR THE FUTURE

During the last 50 years India has developed a large government health infrastructure with more than 150 medical colleges, 450 district hospitals, 3000 Community Health Centers, 20,000 Primary Health Care centers and 130,000 Sub-Health Centers. On top of this there are large number of private and NGO health facilities and practitioners scatters though out the country.

Over the past 50 ears India has made considerable progress in improving its health status. Death rate has reduced from 40 to 9 per thousand, infant mortality rate reduced from 161 to 71 per thousand live births and life expectancy increased from 31 to 63 years.

However, many challenges remain and these are: life expectancy 4 years below world average, high incidence of communicable diseases, increasing incidence of non-communicable diseases, neglect of women's health, considerable regional variation and threat from environment degradation. It is estimated that at any given point of time 40 to 50 million people are on medication for major sickness in India. About 200 million workdays are lost annually due to sickness. Survey data indicate that about 60% people use private health providers for outpatient treatment while 60 % use government providers for in-door treatment. The average expenditure for care is 2-5 times more in private sector than in public sector.

India spends about 6% of GDP on health expenditure. Private health care expenditure is 75% or 4.25% of GDP and most of the rest (1.75%) is government funding. At present, the insurance coverage is negligible.

Most of the public funding is for preventive, promotive and primary care programmes while private expenditure is largely for curative care. Over the period the private health care expenditure has grown at the rate of 12.84% per annum and for each one percent increase in per capital income the private health care expenditure has increased by 1.47%. Number of private doctors and private clinical facilities are also expanding exponentially. Indian health financing scene raises number of challenges, which are:

- increasing health care costs,
- high financial burden on poor eroding their incomes,
- increasing burden of new diseases and health risks and
- neglect of preventive and primary care and public health functions due to under funding of the government health care.

Given the above scenario exploring health-financing options becomes critical. Health Insurance is considered one of the financing mechanisms to over come some of the problems of our system.

HEALTH INSURANCE SCENE IN INDIA

Health insurance can be defined in very narrow sense where individual or group purchases in advance health coverage by paying a fee called "premium". But it can be also defined broadly by including all financing arrangements where consumers can avoid or reduce their expenditures at time of use of services.

The health insurance existing in India covers a very wide spectrum of arrangements and hence the latter-broader interpretation of health Insurance is more appropriate.

Health insurance is very well established in many countries. But in India it is a new concept except for the organized sector employees.

In India only about 2 per cent of total health expenditure is funded by public/social health insurance while 18 per cent is funded by government budget. In many other low and middle income countries contribution of social health insurance is much higher.

Table: Percentage of total health expenditure funded through public/social insurance and direct government revenue

Country	Social Health Insurance	Government Budget
Algeria	37	36
Bolivia	20	33
China	31	13
Korea	23	10
Vietnam	2	20
India	2	18

Source: As cited in Naylor et al. 1999.

It is estimated that the Indian health care industry is now worth of Rs. 96,000 crore and expected to surge by 10,000 crore annually. The share of insurance market in above figure is insignificant. Out of one billion population of India 315 million people are estimated to be insurable and have capacity to spend Rs. 1000 as premium per annum. Many global insurance companies have plans to get into insurance business in India. Market research, detailed planning and effective insurance marketing is likely to assume significant importance. Given the health financing and demand scenario, health insurance has a wider scope in present day situations in India. However, it requires careful and significant effort to tap Indian health insurance market with proper understanding and training.

There are various types of health coverages in India. Based on ownership the existing health insurance schemes can be broadly divided into categories such as:

- Government or state-based systems
- Market-based systems (private and voluntary)
- Employer provided insurance schemes
- Member organization (NGO or cooperative)-based systems

Government or state-based systems include Central Government Health Scheme (CGHS) and Employees State Insurance Scheme (ESIS). It is estimated that employer managed systems cover about 20-30 million of population. The schemes run by member-based organizations cover about 5 per cent of population in various ways. Market-based systems (voluntary and private) have Mediclaim scheme which covers about 2 million of population.

There are many employers who reimburse costs of medical expenses of the employees with or without contribution from the employee. It is estimated that about 20 million employees may be covered by such reimbursement arrangements. There are several government and private employers such as Railway and Armed forces and public sector enterprises that run their own health services for employees and families. It is estimated that about 30 million employees may be covered under such employer managed health services (Ellis et al. 1996).

General Insurance Corporation (GIC) and its four subsidiary companies and Life Insurance Corporation (LIC) of India have various health insurance products. These are Ashadeep Plan II and Jeevan Asha Plan II by Life Insurance Corporation of India and various policies by General Insurance Corporation of India as under: Personal Accident Policy, Jan Arogya Policy, Raj Rajeshwari Policy, Mediclaim Policy, Overseas Mediclaim Policy, Cancer Insurance Policy, Bhavishya Arogya Policy and Dreaded Disease Policy (Srivastava 1999).

The health care demand is rising in India now days. It is estimated that only 10 per cent of health insurance market has been tapped till today. Still there is a scope of rise up to 35 per cent in near future. The most popular health Insurance cover is Mediclaim Policy. This policy is discussed below.

MEDICLAIM SCHEME

The government insurance companies started first health insurance in 1986, under the name mediclaim; thereafter Mediclaim has been revised to make it attractive product. Mediclaim is a reimbursement base insurance for hospitalization. It does not cover outpatient treatments. First there is used to be category-wise ceilings on items such as medicine, room charges, operation charges etc. and later when the policies were revised these ceilings were removed and total reimbursements were allowed with in the limit of the policy amount. The total limit for policy coverage was also increased. Now a person between 3 months to 80 years of age can be granted mediclaim policy up to maximum coverage of Rs. 5 lakh against accidental and sickness hospitalisations during the policy period as per latest guidelines of General Insurance Corporation of India. This scheme is offered by all the four subsidiary companies of GIC. Mediclaim scheme is also available for groups with substantial discount in premium.

The current statistics on health insurance indicate that out of 1 billion population only about 2 million of population is covered by Mediclaim scheme. The reason for lack of popularity of this scheme could be several. The health insurance products are generally complicated and it is suggested that GIC and its subsidiary companies who deal in non-life insurance market which is dominated by mandated insurance such as accident, fire and marine, do not have expertise in marketing health insurance and therefore this scheme is not popular. Health insurance also represents very small percentage of overall business of GIC and its subsidiaries hence they have also not focused their attention in this area. The GIC companies have little interest and means to monitor the scheme. It should also be recognized that because of technicalities of health service business there are number of cumbersome rules which have hampered the acceptance of the scheme. It is also reported that in number of cases the applicants of older ages have been refused to become member of mediclaim scheme due to unnecessary conservatism of the companies.

Another area of less popularity of the. Mediclaim is the lack of appropriate marketing efforts in selling these products. To popularize the schemes It IS Important that proper marketing is done. To make the scheme more acceptable government has exempted the premium paid by individuals from their taxable income. This provides 20-40% subsidy on the premium to taxpayers.

Mediclaim has provided a model for health insurance for the middle class and the rich. It covers hospitalization costs, which could be catastrophic. But given the the premium is on higher side it as remained limited to middle class, urban tax payers segment of the population. There are also problems and negative unintended consequences of this scheme. There are reported fraud and manipulation by clients and providers, which have implications for the growth and development of this sector. The monitoring systems are weak and there are chances that if the doctor and patient collude with each other, they can do more harms to the system. There is also element of adverse selection problem as the scheme is voluntary. As the scheme reimburses charges without limit it also will pushed up the prices of services in the private sector. Our analysis of mediclaim data from one center indicates wide variation of charges for same operation in the same city. Anecdotal evidence from doctors also indicates that charges are increased if patients are insured. All these effects will tend to increase the prices of private health care thus hurting the uninsured.

EMPLOYEE STATE INSURANCE (ESI) SCHEME

Under the ESI Act, 1948 ESI Scheme provides protection to employees against loss of wages due to inability to work due to sickness, maternity, disability and death due to employment injury. It also provides medical care to employees and their family members without fee for service. When implemented for the first time in India at two centres namely Delhi and Kanpur simultaneously in February 1952, it covered about 1.2 lakh employees. Presently the scheme is spread over 22 states and Union territories across India covering 91lakh employees and more than 350 lakh beneficiaries. The Act compulsorily covers: (a) all power using non-seasonal factories employing 10 or more persons; (b) all non-power using factories employing 20 or more employees and (c) service establishments like shops, hotels restaurants, cinema, road transport and news papers are covered. ESIC is a corporate semi-government body headed by Union Minister of Labour as Chairman and the Director General as chief executive. Its members are representatives of central and state governments, employers, employees, medical profession and parliament.

The financing of the scheme is done by Employees State Insurance Corporation (ESIC) which is made up of contributions from: (a) employees who contribute at the rate 1.75 per cent of their wages (if daily wage is Rs.25 or less, his contribution is waived); (b) employers who contribute at the rate of 4. 75 per cent of total wage bills of their employees to contribution on behalf and for employees having daily wage ofRs. 25 or less; and (c) State Governments contributes 12.5 per cent of total shareable expenditure worked out by prescribed ceiling on expenditure which is Rs. 600 per insured person per annum and expenditure incurred outside/ over and above the prescribed limit.

The State Government runs the medical services of this scheme of social insurance meant for employees covered under the ESI Act 1948. This scheme-compulsory and contributory in nature-provide uniform package of medical and cash benefits to insured persons is implemented through special ESI hospitals and diagnostic centers, dispensaries and panel doctors.

The delivery of medical care is through service (direct) system and/or panel (indirect) system. It provides allopathic medical care, but medical care by other systems like ayurvedic and homeopathy in the states is also provided as per the state government decision. The medical care consists of preventive, promotive, curative and rehabilitative types of services are provided by the scheme through its own network or through arrangements with reputed government or private institutions by concept of proper referral system and regionalisation.

Table : Existing infrastructure under ESIS in India

Particulars	
No. of Centers	632
No. of Insured Persons/Family Units	84,45,000
ESI Hospitals	125
Number of ESI Hospital Beds	23,334
ESI Dispensaries	1,443
Insurance Medical Officers	6,220
Insurance Medical Practitioners	2,900

Preventive services include immunization, maternal and child health, family welfare services. Promotive services include health education and health check-up camps. Curative services include: dispensary care, hospital care, maternity care, supportive services including diagnostic centre, drugs, dressings, surgical procedures, dental care; prosthesis and other appliances. Rehabilitative services include: physical rehabilitation, economical rehabilitation, and provision of artificial aids (social, psychological rehabilitation). Even though the scheme is formulated well there are many problem areas in managing this scheme. Some of the problems are:

- large number of employers try to avoid being covered under the scheme,
- a large number of posts of medical staff remains vacant because of high turnover and lengthy recruitment procedures,
- there is duality of control,
- rising costs and technological advancement in super specialty treatment
- management information system is not satisfactory.
- there is low utilization of the hospitals
- the workers are not satisfied with the services they get.
- in rural area the access to services is also a problem.

Some of the state governments have to subsidize the scheme heavily even though the ESI Corporation, which is the financial arm of the system, has much surplus funds. All these problems indicate an urgent need for reforms in the ESI scheme (Vora, 2000).

Some of the options for reforms in ESI scheme could be: making the scheme autonomous-managed by workers and employers while government only retails controls through a guiding framework as is the case with German Sickness Funds. Secondly the scheme should be made open for non-organized sector through fixed income based contribution. This will extend the benefits of the scheme to many more people. The government should set the patient care standards and monitor outcomes as well as patient satisfaction. The management of the health facilities also needs to be improved substantially. The financial management of the scheme also needs improvement.

HEALTH INSURANCE FOR POOR BY NGOS

With 70 per cent of population in India living in rural areas and 95 per cent of work-force working in unorganized sectors, and disproportionately large percentage of these populations living below poverty line, there is strong need to develop social security mechanisms for this segment of population. This need for security is further increased because the poor are the most vulnerable for ill health, accidents, death, desertion, social disruptions such as riots, loss of housing, job and other means of livelihood. There are some efforts in this direction of providing social security to the poor by a few NGOs. The most prominent among them is that of Self-Employed Women's Association (SEWA). The other scheme by government insurance companies developed to focus on poor is called Jan Arogya Bima Policy which was introduced in 1995 and covers expenditure up to Rs. 5000 for a premium of Rs. 70 per annum.

It is estimated that about 5 million people are covered under various NGO insurance schemes. The experience from other countries suggest that in developed countries such as USA, UK, the health insurance have grown out of small non-profit schemes. A large share of health insurance market in USA is in not-for-profit sector. There is need in India to promote these schemes as they address the needs of the poor. Over the last few years in India small and big NGO's like Tribhuvandas, SEW A, ACCORD etc. have implemented the insurance schemes. Many of these schemes are designed to meet the needs of the poorer segments of the community. They have developed several innovations such as

- mechanism of monitoring the performance,
- pricing of various services,
- integration of various risks in one single product,
- linking of insurance schemes with savings,
- coverage of many services not included in market based schemes such as maternity services, transportation, coverage of risks such as from riots, floods etc.

Some NGOs have developed special linkages with public health systems, private facilities and also accessed resources through insurance companies.

SEWA's Health Insurance and Social Security Schemes for the Poor

Poor women are the most vulnerable sections of a developing society. SEW A-a membership based women workers' trade union, has developed an initiative to protect the poor women from financial burdens arising out of high medical costs and other risks. Each member has option to join the programme by paying Rs. 60 per annum and it provides limited cover for risks arising out of sickness, maternity needs, accidents, floods and riots, widowhood etc. The scheme is also linked with saving scheme. Members have the option to either deposit Rs. 500 in SEW A Bank and interest on this deposit will cover the annual premium or pay annual premium of Rs. 60. The scheme has 30,000 members and is expected to grow to 50000.

In the beginning the SEW A started this programme with the support of one of the public sector insurance companies. The experience of SEW A has been that the insurance companies are not well equipped to handle the present day complexities of health insurance particularly in context of lower income group needs. Given the bureaucratic rigidities in settling the claims, procedures, which one has to follow, and poor monitoring mechanisms make it difficult for the poor to continue with these schemes. For example, the patients belonging to lower income groups opting for the schemes would need systems which are simple, flexible, prompt, relevant, having less paper work and have fewer tiers. The design of the product including what it covers, scope of coverage and at what premium are important considerations for people belonging to lower income groups.

SEWA experience suggests that the design of the insurance products have to be integrated with several add-ons that may be priced differently. For example, health risk coverage should include sickness as well as maternity aspects. SEW A experience illustrates that other aspects of risk which need coverage include natural and accidental death of women and her husband, disablement, loss because of riots/flood/fire/ theft etc. The overall premium has to be low. There has been lot of emphasis and education in the community on understanding the concept of insurance. This awareness is growing. The linkage with the providers has been critical aspect in keeping this cost of scheme down. At the same time the member has complete choice in selecting the provider but the reimbursement is limited. It has been observed that costs in private are more than 5 times than what they are in public sector hence developing linkages with the public facilities are therefore critical.

This also depends on quality of care at public facilities. The overall experience of SEW A's health insurance has been encouraging. Women have started to seek health care and have been asking to enlarge the scope of the scheme. The scheme has tried to address the special needs of women health by allowing the other systems of medicine, which is quite popular in various places and paying for maternity related expenses which are not covered by Mediclaim scheme. The scaling up of the scheme and increasing the coverage is the most important management and organizational challenge. Recent study of the members of the SEW A scheme by Gumber and Kulkarni (2000) also indicate its usefulness.

Other NGO Health Insurance Schemes

Over the last several year there has been efforts to develop health insurance by various small NGOs. Some of the prominent among them have been ACCORD in

Karnataka, Tribhuvandas foundation, Aga Khan Health Services, India (AKHSI) and Nav-sarjan in Gujarat, and Sewagram medical college Maharashtra. -ACCORD works with tribal population in forested areas ofKarnataka, AKHSI works with Ismaili population in North Gujarat, Tribhuvandas Foundation works in villages of Kheda district where there are strong milk producing unions of Amul Dairy Cooperative, Nav-sarjan works with schedule castes in 2000 villages of Gujarat. Ranson (1999) has reviewed NGO efforts in India in this field. There are some common features of NGO schemes.

The coverage of these schemes vary and most use their own health workers to provide primary care and have tied up with a hospital to provide secondary care. Premiums are low, generally fixed and not related to risk. Most schemes have limited coverage and some also provide wider services besides health and treatment. All these organizations had good track record of services in the community and then added on health insurance on their existing activities hence they did not have to establish credibility with the community. The key feature among them was low premium and low coverage. These NGOs have shown that it is possible to develop a model of health insurance for the poor without much subsidy. The experience also suggests that if a credible NGO exists then it is not difficult to develop health insurance as an add on benefit. What is unclear and need to be researched is that what amount of total health expenditure does these scheme covers for the poor given that their coverage is limited.

CONSUMER AND SOCIAL PERSPECTIVE ON HEALTH INSURANCE

With the liberalization of insurance and entry of private companies in this business it is very important that specific interventions are developed which focus on increasing the consumer awareness about insurance products. One of the major challenges after privatization of insurance would be how to develop such mechanisms, which help making consumers aware about the various intricacies of insurance plans. As of now information, knowledge and awareness of existing insurance plans is very limited. This is also shown by the study of Gumber and Kulkarni (2000) among the members of SEWA, ESIS and mediclaim schemes. With Consumer Protection Act coming in force it has become easy for aggrieved consumers to complain and seek redressal for their problems. Consumer organizations such as CERC of Ahmedabad have been helping consumers to get due justice in disputes with the insurance companies. Their experience would be varying valuable in guiding development of health insurance plans that are transparent and just.

Many a times the insurance claims are rejected due to some small technical reasons. This leads to disputes. Most of the time the conditions and various points included in insurance policy contracts is not negotiable and these are binding on consumers. There is no analysis on what is fair practice and what is unfair practice. Given that insurance companies are large and almost monopoly setting the consumers is treated as secondary and they do not have opportunity to negotiate the terms and conditions of a contract. Many times insurance companies do not strictly follow the conditions in all cases and this create confusion and disputes. (Shah M 1999)

The most important area of dispute and unfair treatment is the knowledge and implications of pre-exiting conditions. A number of cases of litigation are disagreement on these pre-existing conditions. These problems also arise because of lack of specification of number of areas and properly spelling out the conditions. This is also because some chronic conditions such as high blood pressure and diabetes can increase the risk of may other disease of organs such as heart, kidney, vascular and eyes diseases. The patients with these pre-existing conditions are denied claims for treatment of complications. This is not fair and leads to disputes.

Health insurance is typically annual and has to be renewed yearly. Policy, which is not renewed in time lapses and a new policy has to be taken out. Medical conditions detected during the interim period are treated as pre-existing condition for the new policy, which is not fair. This is seen as major issue as it changes the conditionalities about what constitutes pre-exiting conditions. Courts, however, have ruled that even if there is delay in renewing the policies it should be considered as renewed policy. In case two doctors give different reports one favouring consumer and other insurance company, the insurance company generally follows the later opinion. There are several such consumer-related issues, which need to be addressed in health insurance.

One of the planks on which the insurance has been deregulated is the gain in efficiency and passing on these benefits to the consumers. It is very unrealistic to assume that insurance companies will be able to gain efficiency, which helps them to reduce the price of schemes. At least one should not be expecting this thing happening in the short-run. But providing full information to the consumer and dealing with claims in a just and expeditious manner is the minimum expected outcome of the deregulation process. Consumer organizations have to play very active role in future development of the health insurance sector in India.

There are several social issues such as exclusions of sexually transmitted diseases, AIDS, delivery and maternal conditions etc. These are not socially and ethically acceptable. "Insurance companies much take care of all the risks related to health. The companies may charge additional premium for certain conditions. Secondly the present mediclaim policy premiums are high and do not differentiate between people living in urban and rural areas where the costs of medical care are different. Thus the present policy is less attractive to poor and rural people. The tax subsidy provided to the mediclaim is also going largely to the rich who are the taxpayers. The newer health insurance policies have to improve upon the shortcoming of the existing policies.

IMPACT OF HEALTH INSURANCE ON STRUCTURE AND QUALITY OF PRIVATE PROVISION

The experiences in liberalizing the private health insurance suggest that it has undesirable effects on the costs of health care. The costs of care generally go up. Given the present system of fee for service and current scenario of health infrastructure in private sector, the development of insurance will need improvements in quality and change in structure. The new investments to improve quality will result into high cost and therefore increase in prices of insurance products. There would be developments in the direction of exploring options of managed care, which would help in reducing the costs. The developments would be needed in the direction of strong information base and accreditation system for providers. The structure of the health sector will have to change from multiple-single doctor hospitals and clinics to larger hospitals and polyclinics, which provide services of multiple specialities and can operate at larger scale. This will allow them to provide high quality professional care at competitive prices. As one of the responses to these issues Third Party Administrators (TPA) are rapidly emerging in India. Here we can learn from the models, which have emerged elsewhere. But their applicability to Indian situation needs to be examined carefully. These aspects of the health sector will need detailed study.

We lack adequate information base to operate insurance schemes at large scale. The insurance mechanism prevalent in many developed countries has their history. Health reforms experiences in many countries are replete with the suggestion that the systems cannot be replicated easily. Self-regulation is an important in any market driven system. The regulation from outside does not work. Implementation of regulation in this sector is difficult. We significantly lack mechanisms and institutions, which would ensure self-regulation and continuing education of provides and various stakeholders. The accreditation systems are hard to implement without mechanisms to self-regulate. For example it took 35 years in US to put the accreditation system effectively in place. For example, it has been difficult for many States in India to put nursing homes legislation in place. Given the deterioration on standards in medical education, lack of regulation by medical council and rising expectations of the community it is difficulty to ensure quality standards in Indian health care system. Given this situation health insurance systems will have to deal with this complex issue of quality of care in years to come.

ROLE OF REGULATORS

The government has established Insurance Regulatory and Development Authority (IRDA) which is the statutory body for regulation of the whole insurance industry. They would be granting licenses to private companies and will regulate the insurance business. As the health insurance is in its very early phase, the role of IRDA will be very crucial. They have to ensure that the sector develops rapidly and the benefit of the insurance goes to the consumers. But it has to guard against the ill effects of private insurance. The main danger in the health insurance business we see is that the private companies will cover the risk of middle class who can afford to pay high premiums. Unregulated reimbursement of medical costs by the insurance companies will push up the prices of private care. So large section of India's population who are not insured-will be at a relative disadvantage as they will, in future, have to pay much more for the private care. Thus checking increase in the costs of medical care will be very important role of the IRDA.

Secondly, IRDA will need to evolve mechanisms by which it puts some kind of statue in place that private insurance companies do not skim the market by focusing on rich and upper-class clients and in the process neglect a major section of India's population. They must ensure that companies develop products for such poorer segments of the community and possibly build an element of cross-subsidy for them. Government companies can take the lead in this matter and catalyze new products for the poor and lower middle class as they have done in the past. Thirdly the regulators should also encourage NGOs, Co-operatives and other collectives to inter into the health insurance business and develop products for the poor as well as for the middle class employed in the services sector such as education, transportation, retailing etc and the self employed. This could be run as no-profit-no loss basis similar to the scheme pioneered by Indian Medical Association for its members. Special licenses will have to be given to NGO for this purpose without insisting on the minimum capital norms, which are for commercial insurance companies.

EXPERIENCE OF HEALTH INSURANCE IN OTHER COUNTRIES: US & GERMANY

Various developed countries have differing insurance system to cover health risks. It is useful to contrast the American private health insurance system to German Social health insurance system. Table gives this comparison. It is clear from the above that the German system is clearly superior to the American system. German system is social health insurance based on some key principles of solidarity, delegation and free choice, while American system is based on private market philosophy (Reinhard 1999, Stierle 2000). Thus the German system is much more suited to the needs of the developing countries.

Table

Key Features	American system	German System
Owners of health insurance	Private companies	Sickness funds composed of Members who are workers of one type - as in a cooperative
Coverage, and access to health care	70 % of population covered, access to health care unequal	99.5% of population covered and access to every one is equal
Premium based on	Actuarial risk (Age, sex, disease)	Income - % of pay roll. Shared equally by employer and employees
Selection and refusals	Do occur	Not allowed by law
Reimbursement to providers	Based on costs and per cases/procedure basis	Outpatient is on prospective per capita basis, in-patient per day, per case basis.
Nature of subsidy (risk pooling)	From healthy to sick	Healthy to sick, high income to low income, young to old, small families to big families
Choice of providers	Yes - but being restricted in HMO system	Yes - wide choice
Coverage & co-payments	Limited to medical care and co- payments high	Coverage very wide and co-payment low
Nature of competition	Between companies	Not much - recently between sickness funds.
Nature of regulation	Minimal by government, mostly by market forces	Self-regulation by autonomous bodies under overall framework of social legislation
Effect of medical costs	Highly inflationary - recently this effect is reduced due to various controls	Inflationary effect limited due to prospective per capita payment.

But some of the prerequisites of the German system are not present in India. For example for social health insurance to work the work force has to be organized and working in formal sector so that their incomes are clear and there is a mechanism for payroll deduction of the contribution. It also needs a well-developed regulatory framework and culture of solidarity and self-regulation so that well off section of the community is willing to pay for the costs of sickness. Universal compulsory social health insurance is not possible in India at this stage but NGOs and workers in the formal sector can for organizations to try out such social health insurance in India. Experiences from other countries such as Malaysia and Philippines needs to be studies (Malayasia 1999, Philippines 1999); so that we can develop a model based on good innovations from various countries while keeping the realities of Indian health system.

CONCLUSION

In India has limited experience of health insurance. Given that government has liberalized the insurance industry, health insurance is going to develop rapidly in future. The challenge is to see that it benefits the poor and the weak in terms of better coverage and health services at lower costs without the negative aspects of cost increase and over use of procedures and technology in provision of health care. The experience from other places suggest that ifhealth insurance is left to the private market it will only cover those which have substantial ability to pay leaving out the poor and making them more vulnerable. Hence India should proactively make efforts to develop Social Health Insurance patterned after the German model where there is universal coverage, equal access to all and cost controlling measures such as prospective per capita payment to providers. Given that India does not have large organized sector employment the only option for such social health insurance is to develop it through co-operatives, associations and unions. The existing health insurance programmes such as ESIS and Mediclaim also need substantial reforms to make them more efficient and socially useful. Government should catalyze and guide development of such social health insurance in India. Researchers and donors should support such development.

9

MICRO-INSURANCE IN INDIA: TRENDS AND STRATEGIES FOR FURTHER EXTENSION

Microfinance phenomenon is one of the most remarkable socio-economic developments of our times. For a long time the poor, because of their economic circumstance, were considered non-bankable. However, the "micro-credit phenomenon" has shown that the poor can be made creditworthy if they are organized in small groups. This clearly has profound implications not just from a finance perspective but, more importantly, from the perspective of poverty alleviation.

Inspired by the Grameen experiment that started in Bangladesh around mid-70s, micro-credit has quickly spread in other parts of the developing world, including India. Micro-credit in India really started in a big way in the early 90s with the recognition of self-help groups as conduit for providing credit to the poor. In the late 90s, numerous agencies involved in micro-credit operations in India started adding other financial services, including micro-insurance to its micro-credit operations. Microfinance is surely coming of age in India.

The importance of microfinance must be looked against the fact that even with wide network of banks in India, the low-income people especially in rural areas, have been largely bypassed by the formal banking system. The government of India has been involved in its promotion in a variety of ways. This movement needs further guidance and direction from government.

This paper provides an overview of the micro-insurance scene in India and suggests strategies for its further extension. The paper should be useful for all those involved in microfinance.

INTRODUCTION

Micro-insurance, the term used to refer to insurance to the low-income people, is different from insurance in general as it is a low value product (involving modest premium and benefit package) which requires different design and distribution strategies such as premium based on community risk rating (as opposed to individual risk rating), active involvement of an intermediate agency representing the target community and so forth. Insurance is fast emerging as an important strategy even for the low-income people engaged in wide variety of income generation activities, and who remain exposed to variety of risks mainly because of absence of cost-effective risk hedging instruments.

Although the type of risks faced by the poor such as that of death, illness, injury and accident, are no different from those faced by others, they are more vulnerable to such risks because of their economic circumstance. In the context of health contingency, for example, a World Bank study (Peters et al. 2002), reports that about one-fourth of hospitalized Indians fall below the poverty line as a result of their stay in hospitals. The same study reports that more than 40 percent of hospitalized patients take loans or sell assets to pay for hospitalization. Indeed, enhancing the ability of the poor to deal with various risks is increasingly being considered integral to any poverty reduction strategy (Holzmann and Jorgensen 2000, Siegel et al. 2001).

Of the different risk management strategies, insurance that spreads the loss of the (few) affected members among all the members who join insurance scheme and also separates time of payment of premium from time of claims, is particularly beneficial to the poor who have limited ability to mitigate risk on account of imperfect labour and credit markets.

In the past insurance as a prepaid risk managing instrument was never considered as an option for the poor. The poor were considered too poor to be able to afford insurance premiums. Often they were considered uninsurable, given the wide variety of risks they face. However, recent developments in India, as elsewhere, have shown that not only can the poor make small periodic contributions that can go towards insuring them against risks but also that the risks they face (such as those of illness, accident and injury, life, loss of property etc.) are eminently insurable as these risks are mostly independent or idiosyncratic. Moreover, there are cost-effective ways of extending insurance to them. Thus, insurance is fast emerging as a prepaid financing option for the risks facing the poor.

DEVELOPMENT OF MICRO-INSURANCE IN INDIA

Historically in India, a few micro-insurance schemes were initiated, either by nongovernmental organizations (NGO) due to the felt need in the communities in which these organizations were involved or by the trust hospitals. These schemes have now gathered momentum partly due to the development of micro-finance activity, and partly due to the regulation that makes it mandatory for all formal insurance companies to extend their activities to rural and well-identified social sector in the country (IRDA 2000). As a result, increasingly, micro-finance institutions (MFIs) and NGOs are negotiating with the for-profit insurers for the purchase of customized group or standardized individual insurance schemes for the low-income people. Although the reach of such schemes is still very limited---anywhere between 5 and 10 million individuals---their potential is viewed to be considerable. The overall market is estimated to reach Rs. 250 billion by 2008 (ILO 2004).

The insurance regulatory and development authority (IRDA) defines rural sector as consisting of (i) a population of less than five thousand, (ii) a density of population of less than four hundred per square kilometer, and (iii) more than twenty five per cent of the male working population is engaged in agricultural pursuits. The categories of workers falling under agricultural pursuits are: cultivators, agricultural labourers, and workers in livestock, forestry, fishing, hunting and plantations, orchards and allied activities.

The social sector as defined by the insurance regulator consists of (i) unorganized sector (ii) informal sector (iii) economically vulnerable or backward classes, and (iv) other categories of persons, both in rural and urban areas.

The social obligations are in terms of number of individuals to be covered by both life and non-life insurers in certain identified sections of the society. The rural obligations are in terms of certain minimum percentage of total polices written by life insurance companies and, for general insurance companies, these obligations are in terms of percentage of total gross premium collected. Some aspects of these obligations are particularly noteworthy. First, the social and rural obligations do not necessarily require (cross) subsidizing insurance. Second, these obligations are to be fulfilled right from the first year of commencement of operations by the new insurers. Third, there is no exit option available to insurers who are not keen on servicing the rural and low-income segment. Finally, non-fulfillment of these obligations can invite penalties from the regulator.

In order to fulfill these requirements all insurance companies have designed products for the poorer sections and low-income individuals. Both public and private insurance companies are adopting similar strategies of developing collaborations with the various civil society associations. The presence of these associations as a mediating agency, or what we call a nodal agency, that represents, and acts on behalf of the target community is essential in extending insurance cover to the poor. The nodal agency helps the formal insurance providers overcome both informational disadvantage and high transaction costs in providing insurance to the low-income people. This way microinsurance combines positive features of formal insurance (pre paid, scientifically organized scheme) as well as those of informal insurance (by using local information and resources that helps in designing appropriate schemes delivered in a cost effective way). In the absence of a nodal agency, the low resource base of the poor, coupled with high transaction costs (relative to the magnitude of transactions) gives rise to the affordability issue. Lack of affordability prevents their latent demand from expressing itself in the market. Hence the nodal agencies that organise the poor, impart training, and work for the welfare of the low-income people play an important role both in generating both the demand for insurance as well as the supply of cost-effective insurance.

SUPPLY AND DEMAND SIDE DEVELOPMENTS

Supply of Micro-insurance

Recently, the ILO (2004a) prepared a list of products of all insurance companies, public as well as private, for the disadvantaged groups in India. Some of the observations made on the basis of the list are presented below:

Out of 80 listed insurance products, 45 (55%) cover only a single risk. The other products, covering a package of risks, mostly focus on 2 (20%) or 3 (18%) risks. The available products cover a wide range of risks. However, the broad majority of the insurance products cover life (40 products or 52%) or accident-related risks. The health coverage remains very limited (12 products).

Most life insurance products (23 out of 42) are addressed to individuals. However, some products may be bought both by individuals and groups.

Most life insurance products (55%) have been designed to cover anextended contract duration ranging from 3 to 20 years.

Out of 42 life insurance products, 23 are pure risk products. The other 19 products propose various types of maturity benefits.

Out of the 12 currently available health insurance products, 7 have been designed and are restricted to groups.

Out of the total 12 health products, 7 products propose the reimbursement of hospitalization expenses while the other 5 have chosen to narrow down the coverage to some specific critical illnesses.

Most of the health insurance products specifically exclude deliveries and other pregnancy-related illnesses. Most of these products also mention amongst their exclusion clauses, HIV/AIDS.

Most products whether life or non-life require a single payment of premium (i.e., a one-time payment) upon subscription.

Private insurance companies have three times more products than the public companies.

As per the IRDA statistics, the public insurance companies still play a predominant role in the present coverage of the rural and social sectors. This is only to be expected since the incumbent public insurers have been in the market for a number of years now.

Demand for Micro-insurance

On the demand side too, the ILO (2004b) has recently prepared an inventory of micro-insurance schemes operational in India. Based on this list some of the observations are made below:

The inventory lists 51 schemes that are operational in India.

Most schemes are still very young, having started their operations during the last few years. Of the 39 schemes for which this information is available, around 24 schemes came up during the last 4 years, and about 7 schemes have operated for more than a decade.

As regards the beneficiaries, the 43 schemes for which the information is available cover 5.2 million people.

Most insurance schemes (66%) are linked with micro finance services provided by specialized institutions (17 schemes) or non-specialized organizations (17 schemes). Twenty two percent of the schemes are implemented by community based organizations, and 12% by health care providers.

Life and health are the two most popular risks for which insurance is demanded: 59% of schemes provide life insurance and 57% of them provide health insurance.[8] In SEWA's[9] experience health insurance tops the list of risks for which the poor need insurance.

Twenty-five out of 37 schemes received some external funds to initiate their schemes. Twenty out of 32 schemes received external technical assistance in the form of advisory services, technical services, training or even referral services for their schemes.

In the majority of the schemes special staff had been recruited to manage the insurance activities. The other schemes kept relying on their regular staff while recognizing them the additional responsibilities linked to the management of the scheme.

Most schemes (74%) operate in 4 southern states of India: Andhra Pradesh (27%), Tamil Nadu (23%), Karnataka (17%) and Kerala (8%), and the two western states (Maharashtra (12%) and Gujarat (6%)) account for 18% of the schemes. 56% of schemes deal with one single risk.

Most schemes require single yearly premium at the time of subscription. Of the 43 schemes, 6 use a monthly payment for their contribution, while 2 others have linked the contributions to some other activities developed with their members (disbursement of loan etc.).

Most of the schemes (27) rely on voluntary contribution, while 10 schemes imposed compulsory contributions, and 7 adopted a mix of voluntary and compulsory contributions (based on the type of service provided).

Any nodal agency keen on buying insurance for their members now have a choice of insurers and approach those who offer them the best deal. According to the ILO inventory, 8 schemes have already entered into partnerships with at least 2 insurance companies (public or commercial), and 3 schemes have already entered simultaneous partnerships with both public and commercial insurance companies.

Clearly, health and life are two most important risks for which insurance is demanded. Indeed, at low-income level, when much of the income goes into meeting basic needs, the scope of having varying priority needs is very limited. On the supply side we observe that out of 80 odd products only 7 products are health insurance products that provide for reimbursement of hospital expenses. Admittedly, compared to life insurance, which is a relatively straightforward business, health insurance is a much more complex service as it involves addressing the provision of healthcare that is location specific. The design and sale of products are currently driven by the objective of meeting the regulatory obligation and the making of profits or reducing losses. In this situation, there is a danger of certain priority needs getting neglected by the insurance companies. Most products require single yearly premium at the time of subscription. It is well known that rural incomes are irregular and uncertain to enable payment of premium in one go, and more so when only a part of the remuneration is paid in cash. In the above, we find only a few schemes offer flexibility in paying premium. This could act as a serious drawback in increasing the membership.

We find that most of the schemes are concentrated in the southern region of the country. The southern regions are well known for the social mobilization of low-income people. In contrast, the northern region is bereft of such mobilization as the nodal agencies are either non-existent or dysfunctional. Creating and nurturing nodal agencies can be quite involved and can take a long time to develop. Local government, that can also perform the role of nodal agency, will take a long time to strengthen as a result of decentralization process currently underway in most Indian states. There has to be alternative approaches to extending insurance in regions where nodal agencies do not exist.

Even before insurance is bought for all important contingencies, affordability constraint is likely to kick in, especially for the low-income people. The issue then is how to cover for these other important contingencies. One of the ways suggested is to impose a tax at industry level (this could be on the turnover or profits of the industry), and use the tax proceeds for the benefit of workforce involved in activities peripheral to the industry. Finally, the type of contingency and the number of people covered under it are important parameters, but so is the extent of benefit provided should the contingency happen. Currently, the benefit or protection provided under some insurance schemes is quite shallow.

The attitude of insurers on these obligations has been mixed. Some have taken a positive view of the regulatory obligations and have made a genuine attempt to understand the rural and low-income segment of the market. Indeed, a few insurers have actually surpassed their obligations by a wide margin. These companies have realised that there is potential in the rural and low-income segment but tapping that potential requires a different kind of approach. In some cases, insurance companies have actually cross10 subsidised their micro-insurance products while in other cases insurers have been able to find a donor for paying premium, at least in part, on behalf of the low-income people. The impact of rural and social obligations on extending insurance to the intended people has been positive. However, development of micro-insurance needs further guidance from the insurance regulator by way of supplementary provisions. Sensing this, the insurance regulator has already come out with a concept paper on micro-insurance in which it has spelled out its thinking on what these supplementary provisions could be.

ON EXTENDING MICRO-INSURANCE

Prior to the introduction of social and rural obligations, insurance to the lowincome people took the form of (i) a nodal agency tying up with one of the public insurance companies (the intermediate model), and (ii) a nodal agency itself underwriting risk i.e., performing the role of an insurance company (the insurer model). However, with the social and rural obligations the insurer model is becoming less common and is getting subsumed in the intermediate model. To further promote this model, the IRDA is thinking of introducing supplementary provisions outlined in its concept note on micro-insurance in which it defines 'micro-insurance' and 'micro-insurance agent'. The concept note suggests how a single insurance company can offer composite insurance product to the low-income people, sets a ceiling on the commission that can be paid to insurance agents, minimum coverage to make insurance meaningful, and so forth.

At a time when the supplementary provisions on micro-insurance are still under consideration by IRDA, two aspects that need to be considered are: (i) the role of flexibility in premium collection, and (ii) micro-insurance taken up by MFIs as distinct from non-MFIs. We elaborate each of these two points below.

Flexibility in Premium

In the IRDA's concept note on micro-insurance there is no provision that explicitly calls for allowing flexibility in premium collection which is necessary for extending the reach of micro-insurance. Although some micro-insurance products allow for half-yearly, quarterly and even monthly payment of premium, most products whether life or non-life require single, yearly payment of premium upon subscription. This can be a serious drawback in extending the reach of insurance to the low-income people, especially in rural areas. Often nodal agencies adopt several methods to facilitate premium collection. These methods may take the form of soft loans for paying premium, collecting premium in kind, collecting smaller amounts but more frequently, having insurance contract of shorter durations and so forth. Where a nodal agency collects annual premium in one go, there is not much involvement of the agency. Rural incomes display seasonality. Moreover, for the low income people premium constitutes a significant proportion of their income. Therefore, flexibility in premium collection has a bearing on their joining or not joining an insurance scheme, and hence, on the membership size. The literature on micro-insurance cites the importance of appropriate 'timings' for premium collection. In particular, premium collection schedule should match with the cash flows.

The cash flow varies for different categories of workers. For example, the cash flows in case of farmers would depend on the number of crop cycles in a year as well as on the timings of harvest whereas a self-employed household worker may have a more stable income stream. Therefore, synchronizing premium collection with the harvest time is necessary for farmers whereas for selfemployed household workers paying premium in small but regular installments may be easier. Also, cash flows for the rural poor may be different from those of the urban poor. The 'type' of flexibility needed in premium collection would depend very much on (i) the pattern of income stream of the target population, and (ii) the spread of risk for which insurance is sought. As noted above the former is necessary for increasing the membership. The latter is needed to induce insurance company to allow for flexibility in premium collection.

To elaborate on this, supposing for a one year insurance contract, premium is collected twice a year in equal installments. If the risks for which insurance is bought are unevenly distributed between the two sub-periods that make up a year then the interest of insurance company needs to be protected against the possibility of greater outflow (on account of higher claims) than the premium inflow in the first sub-period. The protection could come when either the nodal agency provides for some implicit guarantees or when the insurance contract is initiated in a sub period having lower risk or when flexibility in premium collection is built taking this fact into account. Thus, flexibility in premium collection needs to be appropriate from the viewpoint of both the insurer and the insured. An explicit provision in this respect in the concept note would be a significant step forward.

Formally, we demonstrated this below:

Supposing in a single period case, a risk averse, utility maximizing agent faces two states of nature: a good state, whose probability is denoted by (1-p), yields income y, and a bad (loss) state, with probability p, yields income denoted by y-L. Faced with these uncertain income prospects, the agent's expected utility is given as:

$$(1-p)\ u(y) + p\ u(y-L)$$

To convert this uncertain prospect into a certain prospect, supposing the agent has the option of buying insurance at an actuarially fair price.15 Faced with this option, the standard result in insurance theory suggests that the agent would buy full insurance (see Mas-Colell et al. 1995, pp. 187-188). The utility the agent would get after buying full insurance is given as: u(y-pL), where pL denotes actuarially fair premium paid by the agent. This stylized result holds when the agent in question has sufficient income to buy insurance. In case of the poor, who often live on day-to-day basis, the analysis needs to be modified. While the poor may be able to afford premium on the basis of his average annual income, he may not be able to pay premium in a single installment.

That is, while $y\text{-}p\ L > c$, (the aggregate income less the premium is greater than the basic consumption denoted by c), he may not be able to pay premium in one go, if this aggregate income y is earned in different periods, whereas the insurance contract is for the entire period. In particular, if the agent earns his income y, in two equal installments, and his consumption is also split evenly over this two periods, then assuming that risk is also spread evenly, the more appropriate representation of his expected utility is not (1-p) u(y) + p u(y-L) as assume above, but rather 2 {(1-p/2) u(y/2) + p/2 u(y/2-L)}, that is, two times the utility the agent gets in a sub-period (the expression in the curly braces represents utility in a sub-period).

Notice that we cannot split the loss in the two sub-periods in the same way as we do for income and consumption because of the lumpiness of it (the bad state is defined as the state in which agent's experiences loss, L).

We continue to assume that the agent earns this total income in two sub-periods, while the insurance contract is for the entire two periods. It is easy to check that the best strategy would be to collect premium in two installments. In the absence of savings the agent may not be able to pay premium if it is collected in one installment. That is, if y/2-pL< c/2, the agent would not be able to pay premium and hence not buy insurance.

However, if the agent is charged premium in two equal installments he may be able to buy insurance. We demonstrate this below. Expected utility of agent when he is fully insured and the premium is spread over two sub periods is:

u((y-pL)/2) + u((y-pL)/2) or 2u((y-pL)/2)

That the agent is better off with insurance than without it (that is, u((y-pL)/2) > {(1-p/2) u(y/2) + p/2 u(y/2-L)}), follows straightaway from the fact that insurance at actuarially fair price makes risk averse agent better off. This suggests that periodicity in premium collection should match the income schedule of the target community under consideration. In the above we assumed symmetry with respect to risk as well as income. We allow for asymmetries in risk and income below. In particular we consider two cases: case (i) when risk is asymmetric, and case (ii) when income is asymmetric.

Case (i): When Risk is Asymmetric

Supposing now that the risk over these two sub-periods is not spread evenly. Let's assume that the risk is higher (2p/3) in the first sub-period than in the second sub-period (p/3). In the absence of insurance, agent's expected utility would be given as:

$$\{(1-2p/3)\ u(y/2) + (2p/3)\ u(y/2-L)\} +$$
$$\{(1-p/3)\ u(y/2) + (p/3)\ u(y/2-L)\}$$

The two expressions in the curly braces represent agent's utility in each of the sub-periods.

In this case too if insurance premium is spread out evenly, agent's expected utility continues to be the same as in the previous case (2 u(y-pL)/2)). However, if the premium is spread out evenly, the insurer may actually stand to lose if the agent, having lived the first (more risky) sub-period, fails to pay second installment. In this situation, from insurer's viewpoint the premium collection in the first sub-period (pL/2) will fall short of the claims (2pL/3). For this reason, the insurer is likely to oppose the collection of premium in two equal installments in each of the sub-periods. Alternatively, insurer may prefer to initiate insurance contract during the sub-period when the agent has lower risk (because the premium collection (pL/2) would exceed claims (pL/3), and therefore insurance company faces no risk of losing out in case agent fails to repay during the second sub-period).

Case (ii): When Income is Asymmetric

Consider another situation where the asymmetry between the two sub-periods is not in terms of risk but in terms of income. Supposing that now the agent earns 2/3 rd of his income in the first sub-period and the remaining in the second sub-period. In the absence of insurance his utility is:

$$\{(1\text{-}p/2)\ u(2y/3) + (p/2)\ u(2y/3\text{-}L)\} +$$
$$\{(1\text{-}p/2)\ u(y/3) + (p/2)\ u(y/3\text{-}L)\}$$

His utility in case of insurance when the premium is distributed evenly is;

$$u(2y/3\text{-}pL/2) + u(y/3\text{-}pL/2)\}.$$

From the agent's perspective it is better to pay higher premium when his income is higher. (The agent is unlikely to pay half the premium amount in the second sub-period when his income is lower.) From an insurer's perspective, it is better to collect premium in equal installments since risks are distributed evenly. Collecting premium in two unequal installments (lower installment when the agent's income is lower) gives rise to the same problem as discussed above: that the agent may not pay the second installment. A way to get around this problem is to collect premium in two unequal installments but beginning from higher installment in the period in which agent has higher income.

The above analysis highlights the need for having flexibility in premium collection and, moreover, the type of flexibility depends very much on the risks and the income of the target community. Thus, appropriately flexible mechanism from the viewpoint of both the insurer and the insured is essential for ensuring higher membership in micro-insurance scheme.

Micro-insurance and Micro-finance

Micro-finance activity in the country is leading to the spread of micro-insurance among its members/clients. For MFIs, integrating insurance with their credit and savings activities makes logical sense as it helps them to reap scale economies in financial management, provides them with a captive market, and enables them to use their existing network and distribution channels to sell insurance. Besides, linking micro-insurance with micro-credit makes it cheaper for the borrower to have both these financial services. Indeed, the natural linkage between micro-insurance and micro-finance is well reflected in the ILO inventory referred to earlier. Not only are the specialized microfinance organizations the most numerous in initiating the micro-insurance schemes, but many organizations involved in other activities are also providing micro-finance services to their target groups. Since most of the larger micro-finance organizations operate in the three southern states of Andhra Pradesh, Tamil Nadu and Karnataka, the existence of micro-insurance schemes in the south appears directly proportional to the growth of micro-finance activities in that part of the country.

Insurance helps in reducing interest rate charged on credit. With insurance interest rate together with the premium may be lower than interest rate charged in the absence of insurance. The intuition runs as follows: contingencies such as illness, accident, life etc. have a bearing on project performance and thereby on loan recovery. Health insurance, for example, by improving financial access to medical care of the insured who takes loan/credit, reduces disruption in the economic activity for which loan is taken, and thereby enables the borrower to repay loan. Higher loan recovery is an important determinant of interest rate charged by a lending agency. The higher the loan recovery, the lower is the interest rate charged by a lender. Thus, insurance, by reducing the risk of loan default due to the contingency against which insurance is bought, reduces interest rate charged by the lender. For this reason it makes better sense for micro credit organizations to introduce micro-insurance. Important here is to stress that when insurance is integrated with credit the total amount charged (i.e., interest plus premium) may be lower than the interest charged in the absence of insurance.

Below we formally demonstrate why integrating micro-insurance with micro finance makes better sense.

Let us first look at the issue from a borrower's perspective. Supposing u (y) denotes the utility that a risk averse agent (characterised by standard concavity assumptions made on the utility function) gets from his income, y. Supposing in a twoperiod setting, the agent's income in the first period is y, and he runs the risk of not being able to earn this usual income in the second period if he, for example, falls sick. In the event of sickness, whose probability for the sake of simplicity is 0.5, his income reduces by z. His 2-period utility is given as:

$$u(y)+(1/2)[u(y)+u(y-z)]$$

Note that, we have assumed the discount rate to be 1 (this is a simplifying assumption). If the agent has access to insurance he would be better off with insurance than without it as his utility with insurance would be strictly greater than without it i.e., $[u(y-z/2)+ u(y)] > u(y)+(1/2)[u(y)+u(y-z)]$. But our starting point is the case when the agent (or the borrower) does not have access to insurance.

Against this backdrop, let's examine the case in which the agent takes credit for some productive activity in period 1. Let L denote the loan amount, R denote the return the borrower generates on the investment made from the loan amount, and r denote the rate of interest the borrower has to pay to the lender. We assume that the activity for which loan is taken is per se risk free i.e., there is no inherent risk in the project for which the loan is taken. This is a simplifying assumption motivated by the fact that the risk of the failure of micro enterprises (distinct from that of loan default) is negligible. We further assume that the loan default occurs if the individual falls sick, in which case he neither repays the loan amount nor gains from the borrowed loan. Under these assumptions, his two-period utility would be:

$$u(y)+(1/2)[u(y+(R-r)L)+u(y-z)]$$

We have assumed that the loan taken in the first period cannot bc used as consumption loan. It has to be strictly invested in an income generating activity (hence L does not figure in the first period utility). The borrower reaps the benefit from the activity only in the second period if he stays healthy. However, if he falls sick, the value of the income generating activity depreciates. For simplicity we assume that this value becomes nil (i.e., L=0) so that neither the lender nor the borrower is able to recover anything from the investment.

Supposing that the agent has an option of buying insurance by paying actuarially fair premium in the first period. Since insurance is available at actuarially fair premium (z/2), the standard result in the literature shows that the agent would go for full insurance cover.

His utility after purchase of insurance would be:18

$$u(y-(z/2))+u(y+(R-r)L)$$

From lender's perspective there are two cases:

Case I: when the agent (the borrower) doesn't have insurance

In this case, the lender would charge interest rate so that the amount he gets back is greater than (or equal to) the amount he has to pay i.e., the cost of credit to the lender denoted by s. This condition is shown below.

r0 L/2 sL, where r0 is the interest rate charged by the lender

=> r0 2s. ....(1)

In equilibrium, this inequality will hold as equality.

Case II: when the agent (the borrower) has insurance

In case the agent has insurance, the probability of loan default is zero in which case the lender is able to recover full amount he lends. So the rate of interest he charges is greater than the cost of funds to the lender i.e.,

r1 L s L. ....(2)

where r1 is the interest rate charged by the lender

In equilibrium this inequality will hold as equality.

From (1) and (2), it is straightforward to check that r0>r1.

From the borrower's perspective it would be better to have insurance when the interest rate plus the premium that he is lower than the interest rate charged in the absence of insurance. This would be the case if r0>r1+z/2. Substituting the equilibrium values of r0 and r1 yields the condition: 2s > s+z/2 or 2s>z. Thus from borrower's perspective it may make good sense to buy insurance along with loan only when the above condition holds.

The lender whose clients do not have access to insurance would end up charging higher rate of interest and this would tend to turn his borrowers away from him and towards the lender who also provides insurance. So, from the lender's perspective it makes good sense to integrate insurance with their finance operations.

Given the beneficial outcome of integrating micro-insurance with micro-finance, it is necessary to have a pro-active policy that would promote such integration. Currently, the MFIs are not even regulated and therefore the scope of public policy in promoting this integration or even promoting micro-insurance in general is very limited. Furthermore, besides MFIs, microcredit is also being extended by the government through several programs. It becomes imperative for the government to have a clear thinking on how to promote micro-insurance on the one hand and microcredit with its positive impact on poverty reduction and empowerment on the other. At present, the concept note does not make any distinction between micro-insurance through micro-finance institutions and micro-insurance through other agencies.

CONCLUSIONS

Policy-induced and institutional innovations are promoting insurance among the low-income people who form a sizable sector of the population and who are mostly without any social security cover. Although the current reach of 'micro-insurance' is limited, the early trend in this respect suggests that the insurance companies, both public and private, operating with commercial considerations, can insure a significant percentage of the poor. Serving low-income people who can pay the premium certainly makes a sound commercial sense to insurance providers. To that extent imposing social and rural obligations by insurance regulator (IRDA) is helping all insurance companies appreciate the vast untapped potential in serving the lower end of the market.

However, it is becoming increasingly clear that micro-insurance needs a further push and guidance from the regulator as well as the government. IRDA has already come up with the concept note on micro-insurance, which suggests the regulator's bias towards insurer-agent model. Even so, two areas in which having explicit provisions would aid the development of micro-insurance are: one, flexibility in premium collection, and two, encouraging micro-insurance among micro-finance institutions (MFIs).

Given irregular and uncertain income stream of the poor, flexibility in premium collection is needed to extend the micro-insurance net far and wide. Moreover, MFIs are playing a significant role in improving the lives of poor households. Quite apart from this, linking micro-insurance with micro-finance makes better sense as it helps in bringing down the cost of lending. Given this, there is a case for strengthening the link between micro-insurance and micro-credit. At present microfinance business in the country is unregulated. Regulation of MFIs is needed not only to promote micro-finance activity in the country but also to promote the linking of micro-insurance with micro-finance which as demonstrated in the paper makes a good sense.

KARNATAKA HEALTH INSURANCE SCHEME FOR RURAL FARMERS & PEASANTS

This is a case study of the Yeshasvini Health Insurance Scheme for rural farmers and peasants in Karnataka. The scheme, now in its second year of operation, covers 2.2 million farmers and peasants who pay an annual premium of Rupees 60 ($1.50) for comprehensive coverage of all surgical procedures and outpatient care. The scheme is unique in that it has overcome many of the problems associated with health insurance schemes for the poor (such as low levels of coverage and benefits). These features raise the potential of the scheme to be a model for developing countries in providing a modicum of health security for their citizens. In this case study we describe the origins and functioning of the scheme and analyze its performance todate, with a view to assessing the generalizability of this model of health insurance to other populations and countries. We find support for transferability to several other states in India, particularly those with a reasonable network of private hospitals. We also identify the institutional conditions that influence success of a scheme like this, while discussing some of the critical problems that occurred during the scheme's first year of operations.

This is a case study of the Yeshasvini Health Insurance Scheme introduced throughout rural Karnataka in 2003. In its first year of operation, the scheme covered 1.6 million rural farmers and peasants dispersed throughout Karnataka state. For a premium payment of only Rs 5 per month or Rs. 60 per year, participants are covered for all surgical interventions, major or minor, and for outpatient services (OPD) at a network of private hospitals. At the end of the first year of operations in June 2004, 9,039 surgeries had been performed, and 35,814 patients had received outpatient consulting services. A significant proportion of total surgeries were classified as "major" (e.g. cardiac surgery) without which the patient would not have survived. The Yeshasvini scheme (hereinafter referred to as "the scheme") is the world's largest health insurance scheme for the rural poor. Given its remarkable success in the first year of operations, the increased number of people covered in its second year (2.2 million), and replications and extensions of the scheme in Gujarat and in other parts of Karnataka, the scheme is already becoming an important model of health insurance for disadvantaged populations within and outside of India.

The aim of this chapter is to document and analyze the Yeshasvini case. It has not been studied previously. As the scheme breaks new ground on several different fronts in providing health insurance to large rural populations, we will describe the origins of the scheme, the process of its establishment, the rational for decisions taken along the way, the major problems and drawbacks that need to be addressed for the future, and the lessons for transferability to other populations within Karnataka, the rest of India and the world. The section below briefly highlights the urgent need for health insurance coverage for poor, rural and informal sectors, and through a brief survey of six selected typical experiments around the world, identifies the key challenges in providing such health care coverage.

Thereafter, we discuss various aspects of the Yeshasvini scheme, with specific reference to its origins and how it has overcome many of the challenges that have plagued health insurance schemes in other places. Then,, we look at some representative data, and some case studies of individuals and hospitals to get a "feel" for how the scheme operates in practice. Finally, we examine reasons for success and evaluate the potential transferability of this model to other populations within India, and across the world.

THE CRITICAL NEED FOR HEALTH INSURANCE FOR POOR, RURAL, AND INFORMAL SECTOR POPULATIONS

Providing health insurance or health security for poor people continues to be one of the most important unresolved policy issues for the world. Most rural and informal sector workers in the world do not have any form of health insurance. And in most developing countries, the rural and informal sectors constitute the bulk of the population. In India, for example, estimates suggest that 90% of India's families earn their livelihood from the unorganized sector, contributing 40% of the nation's GDP (Jhabvala and Subrahmanya 2000). However, they are poor, most of them are not in employer-employee relationships, they do not have any form of insurance or security (e.g. maternity benefits, retirement, health insurance), nor do they have representative organizations that might help them fight for these benefits (Ahmad et al. 1991, Gumber & Kulkarni 2000).

The poor are particularly vulnerable to the lack of health security. Studies show that the poor spend a greater percentage of their budget on health related expenditures (this varies between 6-8% in various studies see Sheriff et al 1999). The burden of treatment is particularly devastating for major health issues, and particularly when they seek "in-patient" care (hospitalization). Further, the high incidence of sickness (morbidity in technical terms) cuts into their budget in two different ways, i.e. they need to spend large amounts of money for treatment and are unable to earn money while under treatment. In fact, healthcare costs are one of the primary reasons for rural indebtedness and poverty (Gumber 1997). It is estimated that at least 24 per cent of all Indians hospitalized fall below the poverty line because they are hospitalized, and that out-of-pocket spending on hospital care raises by 2% the proportion of the population in poverty (Peters et al. 2001, 2002).

Moreover, there is the issue of accessability....given that a majority of poor households reside in remote rural areas where no government or private medical facilities are available. Obtaining treatment at a town or district level hospital involves travel costs, which are not insignificant. Thus for many, simply accessing health care is by itself, an expensive proposition. See for example, Subrahmanya and Jhabvala (2000) and Gumber and Kulkarni (2000) for a more extensive analysis and documentation of the various studies that highlight health security concerns of a majority of the world's population.

However, a common perception is that the poor are too poor to buy health insurance. While it might be true for the poorest of the poor who struggle for survival every day, it need not be true for those living close to the poverty line (Martin et al. 1999, Zeller and Sharma 1998). Moreover, there is substantial evidence that if provided with the opportunity, the poor would be willing to pay for health insurance. A recent study by Gumber and Kulkarni (2000) suggest that the rural respondents in Gujarat were willing to pay an annual premium of Rs. 80 and Rs. 95 for coverage for hospitalization, chronic ailment, and specialist consultation and an additional 16% if there was coverage of transport costs, medicine costs and diagnostic charges.

However, a large number of the existing schemes for poor people still involve part or full subsidies by the governments of various-countries.

Several obstacles stand in the way of providing health insurance to the rural poor and informal sectors (Van Ginneken 1999). First, the rural and informal sector is not a homogenous category, so it is difficult to organize them. Second, they are geographically dispersed. Third, there are no employers or it is difficult to identify employers. Fourth, providing health insurance to this section of the population is a daunting task, because rural and unorganized workers often need employment, income and social security simultaneously, which is hard to provide. As a result, for example, overall health insurance coverage is low in India (Gumber 2002). Estimates suggest that less than 10% of people in India have access to health insurance, and a majority of them belong to organized sector (Gumber 1998, Ellis et al 2000). Obviously, the demand for health care for the rural and unorganized sector has largely been unmet.

Commercial insurance companies so far have showed little interest in providing health insurance for rural farmers and workers in the informal sector because of potentially low profitability and high risk. It is non-government organizations (NGOs) and charitable institutions (not-for-profit) that have played an important role in the delivery of affordable health services to the poor. However, the coverage of these schemes have been very limited, and the record has been mixed. A recent review of 83 NGO provided health insurance schemes for the informal sector suggest issues of poor design and management, affecting their sustainability (Bennett, Creese and Monasch 1998). We reviewed several initiatives and experiments, which, despite the problems, provided us valuable experience and lessons. These include SEWA's comprehensive approach to security for its members (Gumber 2002, McCord et al 2001), ACCORD for the tribal people of Gudalur in Tamil Nadu (Eswara Prasad 1998, Devadasan et al 2004), and some micro-level schemes including NHHP (McCord 2000), UMASIDA (Van Ginneken 1999, McCord, 2000), and GRET (McCord 2001). In addition, the comprehensive social welfare schemes (which include health insurance) through welfare funds in Kerala (see Kannan 2002 for a detailed evaluation) has also received research attention.

Since these schemes have been reviewed elsewhere, we only summarize the lessons that we have learnt from the various analyses.

a) Restriction in Scope

Most health insurance schemes for poor people are limited in scope. They cover at best a very small percentage of the targeted population. In many cases, they are restricted to a single defined geographic area, or to a small subset of the population (e.g., ACCORD and the various micro-credit based schemes such as NHHP and GRET) or to a defined small population (e.g., SEWA members). From the table above, it is clear that the coverage of target population of these schemes differs significantly, ranging from 625 to 29,140 people. Similarly, Gumber's (2002) review of selected NGO managed health insurance schemes also show a large variation in the population served by the schemes. This ranges from as little as 1,247 persons in the Goalpur cooperative health society in Shantiniketan to the relatively large Raigarh Ambikapur Health Association in Madhya Pradesh which serves 400,000 people. The most studied scheme, that of SEWA in Ahmedabad serves 63,000 people.

Even the various highly regarded welfare fund schemes for unorganized sector workers in Kerala reach less than 29% of the target population. In general, keeping the scheme small and defined in terms of coverage (geographical or population) facilitates the organization of the scheme, collecting premiums, and providing access to health insurance via clinics and dispensaries (most schemes create their own clinics).

Thus, the restricted scope problem is a key issue that needs to be overcome if the goal of health insurance for the masses is to be realized. There are no examples where large sections of the rural population have been mobilized for health insurance purposes. Such mobilization is key to the success of health insurance schemes that purport to cover significant chunks of the target population.

b) Restrictions in Benefits

The second problem is the relatively restricted scope of the benefits offered. The scope of benefits is limited largely because the premiums for health insurance schemes for poor people have to be limited. Thus, the financing of health insurance is a key constraint. In fact, most schemes for the poor focus heavily on primary health care (e.g., SEWA) or have strict ceilings on hospitalization costs. For example, benefits coverage in the SEWA scheme is for a maximum of Rs. 1200 per annum, which covers only 20% of medical costs. In programs like ACCORD, the premium for the tribal people is Rs 60 per annum (for a five person family), and the maximum available for hospitalization is Rs 1500. Some commercial schemes may have a higher coverage.

For example, Mediclaim, a new insurance introduced by the General Insurance Corporation in India covers only hospitalization upto a maximum of Rs 300,000. But, unfortunately, Mediclaim is quite an urban and upper-class phenomenon. While poorer people are able to take advantage of these commercial schemes for illnesses and sometimes for hospitalization, the schemes are of little use for major health issues. Moreover, the lowest known cost of a cardiac by-pass operation in India is Rs. 75,000.

No rural or unorganized sector person will be covered by existing schemes for a cardiac operation. And this is the case for other common operations as well. The Kerala Welfare funds for informal sector workers solve this problem partially, because the cost of financing is imposed on the whole industry e.g., beedi workers via a cess on the total produce of the industry, but they also have ceilings on benefits. Thus the whole issue of financing underlies the key issue to be solved, that of restricted benefits. These problems are evident in schemes that operate outside of India as well. For example, the health insurance scheme in GRET, Cambodia only covers basic in-home care, with 15.6% average coverage of medical costs. Although UMASIDA's scheme in Tanzania provides in-and out-patient 100% coverage, there are many significant exclusions and limitations. More important, UMASIDA's scheme is not sustainable even if it has initial donor funding, since there is no plan for self-financing.

c) *Administrative Issues*

Reviews of various schemes suggest that the administrative establishment underlying the schemes were generally weak, with relatively little attention to quality of health care or efficient delivery. The administrative agencies in the six schemes in Table 1 varied, including an NGO, a unit of a hospital, and bureaucratic organization like a government department. The World Bank survey also found that the administrative operations varied dramatically. In some schemes, the provider of health care was also the administrator, while other schemes kept a division between administrators and providers. In many cases, the local government was the key administrator and responsible for providing benefits. Complaints regarding claims administration have been very high in most schemes. Generally, it was found that the restrictive scope of the scheme and the restricted benefits often co-existed with very high administrative costs, especially since many schemes had to focus on establishing their own dispensaries, care facilities, and hospitals. The high cost and weak administration was most pronounced in the case of the Kerala Welfare Funds (see Kannan 2002).

d) Accessability & Health Care Infrastructure

Last, but not least, there is the issue of accessability. Many schemes are small because of the problem of providing access. For a health insurance scheme to cover the large and highly dispersed rural population in large Indian states, an extensive network of hospitals, dispensaries and care facilities must be built, which is beyond the financial capacity of state and local governments. As we noted, most health insurance schemes like the Kerala welfare funds had their own dispensaries or clinics, some schemes like ACCORD and NHHP even have their own hospitals. Thus, the lack of a HEALTH CARE INFRASTRUCTURE or the expenses involved in creating one has been a factor that has limited the growth of health insurance schemes for the rural poor.

These are not the only problems and issues in creating health insurance for large sections of the rural population, but these are the critical problems. One other criticism that has been levied against most current health insurance schemes for rural and unorganized sector workers has been that they fail to consider the linkage to the broader health care system.......they tend to be close ended schemes with little connection to established institutions. Thus, many problems need to be solved to provide adequate health insurance for rural people.

Van Ginneken (1999) concludes after reviewing many schemes around the world that contributory schemes are more likely to be sustaining. Although the schemes in Table 1 have many problems, they do suggest that microinsurance or community-based health insurance, if properly designed and implemented, can provide an effective mechanism for meeting health care challenges of the poor (also see Jakab and Krishnan (2001), and Preker et al. (2001) for a summary of different case studies on the impact of communitybased health insurance schemes). Below, we discuss the Yeshasvini scheme in terms of how it has solved some of these problems through proper design and implementation.

THE YESHASVINI HEALTH INSURANCE SCHEME

(a) Origins of the Yeshasvini Health Insurance Scheme

The scheme originated in the mind of Dr. Devi Shetty, a cardiac surgeon who has pioneered the spread of telemedicine as well as low cost cardiac operations in India. Dr. Shetty has been acutely concerned with problems of access to sophisticated health care of the rural population. He attempted to solve this problem through the tele-medicine, using local providers and doctors in large urban hospitals connected via the internet. While this is still in the experimental stages in several Indian hospitals, what was clear is that the poor were still unable to afford medical care. Hence he turned to insurance. A pilot study commissioned by his heart Hospital in Bangalore regarding the potential of introducing health insurance revealed some interesting results. First, and as expected, it revealed critical health issues. It was for instance common for aged men to suffer from kidney failure for want of a simple prostrate operation, or from premature blindness that is easily rectifiable by a cataract extraction procedure. Even more important, many middle aged women suffered from excessive bleeding because of a diseased uterus that could be removed by an inexpensive operation. Many children were dying of appendicitis, another easily curable condition.

The study also raised several other issues that has been also uncovered in prior research, i.e., the fact that poor households spend a larger percentage of their budget on healthcare, and the fact that the major chunk of the healthcare budget of rural poor go to earning/male member of the family, followed by children and only then women. The study further revealed that the average poor farmer who perhaps owns two acres of land and maybe a cow would exhaust all of his savings just to get a serious problem diagnosed i.e. including running all diagnostic tests and traveling to a small town. By the time he / she has to go to a larger city hospital for the procedure he / she would be already in debt. This informal survey thus made it clear that it was the capacity of poor people in rural areas to pay for simple operations that was the problem that needed attention. The implications were clear.... any self-financed health insurance scheme for rural poor would have to be based on low premiums but at the same time provide benefits for surgical procedures and hospitalization expenses, as well as cover all of the costs associated with that procedure. In Dr. Shetty's mind, the only solution to this problem was to create a really large health insurance scheme, where the law of large numbers would overcome the basic financing problem associated with the small schemes of the past. This was the basis for the design of the scheme.

Interestingly this pilot study also revealed that there was no (relative) lack of healthcare infrastructure in terms of hospitals and dispensaries. The average occupancy rates in Karnataka's hospitals, was, on average only 35%. The utilization of operation theatres was even lower. At this point, we do not have comparative data for other Indian states, so we do not know whether Karnataka is an exception or the rule. Thus, supply of doctors and hospitals was not the major issue.

Figure 1 below summarizes the unique ways in which the Yeshasvini scheme in solving the four major problems identified previously, i.e. restricted scope, restricted benefits, lack of health care infrastructure and weak administration. We discuss these it in detail in the following sections.

(b) Solving the Restricted Scope Problem: Mobilizing a Large Number of Rural Subscribers

The first step in solving the restricted scope problem was to identify the target population. How does one mobilize a million dispersed rural farmers and informal sector workers in the state of Karnataka (an area of about 191,791 Sq km) with a population of 45 million of which 70% work in agriculture? Mobilization implied three major steps, i.e. communicating the scheme to the farmer, creating a system to collect their premiums, and issuing identity cards for participants. It was obvious to Dr. Shetty and his colleagues that they had to find organizations or institutions which connected rural people. And it was important that everyone in that organization or institution became Yeshasvini members. Otherwise only sick people would have joined the scheme, there would be a problem of adverse selection that would limit the subscriber base and therefore bankrupt the scheme.

The only institution in Karnataka that connected rural farmers and rural peasants were cooperative societies. The cooperative movement has had a long history in Karnataka. The first co-operative society was registered in the year 1905 in Kanaginahal village of Dharward District. Currently over 31000 co-operative societies have been established. The Co-operative movement encompasses developmental sectors like Textiles, Sericulture, Industries, Animal Husbandry, Fisheries, Sugar, Horticulture and Agriculture Credit, Marketing, etc.. Since all cooperatives are required by law to be registered with the Department of Co-operatives, Dr. Shetty initiated discussions with the Principal Secretary of the Department of Cooperatives of Karnataka State. The Principal Secretary was captivated by the novel idea and agreed to cooperate. The Department of Co-operatives oversees the administration and functioning of various co-operative institutions, and also assists the societies financially and provides technical guidance.

The interest showed by the Principal Secretary was beneficial in that an administrative machinery was available that would enable education and enrolment of potential members, using existing channels of communication between the various cooperative societies and the government. The Principal Secretary is assisted by an organization headed by a Registrar of Cooperative Societies, who in turn has deputy Registrars and district level registrars in each district, each assisted by deputy district registrars. Further, other government officers such as the District Collector (the administrative head of each district), the District Health Officer and the District Surgeon could also be involved through the Department of Cooperatives.

Dr. Shetty and his employees went around the state educating the deputy district registrars of cooperative societies about the scheme and the advantages of joining up. He and his colleagues also met with a large number of individual cooperatives, and talked with the secretaries of each society. The process envisaged was that the secretary of each cooperative society would convince the members to join the scheme. Participation in a self-financed insurance scheme must be, perforce voluntary.

However, the government, in its zeal, also got into the mobilization game. The Registrar of Cooperative Societies issued each of the deputy district registrar's a target membership to recruit. Those deputy district registrars issued each cooperative secretary a target for membership. Initially the department decided to focus its attention on cooperatives of farmers. Although there were more than 30,000 cooperatives in the state, the department of cooperatives focused on those with the largest membership, i.e. farmers, milk producers and sugarcane producers. Given this administrative "fiat" each cooperative society secretary followed his/her own methods of signing up members. In some cases, he/she discussed extensively with each individual member and convinced them to sign up. In other cases, the secretary arbitrarily signed up everybody in the society, using their cooperative dues. In yet other cases, all members with outstanding society loans were automatically signed up by the society secretary.

In any case, in this way 16 lakh people (1.6 million) signed on to the scheme and paid their annual premium. These 1.6 million people were spread over 27 districts of Karnataka's 30 districts, although south Karnataka was better represented in terms of membership. Thus, by targeting existing organizations that connected a diverse rural population of farmers, peasants, sugarcane growers, milk producers, the scheme was able to mobilize the large numbers needed for the success of a self funded health insurance scheme for the masses. There are obvious issues here in the negation of free choice for some of the participants in the scheme. In our evaluations we will re-examine this aspect.

There were several benefits to government participation in the scheme, despite the lack of free choice for some participants. For one, the government provided the access to cooperative societies, which was the key. Second the department of cooperatives administrative agency provided a vehicle through which the scheme could be popularized, and communicated to rural farmers. Third, despite the communication effort that focused on how this was private self-financed insurance, since it was popularized by the government it became known as a "govt" scheme. This is a double edged sword, though. In many cases rural farmers told us that they distrusted the government's ability to do anything and would not have joined the scheme. Others talked about agreeing to join only because it was a government scheme. Yet others told us about how the government ran poor quality hospitals, but the fact that they could go to a private hospital to get treatment via a government backed scheme was very attractive. What remains clear however is that without government involvement via its cooperative societies department it would have been impossible to sign up 1.6 million members in its first year of operation,

(c) Solving the Restricted Benefits Problem: Designing the Self Financing Aspects

Given the research results suggesting that rural poor would be willing to pay annual premium ranging from 75-85 Rupees, the premium was fixed at approximately Rs 90 per person per year. Two key assumptions were important. The first assumption was that it would cost Rs 10,000 for a life saving operation, on average. The second assumption was that only 1-2% of any population would require major surgical procedures during the year, an actuarial assumption that is generally used in the West, but not very well supported in India. Given the low premium rates, the success of any scheme would depend on generating a large number of rural subscribers. Again, and completely arbitrarily because the size of the target population was unknown, (and there was very little information about the health record of the target population), it was decided that a minimum of 1 million members (10 Lakh) would be necessary to launch the scheme.

A central tenet of Dr. Shetty's scheme was that health insurance programs for the masses had to be large, but self-financed. However, during the first year, the collaboration with Karnataka state resulted in a violation of this cardinal principle. The Karnataka government, realizing the political advantages of introducing health insurance of this kind, wanted to subsidize the scheme. This became a contentious issue. It soon became clear to Dr. Shetty that government participation in mobilization was tied to its desire to subsidize the scheme to a certain extent. A compromise was evolved where government financial participation was limited to the first year only. It was decided that the premium would be fixed at Rs 90 per annum (2 dollars per year) and each subscriber would pay Rs 60 (1.5 dollars approximately) per year, while the government provided Rs. 30 per subscriber (about .50 cents). It was also agreed that this government contribution would be a one time event for the first cycle year only. Incidentally, during the second year, 2.2 million members have signed up, so the premium has been retained at the Rs 60 level, largely because the first year experience suggested that it might be enough. The Karnataka government would still like to participate financially, but it has not done so.

Once it became clear that the numbers could be mobilized, it was also possible then to think in expanded terms of the coverage. Given the fact that poor people could not pay for hospitalization for both major and minor illnesses, it was decided that all charges associated with any surgical procedure would be covered. Thus a person who needed a heart operation would not be asked to pay any charges for the variety of diagnostic tests that are required before the operation. In fact, other than transportation, the patient would not need to incur any expenses at all.

Table 2 lists the surgical procedures that are covered by the scheme and includes the prices for each procedure that it would reimburse the hospitals (we will discuss this reimbursement process aspect later in the paper). Over 1,700 different operations are covered. However, there are significant exclusions. These include implants including Valves, Grafts Mesh, Stents, Nails, Screws and Joint Replacement surgeries, Liver transplants, and dental surgeries. The scheme also does not cover follow up investigations (unless it can be proved that there was some negligence on the part of the hospital). Each person is entitled to a maximum coverage of Rs. 200,000 per year. Typically, this would include 2 cardiac by-pass operations (Rs, 150,000) and several other smaller operations.

In addition to coverage for surgical procedures, the scheme also covers outpatient consulting at the network of hospitals. This primarily includes doctor's fees. Investigations (diagnostics and X-rays) as part of the outpatient consulting are discounted for Yeshasvini patients, i.e., done at 70% of the total costs. The scheme does not cover any type of medical treatment for the beneficiaries where surgical intervention is NOT required. We found on average that each rural person we talked to went for outpatient services about three times a year. In Mandya district, for example, the average outpatient consultation fee was Rs. 20 per visit. Thus, the cost of the premium (Rs.60) would easily be recovered with three outpatient visits alone, apart from having free surgery and related costs. This was a significant advantage of the scheme.

In this way the scheme was able to provide very wide coverage for most surgical procedures and outpatient services, to a large number of people paying very low premia, and with very large ceilings on maximum coverage (Rs. 200,000 per year). No contemporary health insurance scheme for poor /rural people anywhere in the world has such a high rate of coverage with such a low premium...the closest was the Mediclaim policy by the GIC in India that covered people for a maximum of Rs.15,000 (with a premium ranging from Rs.175 to Rs.330) to Rs.300,000 (with a premium ranging from Rs.2,825 to Rs.5,770) per year and that scheme was not primarily for the rural poor. SEWA only offers a maximum coverage of Rs 1200 per annum.

(d) Solving the Access Problem: Creating a Health Care Infrastructure through a Network of Hospitals

It was clear that to provide rural people with access to hospitals would require the active participation of the private sector. The Government has a network of hospitals, to be sure, but as is often the case, they are inefficiently run, and most patients have to pay for "free" care at government hospitals. More importantly, they are under-funded and do not always have the required equipment.

The private hospitals were not easy to convince however, as they had no means of estimating how much additional revenue participating in the network would bring. Not many hospitals could understand how a system based on individuals paying such low premium levels would work. However, given low capacity utilization rates, about 30-40 hospitals agreed to participate, but once the scheme commenced and the number of patients grew, more hospitals were coming forward. By March 2004, when this evaluation commenced about 92 hospitals were on board. By June 2004, 118 hospitals were certified to participate.

A formal process was established for evaluating hospitals before they could join the network. The administrator of the Yeshasvini scheme, (to be discussed below) established the process shown here in Figure 3. Essentially, a hospital sends its application to the District Collector, the Chief Administrative Officer of the district. The District Collector, the District cooperative Registrar, the District Health Officer and the District Surgeon visit the hospital. They then send a report FHPL. The district FHPL coordinator visits the hospitals again, to examine the quality of care at the hospital. Only hospitals with a certain level of infrastructure are allowed to be part of the network. They also obtain the rates charged by that hospital for various operations. Based on a comprehensive survey of rates charged by different hospitals in Karnataka, a rate sheet for various operations and treatments was developed. These rates are listed in Table-2. Tariffs for the most commonly performed diagnostic tests have also been fixed.

As of March 1994, only district level hospitals are part of the system. In terms of access, rural villagers will have to travel at a maximum about 100 km to get surgical care at a district level hospital. The average distance is 40 kilometres. Now, taluk level hospitals want to join, but they will have to improve their infrastructure quite dramatically over the next few years to be eligible.

(e) Solving the Administrative Problem: Professional Administration Processes and Third Party Administrators Administration

The Scheme is administered by the Yeshasvini trust, which is composed of 11 board members, drawn from the medical community and the Department of Cooperation. Currently, the Principal Secretary of the Department of Cooperatives, the Registrar, the Additional Registrar, the MD of the Apex Bank, the Secretary of the Sugar Cane Commission, the Secretary of the Karnataka Milk Federation, and five doctors who are representatives of the network of participating hospitals, are sitting in the board. The government of India's Insurance Development Regulatory Authority (IRDA) mandates that insurance schemes must have a Third Party Administrator (TPA) who will handle the schemes and the claims process, but will not be a part of the organization providing medical services. Although the IRDA does not specify such rules for self-financed schemes, the trust decided to appoint a well established private firm-Family Health Plan Limited (FHPL), a division of Apollo hospital, as the third party administrator. FHPL, with over a decade of experience in administering medical health schemes, is the largest agency in the country in health insurance scheme administration field. Moreover, FHPL is also the first TPA in India to conceptualize, design and implement a Self Funded Scheme (SFS). A representative of the trust sits in the office of FHPL to provide guidance and ensure adherence to the basic elements of the scheme. It is FHPL who devises procedures and systems for managing the scheme.

The total fees paid to FHPL for managing the scheme is Rs. 5,900,000, which translates into roughly 4% of the total subscriptions to the scheme. The total subscriptions (1.6 million subscribers each paying a total of Rs 60, and the state government's contribution of Rs. 30 per head) were Rs. 144,000,000.

Administrative Procedures

When a doctor at a network hospital determines that a Yeshasvini patient requires surgery, that doctor requests FHPL to authorize the surgery. In order for FHPL to do this, the hospital must send FHPL a pre-authorization form, along with a copy of the ID card of the patient and society membership card. They can send it by mail or courier. In cases of emergency they can call and send the documents later. FHPL's resident doctor makes a decision to authorize the operation at the prescribed fee. This is communicated to the hospital. Thereafter the hospital may proceed with the surgery. This process is called Pre-authorization. Once the pre-authorization is issued, the network hospital can proceed with the surgery and then submit the claim to FHPL.

The process is fairly simple. From the patient's point of view, there is very little administrative hassle. From the hospital's point of view as well, it is relatively efficient, and with the internet a lot can be done electronically. There are some problems however. For instance, it is possible that a patient shops at different hospitals, so maybe three pre-authorizations are issued for the same operation. It is also possible that the two hospitals that have not done the operation could also send in fictitious claims (since they have the preauthorization). This may not happen often, since the FHPL doctor is there to check and he may remember having authorized a particular operation for a particular person......but a process of canceling existing pre-authorizations once a claim is sent in by one hospital is still required.

RESULTS OF THE FIRST YEAR OF OPERATIONS

By the end of the first year of operations, a total of 9,039 surgeries had been completed valued at a total of Rs.10.53 crores ($ 2.3 million dollars). However the actual number of pre-authorizations was higher at 10,214 (valued at 11.94 crores or 2.65 million dollars). The difference between the two numbers occurs because pre-authorization are issued, but the surgery does not take place by the end of the fiscal year.

From an accounting standpoint, the scheme turned a profit. The total premium paid by 1.6 million subscribers was Rs 14.4 crores ($ 3.2 million). Subtracting the total number of surgeries (11.94 crores) and the administrative expenses paid to FHPL (Rs.59 Lakhs), the scheme generated a surplus of 1.86 crores, which has been carried forward to the second year of operations. In addition, the number of free outpatient treatments done at various hospitals was large, a total of 35,814 occasions.

We provide below some representative data on the operation of the scheme. These are a snapshot of monthly or weekly activity taken during February of 2004. By March the scheme was into its 9th month of operations.

By the end of February, 7,352 pre-authorizations for surgery had been given. Hysterectomies accounted for the largest percentage of surgeries (24.5%), closely followed by general surgery (23%). Cardiac surgery accounted for 7.35% similar to surgical procedures in cardiology, urology, and orthopaedics. What is key however, is that 99% of the scheme's participants are poor, who would not have been able to afford the expense of cardiac surgery and its associated costs. On average a cardiac operation and assorted care involves a sum of Rs.150-200,000. It is thus safe to say that (assuming that cardiac surgery is only done when life is threatened, and that 99% of the patients having surgery would not have been able to afford it without this insurance scheme) this has been an unqualified success by the sole criteria of human lives saved. But that is not the only criteria of course.

CASE STUDIES OF PATIENTS AND HOSPITALS

While the summery tables provide an overall picture of the operations, we decided to do a few case studies of network hospitals and patients. We interviewed the heads of three hospitals and 4 randomly chosen patients, 2 of whom were in the hospital and 2 were in their villages at Mandya district. More than the summary data, these patient case studies really demonstrate the value of this scheme.

Patients

A.J. Chandrasekhar, Rural Farmer

He is 30 years old and a graduate with a bachelor's degree in agriculture. He has 1.5 hectares of land. He used to grow ragi and bhatta (rice). He has a family of two, and his parents live with him. He has 4 cows and these provide 8-10 litres of milk per day.

In good times, he could make as much as 30,000 rupees per hectare. However, he has stopped both rice and ragi cultivation because of the lack of water in Mandya district.

Thus, he is now living on the income from the sale of milk from his four cows. He is able to make Rs. 2,500 per month on this. His father and mother are both diabetics. The family spends around Rs. 1000 on food, and another Rs. 1000 (on average) for agricultural and dairy inputs. (When he used to grow crops he would earn more but also spend roughly 10-15000 per hectare for sugar and or 5-6000 per 6 month crop of ragi or rice). Another 500 rupees is kept for emergencies and medicine for his parents. He says he spends Rs. 17 per month on entertainment and travel.

He lives about 10-12 km away from Mandya town. To get to Mandya he needs to walk 2 km to the bus stand to catch the one bus a day to Mandya. Occasionally he can get a ride on a 2-wheeler belonging to someone else. He is in the hospital for an operation on his throat. He was told 6 years ago that he needed this operation, but could not afford to do it, since the operation would cost between 5 and 6,000 Rupees. Originally he was not convinced about Yeshasvini when the local secretary of his cooperative society explained the scheme to him. However, when he heard about the benefits of the scheme and assumed that it was run by the government, he took a chance and signed up. That was very good, because his condition got rapidly worse and he needed the operation right away. Now he thinks that it is a really good scheme, and if he can afford it he would sign up all members of his family, especially his parents, since they are diabetics.

Saroja

Diagnosed with supra-renal gland tumour (Adrenal failure). She is 38 years old, and has three children, aged 13, 14 and 17. She does not have a spouse. She works as a coolie. She lives 6 kilometres away from Mandya and travels into the city by bus. Her monthly earnings as a coolie are 600-700 rupees. She has been aware of her medical problem for two years now, but was unable to get treatment because she could not afford it.

She had no idea about the Yeshasvini health scheme, but was told about it by the secretary of the cooperative society when he signed her up without consulting her. Once her illness worsened, he told her to go the hospital for free treatment. She is grateful for the free operations, but argues that she cannot sign up the scheme for the following year because she still cannot afford to. She also feels that now that she has had the operation, she most likely will not need another operation for the next three years.

Deviamma and Shivanna

Deviamma is 38 years of age and the wife of Shivanna, from Degnahally, Tippur Post, KR Nagar Taluk, Mysore. This is located about 70km from Mysore city. They have three children, all teenagers. They own 3/4th of an acre of land, on which they used to cultivate ragi and paddy (rice) but have not done so for some time given that the Cauvery river has dried up. When they were cultivating, they used to earn a profit of Rs. 4,000 per year. For the last three years Shivanna has been working as a coffee picker on a coffee estate. He gets paid 50 rupees per day and works for 20 days per month, resulting in monthly earnings of 1,000 rupees. His wife also works as a casual laborer in the coffee plantation, although her work is occasional. His monthly expenses include Rs. 1,000 for food, about Rs. 100 for entertainment and travel, and for the last year, Rs. 900 per month for a jobrelated course for his eldest son. He has to cut down on the food budget in order to ensure that his son can complete his 8 month course.

He and his wife are both enrolled in Yeshasvini. He was not planning to join the scheme because he did not believe it...it sounded too good to be true. However, he had taken a loan from his cooperative society and the secretary just deducted the subscription fee from his interest payment amounts. He was pleasantly surprised when he found out that his operation and all the expenses associated with it were free. He is determined to enroll in the scheme for the next year for both himself and his wife, but not his children...he does not think that they will get sick.

However, while his wife is in hospital, Shivanna is incurring Rs. 100 per day in expenses. These expenses are connected with his travel to his village and back, and the food along the way, plus some extra nourishment for his wife. In order to finance this, he has taken a loan of Rs. 5,000. He has leased his land for two years for this purpose. He would like to pay back the loan in two years if possible so that he can begin to cultivate the land, provided the water problem has been resolved.

Yashodhamma

Yashodhamma is 58 years old, and lives in Sandkoppaly, KR Nagar Taluk, which is about 70 Km from Mysore. Her husband is Srinivas, a farmer. They have 4 children, three daughters and one son. They have 2 acres of land on which they grow rice. They also have one cow.

Their cow gives 6 litres of milk per day and they earn about 8,000 rupees per year from the cow. They also earn about Rs. 20,000 a year from the rice cultivation. Thus, annual income is 28,000 rupees per year, which is about 2,200 rupees per month.

They are both diabetic. They spend 300-400 rupees per month on medical expenses (medicines) and they also employ a coolie to work on the property for 100 rupees per day for 20 days (which is 2,000 rupees per month). Thus, their household budget is in deficit.

She is in the hospital for a by-pass operation. She went to her local doctor in KR Nagar. After examination, (and fees!) he sent her to Dr. Basappa in Mysore. She was admitted into his clinic with low BP and he kept her under observation for 12 days in the ICU. He also called her folks to tell them that she was near death. But she survived and was then referred to Vikram Hospital. Before coming to Vikram hospital, she has already spent 8,000 rupees, pawning her family jewels for this purpose.

She has survived only because of her participation in Yeshasvini. Vikram hospital charges Rs. 105,000 for a by-pass operation. She is getting it free.

And all of her expenses incurred in the process of testing will also be reimbursed. Given their age, she and her husband are definitely likely to enroll in Yeshasvini for the following year.

Hospitals

Hospital in Mandya: This is a small hospital with a capacity of 60 beds. The regular OPD patients are around 100 per day. Average surgeries before Yeshasvini were about 2-3 per day. Mandya is the district in Karnataka with the highest number of nursing homes per capita. They have 45 nursing homes for a voting population of 8 lakhs and a total population of 13 lakhs.

Mandya was also one of the richest districts in Karnataka...largely because of the sugarcane cultivation. However, now it is one of the poorest. This is because of the lack of water...there is a long running dispute between Karnataka and Tamil Nadu regarding how to share the waters of the Cauvery river, and Tamilnadu is getting the lion's share so there is no water for the sugarcane growers in Mandya. With the decline in income, there is a sharp increase in poverty levels.

Although the doctor was skeptical about the potential of Yeshasvini to bring in new patients, he is now an enthusiastic supporter. On average, his surgical load has increased by 30-40% while his OPD has increased by 32-34%. By and large the largest number are gynecological related...hysterectomy. There is a government hospital in Mandya. Treatment is notionally free there. In his hospital OPD is free but treatment and investigations are not free, unless a surgical intervention is required. Yet, people prefer to come here. This is largely because the quality of care is seen as superior, but also because the government hospital is not really free...one has to bribe everyone there for treatment. There is very little personal care in the government hospital. For example, before Yeshasvini started in Mandya, the government hospital used to do about 100 hysterectomies per month. However, after the four or five Yeshasvini recognized hospitals started, that number has come down to about 25 per month.

This doctor thinks that in the next year signing up people will be no problem. There is a target of 3 lakh people in Mandya for the next year. This doctor feels that he can sign them all up by himself. He lives in the village and is a great propagator.

Incidentally, this doctor also specified the other way of selling Yeshasvini. When faced with the question that many people think that they will not need surgery...so that is one reason why they may not sign up, his response was that even so, they might need medical care. The argument is that typically a consultation fee in Mandya is 20 rupees. With your premium of 60 rupees, you can get three free consultations. That alone ought to be sufficient for more people to sign up.

From the doctor's (nursing home owner's) point of view, being part of Yeshasvini has not only increased revenues, but also has social benefits...it has increased "name and fame". Note also that his hospital benefits from the increased number of patients in other ways. Although OPD is free, at least 30% of the OPD's will get admitted for some other ailment that does not require surgical intervention. They will have to pay for that. So Yeshasvini guarantees an increase in patients, and in revenue, and in terms of fame. In addition, the pre-authorization that they receive is like cash in the bank. GG Hospital Mysore (Gopal Gowda Shantaveri Memorial Hospital) This is a 300 bed hospital with a 30 bed operating theatre.. It's a medium size hospital. It was started as a trust in 1995 but is now expanding into a nursing school, and perhaps a medical college. The owner is closely tied to the political establishment.

While the owner would not necessarily admit that participation in Yeshasvini did not increase the patients he agreed that participation was more like a social responsibility. They do 6-8 operations per day and average 150-200 outpatients per day.

In fact they think that participating in Yeshasvini creates a loss...they provide the example of hysterectomies, where they charge about Rs. 8,000, but Yeshasvini only provides Rs. 5,600. According to them, a typical hysterectomy costs about Rs. 8,000 for the operation, Rs. 2,000 for drugs, and 1,400 for care. Yet they continue to participate. The administrator declines to answer why they did so.

Vikram Hospital: This is a 2 year old, 65 bed hospital, a super specialty hospital for heart care and kidneys. They average about 25 surgeries per month, and about 45 inpatients. OPD's come to about 70/80 per day. They get about 1 or 2 Yeshasvini patients per day. However, since last year they have had about 64 patients from Yeshasvini for a bypass and urological problems. They are enthusiastic supporters of Yeshasvini. All three hospitals talked about the various problems in dealing with Yeshasvini patients. Specifically, patients do not know what is covered by the scheme and what is not covered. They also pointed out that a small percentage of the patients were not poor people i.e., some rich people are also benefiting from the scheme.

DISCUSSION AND EVALUATION

What have we learnt after an examination of the first year of operations of the Yeshasvini health insurance scheme in Karnataka? There are a number of issues to consider in terms of criteria by which one can judge its success. From the perspective of providing coverage for life saving operations for people who would no have been able to afford the operations, the scheme is clearly an unqualified success. It covers a significant percentage of the target population, and has the potential to cover more. The rate of coverage is also very high (Rs. 200,000 per person per year) and the highest compared to any similar schemes for this type of target population anywhere in the world. A clear indicator of success is the number of people benefited in terms of operations.

However, a drawback of the scheme is that it does not cover the poor farmer for all health related issues, but only for outpatient care and all expenses connected with surgery. The things that are not covered (diagnostic tests, and medicines) continue to be a heavy burden on poor rural families, many of which will continue to cause indebtedness. Given however that surgeries are generally required in life threatening situations, the scheme provides a degree of health security for this population that was impossible before. Whether the scheme can cover in future what is not covered now remains an open question. To answer this question, we would need better information regarding the health status of the target population, or at least enough data to develop an accurate actuarial assumption.

A second problem with the scheme is that although designed to be a self-financed scheme, the government of

Karnataka is providing a subsidy of Rs. 2.50 per participant per month during the first year of the scheme. We see government participation as being necessary in the first year but not for the future. Fortunately, the government has not provided for any subsidy in the second year of the scheme.

A third and very important criticism is the fact that not all of the subscribers exercised free choice in joining the scheme. This raises a number of issues that require to be addressed in subsequent years of operation. Clearly, there needs to be a massive education effort of the rural population (an extremely difficult job) but the government cooperation department also needs to be educated about the importance of communication strategies. Simply giving the secretaries of cooperatives target enrolment figures is not the solution. This is a self-financed health insurance scheme which owes its long term success only to the fact that individuals freely chose to join. Our interviews with patients suggest that some of them would not have joined, despite the benefits, had they known the financial commitment. On the other hand, many learnt that they were enrolled only when they went for operations and were grateful. We did not find any support (based on our interviews) for the oftrepeated paternalistic argument that poor peasants do not know what is good for them and do not know how to evaluate such insurance schemes (a justification offered for the lack of free choice). Each of the farmers and peasants we talked with were very clear about the costs and benefits of enrolling in the scheme.

Although we talked with the secretaries of many cooperatives, we are unable to estimate the number of people who may not have exercised free choice in joining the Yeshasvini scheme. Of the patients we interviewed, two deliberately signed up while two did not know that they were members. We also received differing estimates from

Yeshasvini Trust members as well as FHPL administrators. There are some reasons to expect that this may not be as big a problem in future years. First, knowledge of the scheme is spreading in rural areas l through word of mouth from existing patients, and through the network of district hospitals. Second, the department of cooperation and the Yeshasvini Trust are both intending to explore new ways of patient & subscriber education. Given the surplus in the fund after the first year of operations, this issue can and must be addressed. However, there is some indication that word is getting out. For the second year of operations, 2.2 million people have signed up, but for a three year period. And, at least 1.1 million were repeat enrollees. Not all of the increased numbers can be attributed to better education and awareness though, as the department of cooperation has been continuing to issue targets for its officers. However, the element of free choice is going to be a defining variable in the longer term success of self financed health insurance schemes for the poor.

The problem of free choice does not seem to be an issue in the two other areas where Yeshasvini is trying to extend its operations. For the last year, Yeshasvini has been trying to provide health insurance to teachers in state schools, informal workers employed by the municipal corporation of Bangalore, and the entire rural population of Anekal Taluk. In all of these cases, the mobilization of potential subscribers to the scheme is taking a lot of time, as they have to go through an education process to convince people to join. The progress is thus, slow. However they have been very successful in organizing the population in Anekal Taluk. These new extensions overcome many of the problems in the basic Yeshasvini scheme discussed in the paper. Not only is the absence of free choice problem eliminated, but there is relatively no government involvement in the scheme. And there is no subsidy. The fourth drawback is the lack of education amongst the subscribers about what exactly is covered and what is not. In addition, there are a number of small administrative problems, pertaining to administration, the use of identity cards, and the need to have people enroll permanently or at least for a three year period instead of an annual enrolment process. But these are "teehing" issues. Despite of some criticisms, the success of the Yeshasvini scheme is undoubted.

A number of features are responsible for the introduction and success of the scheme. First, the role of the government was key in getting the scheme launched. Not all government departments would have been as responsive as this department in the Karnataka state. Second, the ability to obtain buy-in from state government and private sector hospitals is clearly related to the reputation of Dr. Devi Shetty, whose credibility is great given his record as a cardiac surgeon, philanthropist, educator, telemedicine innovator, and for establishing a state of the art general hospital in Karnataka. Without prodding from him, this scheme would not have got-off the ground. Van Ginneken (1999) suggests that the dependence on the input and charisma of one person or a group of people has been an important factor in the success of several health insurance schemes around the world. That seems to be true in this case as well.

The third important feature is the relatively extensive network of hospitals in Karnataka. We do not have data (at the moment) on the number and distribution of hospitals across and within states, so we do not know whether Karnataka's network is out of the ordinary. It certainly has a more extensive network than West Bengal. Karnataka also has a large number of private medication colleges. Each medical college must have a hospital that meets certain standards, else the college will not be given a license to operate. Although we do not have enough data, some evidence suggests that the number of medical colleges per unit of population is higher in Karnataka than in many other states.

In sum, key individuals like Dr. Shetty, a responsive state department, the identification of organizations that unite widely dispersed rural populations, the network of private hospitals and department of cooperatives' energy were key aspects in establishing a scheme of this magnitude. The issue of free choice and whether more comprehensive coverage can be provided are the two major issues to be considered for the future.

CONCLUSIONS AND IMPLICATIONS

Stepping back, the key story in this model is the law of large numbers being effectively used to provide a high degree of health security to the poorest populations of the world. This is not a new story, to be sure. The key innovative aspect is the success in mobilizing these large numbers, who are geographically dispersed. The key lesson here is that existing organizations that connect people must be drafted as a means through which health security can be introduced. The transferability of schemes like this depends almost entirely on such organizations existing among the target population, and the existence of health care infrastructure of a reasonable kind.

The second key lesson is that there needs to be a methodology by which the subscriptions can be collected from poor people from dispersed rural and informal sectors i.e., we need a system to collect their contributions (which research shows they are more than willing to pay) and to enroll people in the system. Essentially, what is required in each state is a "Health Care Backbone", a system that attracts patients and provides hospitals. One suggestion made by Dr. Shetty is to link the education and collection of premiums to the post offices, perhaps the most decentralized government institution in India.

What we learn from this case is that providing health security to large sections of the population in developing countries depends less on the resources, but more on mobilizing capacity and organization. To be sure a health care infrastructure is a necessary condition, but it is not a sufficient one. And, given a large enough subscriber base, that infrastructure can be built. This is an instance where India's large population, normally seen as a negative, can be a valuable resource increasing social health. Further, given that 70% of the world's population does not have any health security, schemes like this break valuable new ground in providing health security where it is sorely needed. Future research needs to continue to study variants of this scheme that have been introduced in both Karnataka and Gujerat.

10

INSURANCE LAW AND REGULATIONS IN INDIA

The concept of insurance has been prevalent in India since ancient times amongst Hindus. Overseas traders practised a system of marine insurance. The joint family system, peculiar t o India, was a method of social insurance of every member of the family on his life. The law r elating to insurance has gradually developed, undergoing several phases from nationalisation of the insurance industry to the recent reforms permitt ing entry of private players and foreign inves tment in the insurance industry. The Constitution of India is federal in nature in as much ther e is division of powers between the Centre and the States. Insurance is included in the Union List, w herein the subjects included in this list are of the exclusive legislative competence of the Centre. The Central Legislature is empower ed to regulate the insurance industry in India and hence the law in this r egard is uniform throughout the t erritories of India. The development and growth of the insurance industry in India has gone through three dist inct stages.

Insurance law in India had its origins in the United Kingdom with the establishment of a British firm, the Oriental Life Insurance Company in 1818 in Calcutta, followed by the Bombay Life Assurance Company in 1823, the Madras Equitable Life Insurance Society in 1829 and the Oriental Life Assurance Company in 1874. However, till the establishment of the Bombay Mutual Life Assurance Societ y in 1871, Indians were charged an extra premium of up to 20% as compared to the Brit ish. The first statutor y measure in India to regulate the life insurance business was in 1912 with the passing of the Indian Life Assurance Companies Act, 1912 ("Act of 1912") (which was based on the English Act of 1909). Other classes of insurance business were left out of the scope of the Act of 1912, as such kinds of insurance were still in rudimentary form and legislat ive controls were not considered necessary.

General insurance on the other hand also has its origins in the United Kingdom. The firs t general insurance company Triton Insurance Company Ltd. was promoted in 1850 by British nationals in Calcutta. The first general insurance company established by an Indian was Indian Mercantile Insurance Company Ltd. in Bombay in 1907. Eventually, with the growth of fire, accident and marine insurance, the need was felt to bring such kinds of insurance within t he purview of the Act of 1912. While there were a number of attempts to introduce such legislation over the years, non-life insurance was finally regulated in 1938 thr ough the passing of the Insurance Act, 1938 ("Act of 1938"). The Act of 1938 along with various amendments over the years continues till date t o be the definitive piece of legislation on insurance and controls both life insurance and general insurance.

General insurance, in turn, has been defined to include "fire insur ance business", "marine insurance business" and "miscellaneous insurance business", whether singly or in combination with any of them.

On January 19, 1956, the management of life insurance business of two hundred and fort y five Indian and foreign insurers and provident societ ies then operating in India was taken over by the Central Government. The Life Insurance Corporation ("LIC") was formed in Sept ember 1956 by the Life Insurance Corporation Act, 1956 ("LIC Act") which granted LIC the exclusive pr ivilege to conduct life insurance business in India. However, an exception was made in the case of any company, firm or persons intending to carry on life insurance business in India in r espect of the lives of "persons ordinarily resident outside India", provided the appr oval of the Central Government was obtained. The exception was however not absolute and a curious prohibition existed. Such company, firm or person would not be permitted to insure the life of any "person ordinarily resident outside India", during any period of their temporary r esidence in India. However, the LIC Act, 1956 left outside its purview the Post Of fice Life Insurance Fund, any Family Pension Scheme framed under the Coal Mines Provident Fund, Family Pension and Bonus Schemes Act, 1948 or the Employees' Provident Funds and the Family Pension Fund Act, 1952.

The general insurance business was also nationalised with effect from January 1, 1973, through the introduction of the General Insurance Business (Nationalisation) Act, 1972 ("GIC Act"). Under the provisions of the GIC Act, the shares of the existing Indian general insurance companies and undertakings of other exist ing insurers were transferred to the General Insurance Corporation ("GIC") to secure the development of the general insurance business in India and for t he regulation and control of such business. The GIC was established by the Central Government in accordance with the provisions of the Companies Act, 1956 ("Companies Act") in November 1972 and it commenced business on January 1, 1973. Prior to 1973, there were a hundred and seven companies, including foreign companies, offering gener al insurance in India. These companies were amalgamated and grouped into four subsidiary companies of GIC v iz. the

National Insurance Company Ltd. ("National Co."), the New India Assurance Company Ltd. ("New India Co."), the Oriental Insurance Company Ltd. ("Oriental Co."), and the United India Assurance Company Ltd. ("United Co."). GIC undertakes mainly re-insur ance business apart from aviat ion insurance. The bulk of the general insurance business of fire, marine, motor and miscellaneous insurance business is under taken by the four subsidiaries.

Since 1956, with the nationalization of insurance industr y, the LIC held the monopoly in India's life insurance sector. GIC, with its four subsidiaries, enjoyed the monopoly for general insurance business. Both LIC and GIC have played a significant role in the development of the insurance market in India and in providing insurance coverage in India through an ext ensive network. For example, currently, the LIC has a network of 7 zones, 100 divisions and over 2,000 branches. LIC has over 550,000 agents and over 100 million lives are covered.

From 1991 onwards, the Indian Government introduced various reforms in the financial sector paving the way for the liberalization of t he Indian economy. It was a matter of time before this liberalization affect ed the insurance sector. A huge gap in the funds required for infrastructure was felt particularly since much of these funds could be f illed by life insurance funds, being long tenure funds.

Consequently, in 1993, the Government of India set up an eight-member committee chaired by Mr. R. N. Malhotra, a former Governor of India's apex bank, the Reserve Bank of India to rev iew the prevailing structure of regulation and supervision of the insurance sector and to make recommendations for strengthening and modernizing the regulatory system. The Committee submitted its repor t to the Indian Government in January 1994. Two of the key recommendations of the Committee included the privat ization of the insurance sector by permit ting the entry of private players to enter the business of life and general insuranee and the es tablishment of an Insurance Regulatory Authority.

It took a number of years for the Indian Government to implement the recommendations of the Malhotra Committee. The Indian Parliament passed the Insurance Regulator y and Development Act, 1999 ("IRD Act") on December 2, 1999 with the aim "to provide for the establishment of an Authority, to protect t he interests of the policy holders, to regulate, promote and ensure orderly growth of the insurance industry and to amend the Insurance Act, 1938, the Life Insurance Corporation Act, 1956 and the General Insurance Business (Nationalization) Act, 1972". The IRD Act has established the Insurance Regulatory and Development Authority ("IRDA" or "Authority") as a statutory regulator to regulate and pr omote the insurance industry in India and t o protect the interes ts of holders of insurance policies. The IRD Act also carried out a series of amendments to the Act of 1938 and conferred the powers of the Controller of Insurance on the IRDA.

The members of the IRDA are appointed by the Central Government from amongst persons of ability, integrity and s tanding who have knowledge or experience in life insurance, general insurance, actuarial science, finance, economics, law, accountancy, administration etc. The Authority consists of a chairperson, not more than five whole-time members and not more than four part-time members.

The Authority has been entrus ted with the dut y to regulate, promote and ensur e the orderly growth of the insurance and re-insurance business in India. In furt herance of this responsibility, it has been conferred with numerous powers and functions which include prescribing regulations on the investments of funds by insurance companies, regulating maintenance of the margin of solvency, adjudication of disputes between insurers and inter mediaries, supervising the funct ioning of the Tariff Advisory Committee, specifying the percentage of premium income of the insurer to finance schemes for promoting and regulating professional organizations and specifying the per centage of life insurance business and general insurance business to be undertaken by the insurer in the rural or social sector.

The Tariff Advisory Committee ("Advisory Committee") is a body corporat e, which controls and regulates the rates, advant ages, terms and conditions off ered by insurers in the general insurance business. The Advisory Committee has the authority to require any insurer to supply such information or stat ements necessary for discharge of its functions. Any insurer failing to comply with such provisions shall be deemed to have contravened the provisions of the Insurance Act. Every insurer is required to make an annual payment of fees to the Advisory Committ ee of an amount not exceeding in case of reinsurance business in India, one percent of the total pr emiums in respect of facultative insurance accepted by him in India; and in case of any other insurance business, one percent of the total gross premium written direct by him in India.

All insurers and provident societies incorporat ed or domiciled in India are members of the Insurance Association of India ("Insurance Association") and all insurers and prov ident societies incorporated or domiciled elsewhere than in India are associate members of the Insurance Association. There are two councils of the Insurance Association, namely the Life Insurance Council and the General Insurance Council. The Life Insurance Council, through its Executive Committee, conducts examinations for individuals wising to qualif y themselves as insurance agents. It also fixes the limits for actual expenses by which the insurer carr ying on life insurance business or any group of insurers can exceed from the prescribed limits under the Insurance Act. Likewise, the General Insurance Council, through its Executive Committee, may fix the limits by which the actual expenses of management incurred by an insurer carrying on general insurance business may exceed the limits as prescribed in the Insurance Act.

The Ombudsmen are appointed in accordance with the Redressal of Public Grievances Rules, 1998, to resolve all complaints relating to settlement of claims on the par t of insurance companies in a cost-effective, ef ficient and effective manner. Any person who has a grievance against an insurer may make a complaint to an Ombudsman within his jurisdiction, in the manner specified. However, prior to making a complaint, such person should have made a representation to the insurer and either the insurer has rejected the complaint or has not replied to it. Further, the complaint should be made not later than a year from the date of rejection of the complaint by the insurer and should not be any other proceedings pending in any other court, Consumer Forum or arbitr ator pending on the same subject matter. The Ombudsmen are also empowered to receive and consider any partial or total repudiation of claims by an insurer, any dispute in regard to the premium paid in terms of the policy, any dispute on the legal construction of the policies in as much such a dispute relat es to claims, delay in settlement of claims and the non-issue of any insurance document to customers after receipt of premium.

The Ombudsmen act as a counsellor and mediator and make recommendations to both par ties in the event that the complaint is settled by agreement between both the parties. However, if the complaint is not settled by agreement, the Ombudsman may pass an award of compensation within three months of the complaint, which shall not be in excess of w hich is necessary to cover the loss suffered by the complainant as a direct consequence of the insured peril, or for an amount not exceeding rupees two million (including exgratia and other expenses), whichever is lower. Ombudsman within his jurisdiction, in the manner specified. However, prior to making a complaint, such person should have made a representation to t he insurer and either the insurer has rejected the complaint or has not replied to it. Further, the complaint should be made not later than a year from the date of rejection of the complaint by the insurer and should not be any other proceedings pending in any other court, Consumer Forum or arbitrator pending on the same subject matter. The Ombudsmen are also empowered to receive and consider any par tial or total repudiation of claims by an insurer, any dispute in regard to the premium paid in terms of the policy, any dispute on the legal construction of the policies in as much such a dispute relat es to claims, delay in settlement of claims and the non-issue of any insurance document to customers af ter receipt of premium. The Ombudsmen act as a counsellor and mediator and make recommendations to both par ties in the event that the complaint is settled by agreement between both the parties. However, if the

LEGAL & TAX COUNSELING WORLDWIDE

complaint is not settled by agreement, the Ombudsman may pass an award of compensation within three months of the complaint, which shall not be in excess of which is necessary to cover the loss suffered by the complainant as a direct consequence of the insured peril, or for an amount not exceeding rupees two million (including ex gratia and other expenses), whichever is lower. Every insurer seeking to carr y out the business of insurance in India is required to obtain a cer tificate of registration from the IRDA prior to commencement of business. The pre-conditions for applying for such registration have been set out under the Act of 1938, the IRD Act and the various regulations prescribed by t he Authority. The following are some of the import ant general registration requir ements that an applicant would need to fulfil:

(a) The applicant would need to be a company registered under the provisions of the Indian Companies Act, 1956. Consequently, any person intending to carry on insurance business in India would need to set up a separate entity in India.

(b) The aggregate equity participation of a for eign company (either by itself or through its subsidiary companies or its nominees) in the applicant company cannot not exceed twenty six per cent of the paid up capital of the insurance company. However, the Insurance Act and the regulations there under provide for the manner of computation of such twenty-six per cent.

(c) The applicant can carry on any one of life insurance business, general insurance business or reinsurance business. Separate companies would be needed if the intent were to conduct more than one business.

(d) The name of the applicant needs to contain the words "insurance company" or "assurance company".

The applicant would need to meet with the following capital structure requirements:

(a) A minimum paid up equity capital of rupees one billion in case of an applicant w hich seeks to carry on the business of life insurance or general insurance.

(b) A minimum paid-up equity capital of rupees two billion, in case of a person carrying on exclusively the business of reinsurance.

In determining the aforesaid capital r equirement, the

deposits to be made and any preliminary expenses incurred in the formation and regis tration of the company would be included. A "promoter" of the company is not permitted to hold, at any time, more than t wenty-six per cent of the paid-up capital in any Indian insurance company. However, an interim measure has been permitted percentages higher than twent y six percent are permitt ed if the promoters divest, in a phased manner, over a period of ten years from the date of commencement of business, the share capital held by them in excess of twent y six per cent.

An applicant desiring to carry on insurance business in India is requir ed to make a requisition for a registration application t o the IRDA in a prescribed format along with all the r elevant documents.

LEGAL & TAX COUNSELING WORLDWIDE

The applicant is required to make a separate requisit ion for registration for each class of business i.e. life insurance business consisting of linked business, non-linked business or both, or general insurance business including health insurance business.

The IRDA may accept the requisition on being satisfied of the bonafides of the applicant, the completeness of the application and that the applicant will carr y on all the functions in respect of the insurance business including management of investments etc. In the event that the aforesaid requirements are not met with, the Authorit y may after giving the applicant a reasonable opportunit y of being heard, reject the requisition. Thereafter, the applicant may apply to the Authority within thirty days of such rejection for re-considerat ion of its decision. Additionally, an applicant whose requisition for regis tration has been rejected, may approach the Authority with a fresh request for regis tration application aft er a period of two years from the date of reject ion, with a new set of promoters and for a class of insurance business dif ferent than the one originally applied for.

In the event that the Authorit y accepts the requisition for registr ation application, it shall direct supply of the application for registr ation to the applicant. An applicant, whose requisition has been accepted, may make an application along with the relevant documents ev idencing deposit, capital and other requirements in the prescribed form for grant of a certif icate of registration. If, when considering an application, it appears to the Authority that the assured rates, advantages, terms and conditions offered or t o be offered in connection wit h life insurance business are in any respect not workable or sound, he may require that a statement thereof to be submitted to an actuary appointed by the insurer and the Authority shall order the insurer to make such modifications as reported by the actuary.

After consideration of the matters inter alia capital structure, record of performance of each promoters and directors and planned infrastructure of the company, the Authority may gr ant the certificate of r egistration. The Authorit y would, however, give preference in grant of cert ificate of registration to those applicants w ho propose to carry on the business of pr oviding health covers to individuals or groups of individuals. An applicant grant ed a certificate of r egistration may commence the insurance business within twelve months from the date of registration.

In the event that the Authorit y rejects the application for registr ation, the applicant aggrieved by the decision of the Authority may wit hin a period of thirt y days from the date of communication of such rejection, appeal to the Central Government for reconsideration of the decision and the decision of the Central Government in this regard would be final.

An insurer who has been granted a cer tificate of registration should renew the registrat ion before the 31st day of December each year, and such application should be accompanied by evidence of fees that should be the higher of-

- fifty thousand rupees for each class of insurance business, and
- one fifth of one per cent of tot al gross premium writ ten direct by an insurer in India during the financial year preceding the year in which the applicat ion for renewal of certif icate is required to be made, or the application for renewal of certificate is required t o be made, or rupees fifty million Worldwide whichever is less; (and in case of an insurer carrying on solely re-insurance business, instead of the total gross premium written direct in India, the total premium in respect of f acultative re-insurance accepted by him in India shall be taken into account).

This fee may vary according to the total gross premium writ ten direct in India, during the year preceding the year in which the application is required to be made by the insurer in the class of insurance business to which the regis tration relates but shall not exceed one-four th of one percent of such premium income or rupees fift y million, whichever is less, or be less, in any case than fifty thousand rupees for each class of insurance business. However, in the case of an insurer carrying on solely re-insurance business, the total premiums in respect of facultative re-insurance accept ed by him in India shall be taken into account.

The registration of an Indian insurance company or insurer may be suspended for a class or classes of insurance business, in addition to any penalty that may be imposed or any action that may be taken, for such period as may be specified by the Authority, in the following cases:

- conducts its business in a manner prejudicial to the interests of the policy-holders;
- fails to furnish any information as required by the Authority relating to its insurance business;
- does not submit periodical returns as required under the Act or by the Authority;
- does not co-operate in any inquiry conducted by the Authority;
- indulges in manipulating the insurance business;
- fails to make investment in the infrastr ucture or social sector as specified under the Insurance Act.

The Authority, in case of repeated defaults of the grounds for suspension of a certificate of registration, may impose a penalty in the form of cancellation of the certificate. The Authority is compulsorily required to cancel the registration of an insurer either wholly or in so far as it relates to a particular class of insurance business, as the case may be

- if the insurer fails to comply with the provisions relating to deposits; or
- if the insurer fails, at any time, to comply with the provisions relating t o the excess of the value of his assets over the amount of his liabilities; or
- if the insurer is in liquidation or is adjudged an insolvent; or
- if the business or a class of the business of the insurer has been transferr ed to any person or has been transferred to or amalgamated with the business of any other insurer; or
- if the whole of the deposit made in respect of the insurance business has been returned to the insurer;

- if, in the case of an insurer, the standing contract is cancelled or is suspended and continues to be suspended for a period of six months, or
- if the Central Government of India so directs.

In addition to the above, the Authorit y has the discretion to cancel the registration of an insurer

- if the insurer makes default in complying with, or acts in contravent ion of, any requirement of the Insurance Act or of any rule or any regulation or order made or, any direction issued thereunder, or
- if the Authority has r eason to believe that nay claim upon the insurer arising in India under any policy of insurance remains unpaid for three months af ter final judgment in regular course of law, or
- if the insurer carries on any business other than insurance business or any pr escribed business, or
- if the insurer makes a default in complying with any direct ion issued or order made, as the case may be, by the Authority under the IRDA Act, 1999.
- If the insurer makes a default in complying with, or acts in contravent ion of, any requirement of the Companies Act, or the LIC Act, or the GIC Act or the Foreign Exchange Management Act, 2000.

The order of cancellation shall take ef fect on the date on which notice of t he order of cancellation is served on the insurer. Thereafter, the insurer would be prohibited from entering into any new contracts of insurance, but all rights and liabilities in respect of contracts of insurance ent ered into by him before the cancellation takes ef fect shall continue as if the cancellation had not taken place. The Authority may, aft er the expiry of six months from the date on which the cancellation order takes effect, apply to t he Court for an order to wind up t he insurance company, or to wind up the affairs of the company in respect of a class of insurance business, unless the registration of the insurance company has been revived or an application for winding up has alread y been presented to the Court. The Authority has a discret ion, where the registr ation of an insurer has been cancelled, to rev ive the registration, if the insurer wit hin six months from the date on which the cancellation took effect:

- makes the deposits, or
- complies with the provisions as to t he excess of the value of his assets over the amount of his liabilities, or
- has his standing contract rest ored, or
- has the application accepted, or
- satisfies the Authorit y that no claim upon him remains unpaid, or
- has complied with any requirements of the Insurance Act or the IRDA Act, or any rule or regulation, or any order made thereunder or any direct ion issued under these Acts, or
- that he has ceased to carry on any business other than insur ance business or any prescribed business.

The main regulations that regulate the insurance business are the Insurance Act, 1938, the Life Insurance Corporation Act, 1956, the General Insurance Business (Nationalisation) Act, 1982, the Marine Insurance Act, 1963 and the Motor Vehicles Act, 1988. The Indian Contract Act, 1872, governs most of the aspects of the insurance contract. Additionally, the Foreign Exchange Management Act, 2000, Income Tax Act, 1961, Indian Stamp Act and the Hindu and Indian Succession Act govern some aspects involved in insurance. Every insurer should, in respect of the insurance business carr ied on by him in India, deposit with the

Reserve Bank of India ("RBI") for and on behalf of the Central Government of India the following amounts, either in cash or in approved securities est imated at the market value of the securities on the day of deposit, or partly in cash and par tly in approved securities:

- in the case of life insurance business, a sum equivalent to one per cent of his total gross premium written in India in any financial year commencing after the 31st day of March, 2000, not exceeding rupees hundred million;
- in the case of general insurance business, a sum equivalent to three per cent of his total gross premium writt en in India, in any financial year commencing after the 31st day of March, 2000, not exceeding rupees hundred million;
- in the case of re-insurance business, a sum of rupees two hundred million.
- If business done or to be done is marine insurance only and relates exclusively to country craft or its cargo or both, only rupees one hundred thousand should be deposit ed with the RBI.

These deposits will be held by the RBI though for the credit of the insur er and are returnable to the insurer in the event the provisions of t he Insurance Act mandate such return. Interest accr uing, due and collected on deposited securities will be paid to t he insurer, subject to any deductions of the normal commission chargeable for the realization of int erest. In addition, it is import ant to note that the deposits will:

- not be susceptible to any assignment or charge; or
- not be available for the discharge of any liabilit y of the insurer other than liabilities arising out of policies of insurance issued by the insurer so long as any such liabilities remain undischarged, or

- not be liable to attachment in execution of any decree except a decree obtained by a policy-holder of the insurer in respect of-a debt due upon a policy which debt the policy-holder has failed to realize in any other way.

Where the insurer has ceased to carr y on all classes of insurance business in India, the deposit made with the RBI shall, on an application being made to the Court, be returned to the insurer af ter satisfaction of all his liabilities in India in respect of all classes of insurance business. Every insurer is required to invest and keep invested cert ain amount of assets as determined under the Insurance Act. The funds of the policyholders cannot be invested (directl y or indirectly) outside India.

An insurer involved in the business of life insurance is requir ed to invest and keep invested at all times assets, the value of which is not less than the sum of t he amount of its liabilities to holders of life insurance policies in India on account of matured claims and the amount required to meet the liability on policies of life insurance maturing for payment in India, reduced by the amount of premiums which have fallen due to the insur er on such policies but have not been paid and the days of grace for payment of which have not expired and any amount due to the insurer for loans granted on and within the surrender values of policies of life insurance maturing for payment in India issued by him or by an insurer whose business he has acquired and in respect of which he has assumed liability.

Every insurer carrying on the business of life insurance is required to invest and at all times keep invested his controlled fund (other than funds relating to pensions and general annuit y business and unit linked life insurance business) in the following manner, free of any encumbrance, charge, hypothecation or lien:

For the purposes of calculating the investments, the amount of deposits made with the RBI by the insurer in respect of his life insurance business shall be deemed to be assets invested in Government securities. In computing the assets to be inves ted by the insurer, any investment made with reference to the cur rency other than the Indian rupee which is in excess of the amount required to meet the liabilities of the insurer in India with reference to that currency to the extent of such excess and any investment made in purchase of any immovable propert y outside India or on account of any such propert y shall not be taken into account. Further, an insurer should not out of his controlled fund invest any sum in the shares or debentures of any privat e limited company. Where an insurer has accepted reassurance in respect of any policies of life insurance issued by another insurer and maturing for payment in India or has ceded reassurance to another insurer in respect of any such policies issued by himself, the assets to be invested by the insurer shall be increased by the amount of the liabilit y involved in such acceptance and decreased by the amount of the liability involved in such cession.

In case of an insurer incorporated or domiciled outside India or an insurer incorporated in India whose share capital to the extent of one-third is owned by, or the members of whose governing body to the extent of one-third consists of members domiciled elsewhere than in India, the assets required to be invested should, (except to the extent of any part which consists of foreign assets held outside India) be held in India by way of a trust for the discharge of the liabilities.

Every Insurer shall invest and at all times keep invested his segregated fund of unit linked life insurance business as per pattern of investment of fered to and approved by the policy-holders. The insurer is permitted to offer unit linked policies only where the units are linked to categories of assets that are both marketable and easily realizable. However, the total investment in other approved category of-investments should at not time exceed twenty five per cent of the fund. An insurer carrying on general insurance business is requir ed to invest and keep invested at all times his total assets in approved securit ies in the following manner: Every insurer is required to invest and at all times keep invested assets of pension business, general

(a) General Insurance

(b) Pension and General Annuity egal & Tax Counseling Worldwide annuity business and group business in the following manner:

Every re-insurer carr ying on re-insurance business in India is required to invest and at all times keep invested his total assets in the same manner as specified for the general insurance business. An insurer should maintain, at all times, an excess of the value of his assets over the amount of his liabilities of not less than the relevant amount arrived at in the f ollowing manner ("required solvency margin"):

(a) in the case of an insurer carrying on life insurance business, the required solvency margin shall be the higher of rupees five hundred million (one billion in case of re-insurers) or the aggregate sum arrived at based on the calculations specified in the Insurance Act.

(b) in the case of an insurer carrying on general insurance business, the required solvency margin, shall be the highest of the following amounts:-

   (i) rupees five hundred million (rupees one billion in case of a re-insurer); or

   (ii) a sum equivalent to twenty per cent of net premium income; or

(iii) a sum equivalent to thirty per cent of net incurred claims.

This shall be subject to credit for re-insurance in computing net premiums and net incurred claims being actual but a percentage, determined by the regulations, not exceeding fifty per cent.

An insurer who fails to maint ain the required solvency margin will be deemed to be insol vent and may be wound up by the court. An insurer is requir ed under the IRDA (Assets, Liabilities and Solvency Margin of Insurers) Regulations, 2000, to prepare a statement of solvency margin in accordance with Schedule III-A, in respect of life insurance business, and in Form KG in accordance with Schedule III-B, in respect of general insurance business, as the case may be.

Every insurer is required to prepare a statement of the value of assets in accordance with the provisions of the aforesaid regulations. Every insurer should prepare as tatement of the amount of liabilities in accordance with the prov isions of Schedule II-A of the aforesaid regulations, in respect of the life insurance business, and in Form HG in accordance with Schedule II-B, in respect of the general insurance business. The aforesaid forms should be furnished separately for business within India and the total business transacted by the insurer.

In the event that an insurer transacts insurance business in a country outside India and submits the statements or returns or any such par ticulars to a public authorit y of that country, he is required to enclose such particulars along with the Forms specified in the aforesaid regulations and the IRDA (Actuarial Report and Abstract) Regulations, 2000.

An insurer carrying on the business of insurance or reinsur ance in India is required, under the IRDA (Appointed

Actuary) Regulations, 2000, to appoint a person fulfilling the eligibility requirements, to act as an appointed actuary, after seeking the appr oval of the Authority in this regard. It is mandatory for an insurer carr ying on the business of life insurance in India to appoint any actuary.

An appointed actuary has access to all such informat ion and documents of an insurer for the performance of his duties and obligations. An appointed actuary may also attend the meetings of the insurer and discuss matters relat ed to the actuarial advice and solvency of margin.

An appointed actuary, in addition to rendering actuarial adv ice to insurer (in particular in t he areas of product design and pricing, insurance contract wording, investments and reinsurance), is also required inter alia to ensure the solvency of the insurer at all times, certify the assets and liabilities that have been valued and maintain the solvency margin.

In case the insurer is carrying on life insurance business, an appointed actuary should also inter alia-

- certify the actuarial report, abstract and other returns required under the Insur ance Act,
- comply with the provisions with respect to the bases of premium,
- comply with the provisions with respect to recommendation of interim bonus or bonuses payable by the life insurer to policyholders whose policies mature for payment by reason of death or otherwise during the inter-valuat ion period, and
- ensure that the policyholders' reasonable expectations have been considered in the matter of valuation of liabilities and distribution of surplus to the participating policyholders who are entitled for a share of surplus.

In case of an insurer carrying on general insurance business in India, the appoint ed actuary is required to ensure that the rates are fair in respect of those contracts that are governed by the insurer's in-house tariff and that the actuarial principles, in the determinat ion of liabilities, have been used in the calculation of reserves for incurred but not reported claims and other reserves where actuarial advice is sought by the Authority.

Every insurer carrying on life insurance business should every year cause an investigation to be carried out by an actuary with respect to financial condition of the life insurance business, including a valuation of his liabilities and should cause an abstract of the report to be made. This provision shall apply in the event that an investigation into the financial condition of the insurer is made with a view to the distribution of profits or an investigation is made of which the results are made public.

The IRDA (Insurance Advertisements) Regulations, 2000, seeks to regulate and control every insurance advertisement issued by the insurer, intermediary or insurance agent. For this purpose, every insurer, intermediary or insurance agent is required to establish and maintain a system of control over the content, form and method of dissemination of all advertisements concerning its policies and such advertisement should be filed with the Authority as soon as it is first issued. An advertisement issued by an insurer should not fall in the category of an unfair or misleading advertisement. An 'unfair or misleading advertisement' means and includes any advertisement

- that fails to clearly identify the product as insurance;
- makes claims beyond the ability of the policy to deliver or beyond the reasonable expectation of performance;
- describes benefits that do not match the policy provisions;

- uses words or phrases in a way which hides or minimizes the costs of the hazard insured against or the risks inherent in the policy;
- omits to disclose or discloses insufficiently, important exclusions, limitations and conditions of the contract;
- gives information in a misleading way;
- illustrates future benefits on assumpt ions which are not realistic nor realizable in the light of the insurer's current performance;
- where the benefits are not guaranteed, does not explicitly say so as prominentl y as the benefits are stated or says so in manner or form that it could remain unnoticed;
- implies a group or other relationship like sponsorship, af filiation or approval, that does not exist;
- makes unfair or incomplete comparisons with products which are not comparable or disparages competitors.

Every advertisement should disclose the full particulars and identit y of the insurer, and that insurance is the subject matter of solicit ation. In the event that such advert isement describes any benefits, the form number of the policy and the type of coverage should be fully disclosed. In case of Internet advertisements, the website or portal of the insurer or intermediary should contain disclosure statements which outline the site's specific policies vis-à-vis the privacy of personal information for the protection of both their own businesses and the consumers they serve and should also display the registration or license numbers. In addition to these requirements, every insurer or intermediary is also required to follow recognized standards of professional conduct as prescribed by the Advertisement Standards Council of India.

If an advertisement is not in compliance with the aforesaid regulations, the Authority may take action in one or more of the following ways:

- issue a letter to the advertiser seeking information within a specific time, not being more than ten days from the date of issue of the letter;
- direct the advertiser to correct or modify the adver tisement already issued in a manner suggested by the Authority with a stipulation that the corrected or modified advertisement shall receive the same type of publicity as the one sought to be corrected or modified;
- direct the advertiser to discontinue the advertisement;
- any other action deemed fit by the Authority, keeping in view the circumstances of the case, to ensure that he interests of the public are protected.

Every insurer who begins to carry on the business of insurance in India should ensure that he undertakes the following obligat ions to provide life insurance or general insur ance policies, during the first five financial years, to the persons residing in the rural sector or social sector, workers in the unorganised or informal sector or for economically vulnerable or backward classes of the egal & Tax Counseling Worldwide society and other categories of persons and such insurance policies shall include insurance for crops.

A policy of insurance is a contract of a personal nature and hence cannot be transferred by the insured without the consent of the insurer. In the case of life and personal accident insurances, the subject matter of the insurance is a life and is not amenable to transfer. An assignment of the policy in such cases is just an assignment of the right to

receive the proceeds of the policy. The Insurance Act lays down the mode of assignment and transfer of a life insurance policy. An assignment or transfer may be made only on satisfaction of the following conditions:

(i) an endorsement upon the policy itself or by a separate instrument;

(ii) the endorsement or instrument should be signed by the transferor or his agent and should be attested by at least one witness;

(iii) it should specifically set forth the fact of transfer or assignment.

The aforesaid conditions need to be complied with irrespective whether the transfer or assignment is made without consideration or not. The insurer, on being given notice of the assignment or transfer, shall recognize the assignee or transferee as the only person entitled to the benefit of the policy and such a person shall also be subject to all the liabilities and equit ies to which the transferor or assignor was subject to.

Additionally, an assignment may be (a) absolute, or (b) conditional that it shall be inoperative or that the interest shall pass to some other person on the happening of a specific event during the lifetime of the person insured, or (c) in favour of the sur vivor or survivors of a number of persons. However, the term "policy holder" does not include an assignee whose inter est in the policy is defeasible or is for the time being subject to any condition. Hence, an assignee of a policy subject to any condition shall not be entitled to t he rights of a policy holder.

A policy holder of a life insurance policy on his own life has the right, either while effecting the policy or before it matures, to nominate a person to whom the money secured by the policy should be paid in the event of the death of the

policy holder. An insurer is not bound by such nomination unless it is brought to his notice, endorsed on the policy and registered in the records of the policy. It is pertinent to note that a transfer of assignment of a policy automatically leads to cancellation of a nomination. Additionally, these provisions relating to nomination under the Insurance Act do not apply to any policies under the Married Women's Property Act, 1874.

The Reserve Bank of India ("RBI") is the apex bank of India established in 1935 under the Reserve Bank of India Act, 1934. The Exchange Control Department within the RBI is responsible for the regulation and enforcement of exchange controls. Prior to 1999, India had stringent exchange control regulations under the Foreign Exchange Regulation Act, 1973 ("FERA"). The Foreign Direct Investment ("FDI") regime in India has been progressively liberalized in the nineties with the passage of the Foreign Exchange Management Act, 1999 ("FEMA"), which replaced FERA. Most restrictions on foreign investment have been removed and the procedures have been simplified. Non-residents can invest directly in India, either wholly or as a joint venture. Foreign investment is allowed in virtually all sectors including the services sector, subject to Government permission in certain cases.

Insurance companies that are register ed with the IRDA, are permitted to issue general insurance policies denominated in foreign currency and are also permitted to receive pr emiums in foreign currency without the prior approval of the RBI. However, this is permitted only for certain kinds of cases such as marine insurance for vessels owned by foreign shipping companies and chartered by Indian companies, aviation insurance for aircrafts imported from outside India on lease/hire basis for the purpose of air taxi operations etc. Authorised dealers are also permitted to settle claims in foreign curr ency on general insurance policies subject to certain condit ions such as the claim has been made for the loss occurred during the policy period, the claim has been settled as per the surveyors report and other substantiating documents, claims on account of reinsurance are being lodged with the reinsurers and will be received as per the reinsurance agreement, the remittance is being made to the non-resident beneficiary under the policy etc. However, in the case of resident beneficiaries, the claim is required to be settled in rupee equivalent of the foreign currency due and under no circumstances can payment be made in foreign currency to a resident beneficiary.

As per the provisions of the Foreign Exchange Management (Insurance) Regulations, 2000, no person resident in India is permitted to take any general or life insurance policy issued by an insurer outside India. However, the RBI may permit, for sufficient reasons, a resident in India to take any life insurance policy issued by an insurer outside India. However, an exemption has recently been made only for units located in Special Economic Zones ("SEZs") for general insurance policies taken by such units. Therefore, remittances towards premium for general insurance policies taken out by units located in SEZs from insurers outside India are permit ted provided that the pr emiums are paid out of the foreign exchange balances.

A person resident in India but not permanently resident therein is permitted to continue holding any insurance policy issued to him by an insurer outside India, if the premium on such policy is paid out of foreign currency resources outside India. A person resident in India may take a general insurance policy issued by an insurer outside India, provided that, befor e taking the policy he has obtained a no objection certificate from the Central Government of India. Fur ther, a person resident in India is also permitted to cont inue to hold any insurance policy issued by an insurer outside

India when such person was resident outside India, subject to fulfilment of cer tain conditions. A foreign company may enter the insurance business in India in either of the following ways:

" FDI is permitted in India primarily either under the 'automatic route', or with prior government approval. Where FDI does not fall under the 'automatic route', the foreign invest or would require the approval from the Foreign Investment Promotion Board ("FIPB"). Indian companies are generally permitted to accept FDI without prior approval, provided cer tain sectoral policies and investment limits are met. In the insurance sector there is 26% sectoral cap on FDI, subject to obtaining license from the IRDA, which means that a foreign company can invest up to only 26% in an Indian insurance company (calculated in the manner specified in the Insurance Act and regulations thereunder), while 74% would have to be invested by an Indian company."

In the event that a foreign insurance company is not desirous of directly investing in an Indian insurance company, it may, in the beginning, set up a branch or liaison office, subject to the approval of the RBI and/or the Government of India in this regar d. The branch office in India is permitted to under take only a cert ain set of activities such as carr ying our research work for the parent company, representing the parent company in India etc. A liaison of fice is also permitted to under take only a certain set of activities such as acting as a communication channel between the parent company and Indian companies.

Insurance companies and insurance agents, in India, are subject to tax for the premiums and the commissions received by them respectively, under the Indian Income Tax Act, 1963 ("Income Tax Act"). The Income Tax Act deals with the computation of the income of the f ollowing insurance companies:

- Companies carrying on life insurance business which are resident in India;
- Companies carrying on any other kind of insurance business, which are resident in India; and
- Non-resident persons carrying on the business of insurance in India through a branch.

There is no recognized business method of ascertaining the profits derived from life insurance business. This would depend on the actuarial calculations and valuations. The Income Tax Act lays down provisions with respect to the income received by an assessee from the business of insurance, whether the company which receives such business income is resident in India or not. These special provisions exclude the operation of other sections under the Income Tax Act dealing with computation of income. Therefore, the profits and gains from the insurance business are to be computed artificially in accordance with these rules. The First Schedule of the Income Tax Act overrides the other provisions relating to computation of income under separate and distinct heads of income. The income is therefore, not to be computed under the different heads and in accordance with the provisions of the Income Tax Act, but the income from all the sources should be computed as one figure on the basis laid down in this schedule.

The profits and loss of a person carrying on the business of insurance are to be computed separately from the profits and gains from any other business. Though the profits of life insurance business are to be computed separately from the profits of non-life insurance business or other business carried on by the assessee, any loss incurred in life insurance business can be set off against profits of non-life insurance business or other business. In computing the profits of life insurance business, the profits and gains of the business is taken to be the annual average of the "surplus". This surplus is arrived at by adjusting the surplus or deficit disclosed by the actuarial valuation made in respect of the last inter-valuat ion period ending before the commencement of the assessment year. The tax payable, computed in the manner stat ed above, will be reduced by tax withheld at source for income from interes t on securities in respect of annual average of income tax. In computing the profits of any business other than lif e insurance, the profits and gains is taken to be the balance of the profits disclosed in the annual accounts.

In case of non-resident companies carrying on the business of insurance in India, in the absence of reliable data, the profits and gains is taken to be that proportion of the world income which corresponds to the propor tion of the premium income derived from India.

A branch of a foreign insurance company is subject to income tax at the rate of 42% (including 5% surcharge on tax) while a subsidiar y of a foreign insurance company is subject to tax at the r ate of 38.75% (including 5% surcharge on tax).

The Finance Act, 2002 has brought insurance within the service tax net. The insured is thus liable to pay service tax at the r ate of 5%.

The Income Tax Act provides that the income tax payable on the profits and gains arising from the life insurance business will be calculated at the rate of 12.5% of such prof its and gains. An insurance company is required to deposit an amount equal to one-third of the tax, in a Social Securit y Fund as notified by the Central Government. Further, the insurance company is required to deposit an amount of not less than 2.5% of the profits and gains of the insurance business in such a Securit y Fund. Where the insurance company has deposited such an amount, the income tax payable by the insurance company will be reduced by that amount and the amount to be deposited in t he Security Fund would also be calculated on the income tax so reduced.

The Income Tax Act has laid down provisions for the taxat ion of insurance commissions. 'Insurance Commission' has been defined to mean any income (remuneration or reward) by way of commission or otherwise for soliciting or procuring insurance business. The effect of the prov ision is that any person responsible for paying any such income to a resident individual will be r equired to deduct income tax at the prescribed rates. The pr ovision applies only in the event that the individual is a resident of India. This provision is not applicable for an indiv idual who is not a resident of India. Tax for such payments made to a non-resident will have to be deducted under in accordance with the provisions of Section 195 of the Income Tax Act.

An insurance policy needs to be duly stamped in accordance with the stamp dut y prescribed for each kind of policy under the Indian Stamp Act, 1899 ("Stamp Act"). The rates of stamp duty on insurance policies are the same throughout the t erritories of India. Generally, the stamp dut y on a 20 life insurance policy or group insurance is borne by the person effecting t he insurance. In the case of a fire insurance policy, the insurer is liable to bear the st amp duty. Non-payment of stamp dut y, is a punishable offence with a fine w hich may extend up to rupees two hundred if an insur er receives the premium for an insurance policy and does not execute a policy or executes a policy which is not stamped.

All persons who desire to act as an insurance agent for any insurer would have to be regist ered as such under the provisions of the Insurance Act and the IRDA (Licensing of Agents) Regulations, 2000. A license issued under the provisions of the Insurance Act entitles the holder to act as an insurance agent for any insurer.

Any person ("applicant"), desirous of being an insurance agent or a composite insurance agent, may make an application for a license to act as an insurance agent to the Authority. The applicant should possess the minimum qualifications of twelfth standard or equivalent examination conducted by any recognized Board or institution, in cases where the applicant resides in a place with a population of five thousand or more as per the last census; and passed the tenth standard or equivalent examination from a recognized Board or institution if the applicant resides in any other place. Such an applicant should also not suffer from any of the following disqualifications:

- that the person is a minor;
- that he is found to be of unsound mind by a Court of competent jurisdiction;
- that he is found guilty of criminal misappropriation or criminal breach of trust or cheating or forgery or an abetment of or attempt to commit any such offence by a Court of competent jurisdiction.
- Provided that where at least five years have elapsed since the completion of the sentence imposed on any person in respect of such person that his conviction shall cease to operate as a disqualification;
- that in the course of any judicial proceeding relating to any policy of insurance or the winding up of an insurance company or in the course of an investigation of the affairs of an insurer it has been found that he has been guilty of or has knowingly participated in or connived at any fraud, dishonesty or misrepresentation against an insurer or an insured;
- that he does not possess the requisite qualifications and practical training for a period not exceeding twelve months;

- that he has not passed the examination;
- that he violates the code of conduct.

However, any license that had been issued prior to the commencement of the IRDA Act, 1999 shall be deemed to have been issued in accordance with the IRDA (Licensing of Agents) Regulations, 2000 and the provisions of the regulat ion in relation to the pract ical training, qualifications and examination shall not be applicable to such existing insurance agents. No insurance agent can be paid by way of commission or as remuneration, in any form, an amount exceeding,-

- in case of life insurance business, forty per cent of the first year's premium payable on any policy or policies effected thr ough him and five per cent of a renewal premium payable on such a policy. However, the insurer may, during the first ten years of their business, pay f ift y-five per cent of the first years' premium payable on any policy or policies eff ected through them and six per cent of the renewal premiums payable on such policies.
- in the case of business of any other class, fift een per cent of the premium.

An insurance surveyor is a technical expert who inspects the damage or loss of an insurance company. The insurer, based on the estimation of damage of the sur veyor, arrives at the amount of compensation payable to the assured.

Every individual, who int ends to act as a surveyor and loss assessor in respect of the general insurance business, may make an application to the Authorit y for a license. The Authority may grant a license (which shall be valid for a period of five years) af ter he is satisfied that the applicant:

(i) satisfies all the applicable requirements of the Insur ance Act and rules thereunder;

(ii) has furnished evidence of payment of fees for grant of license, depending upon the categorization;

(iii) has undergone a period of practical training, not exceeding twelve months; and

(iv) any other information that may be requir ed by the Authority.

A surveyor and loss assessor is required to spend a major par t of his time in investigating and managing losses arising from any contingency and prepare repor ts. He is required to carry out his duties in compliance with the code of conduct. A surveyor and loss assessor has inter alia the duty and responsibilit y to ensure that he discloses whether he has any int erest in the subject matter in question or w hether it pertains to any of his r elatives, business partners or through material shareholding; or maintaining confidentiality and neutrality without jeopardizing the liability of the insurer and claim of the insured; or conducting inspection and re-inspection of the property in question suffering a loss; or recommending applicability of depreciation, or the percentage and quantum of depreciation etc.

Under the provisions of the IRDA (Third Party Administrators Health services) Regulations, 2001, ("TPA Regulations")the Third Par ty Administrator ("TPA") means a third part y administrator, who has obtained a license from the Authority, and is engaged for a fee or remuneration, as specified in the 24 agreement with the insurance company, for the provision of healt h services. An insurance company may engage more than one TPA and similarly, one TPA may serve more than one insurance company. The TPA is required to maintain professional confidentialit y of records, books, evidence etc. of all transactions that it carries out. In addition, the TPA is required to furnish t o the insurance company and the Authority, an annual repor t and any other return as may be required by the Authority. The TPA is prohibited from charging the policyholders with any separ ate fees. Only a company, with a share capital and register ed under the Companies Act, 1956, can function as a TPA. In addition, the company is also required to fulfil the following conditions to be eligible to act as a TPA:

- The main or primary object of the company should be to carry on business in India as a TPA in the health services, and on being licensed by the Authority.
- The minimum paid up capital of the company shall be in equity shares amounting to rupees ten million.
- The TPA should, at no point of time, have a working capital of less than rupees ten million.
- At least one of the directors of the TPA should be qualified medical doctor registered with the Medical Council of India;
- The aggregate holdings of equity shares by a foreign company shall not at any time exceed twenty-six per cent of the paid-up capital of a third party administrator.
- Any transfer of shares exceeding five per cent of the paid up capital shall be int imated by the TPA to the Authorit y within 15 days of the transfer indicating the names and par ticulars of the transferor and transferee.

Every license granted by the Authorit y shall remain in force for three years. The Authority may revoke or cancel a license gr anted to a TPA for any of the following reasons:

- The TPA is functioning improperly and or against the interests of the policyholders or insurance company.
- The financial condition of the TPA has deteriorated and that the TPA cannot function effect ively or that

the TPA has breached any of the conditions of the TPA Regulation.

- The character and ownership of the TPA has changed significantly since the grant of license.
- The grant or renewal of license was on the basis of fraud or misrepresent ation of facts and that there is a breach on the part of the TPA in following the procedure or acquiring the qualifications under the TPA Regulation.
- The TPA is subject to winding up proceedings under the Companies Act, 1956.
- There is a breach of code of conduct.
- There is violation of any direct ions issued by the Authority under the Insurance Act or the TPA Regulations.

Every insurer re-insures himself t o protect against the risks t o which it subjects himself in the conduct of insurance business. The general insurance company has been designated as the sole re-insurer in India. Every insur er is required to re-insure wit h an Indian re-insurer such percentage of the sum assured on each policy as specified by the Author ity in this regard.

The insurer is free to chose any re-insurer subject t o the condition that such a re-insurer should enjoy a credit rating of a minimum of BBB of Standard and Poor or equivalent rating of any international rating agency. However, the placement of business by the insurer with any other reinsurer can be made only after obtaining the prior approval of the Authorit y. Every insurer is mandatorily required to retain the maximum premium earned in India commensurate with his financial strength and volume of business. Every insurer should draw up a re-insurance programme in respect of all the lives covered by him. However, a programme of reinsurance on an original premium basis can be drawn only after obtaining the approval of the Authorit y. Further, a life insurer is not permitted to make any treaty arrangements with its promoter company or its associate or group company, except on terms, which are commercially competit ive in the market and the prior approval of the Authorit y. The profile of the programme, duly cert ified by the appointed actuary, should be filed with the Authorit y at least fort y-five days before the commencement of each financial year. Additionally, the insurer should also submit the statist ics relating to its reinsurance transact ions with the annual accounts to the Authority. Every insurer who wants to w rite inward reinsurance business should adopt an underwriting policy for the purpose of underwrit ing inward reinsurance business. A note on the underwriting policy indicating the classes of business, geographical scope, underwriting limits and profit objective should be filed with the Authority.

Every insurer is required to maintain a retention, which is commensurate with its financial strength and volume of business. The Authority may require an insurer to justify its retention policy and may give directions to ensure that the Indian insurer is not merely fronting for a f oreign insurer. Every insurer should cede such percentage of the sum assured on each policy for dif ferent classes of insurance writt en in India to the Indian re-insurer as may be specified by the Author ity in accordance with the provisions the Insurance Act. Every insurer is required to submit its reinsurance programme to the Authorit y for the forthcoming year within forth-five day s before the commencement of the financial year. Additionally, the insurer should also file with the Authority a photocopy of every reinsurance treaty slip and excess of loss cover note in respect of that year together with a lis t of re-insurers and their shares in the reinsurance arrangement.

Insurers are permitt ed to place their reinsurance business outside India with only those re-insurers who have over a period of the past five years counting from the year preceding for which the business has to be placed, enjoyed a rating of at least BBB (with Standard and Poor) or equivalent rating of any other international rating agency. It is obligatory for all insurers to of fer an opportunity to other Indian insurers including the Indian re-insurer to participate in its facult ative and treaty surpluses before placement of such cessions outside India. Any surplus over and above the domestic reinsurance arrangements class wise may be placed by the insurer independently with any of the r e-insurers, subject to a limit of ten per cent of the total reinsurance premium ceded outside India being placed with any one re-insurer. In the even that the insurer would like to cede a share exceeding such limit to any par ticular re-insurer, in respect of specialized insurance, the insurer should seek the specific approval of t he Authority in this regard.

LEGAL & TAX COUNSELING WORLDWIDE

Every insurer should also make an outstanding claims pr ovision for every reinsurance arrangement accepted on the basis of loss information advices received from brokers/ cedants and in cases where such advices are not r eceived, on an actuarial estimation basis. In addition, ever y insurer should also make an appropriate provision for IBNR claims on its reinsurance accepted portfolio on actuarial estimation basis. The Indian re-insurer is required to organize domestic pools for reinsurance surpluses in fire, marine hull and other classes in consultation with all insurers and should also assis t in maintaining the retention of business within India. Such arrangements are required to be submitted to the Authority for appr oval. Further, the Indian re-insurer is required to retrocede at least fift y per cent of the obligatory cessions received by it to the ceding insurers after pr otecting the portf olio by suitable excess of loss covers.

Every insurer wanting to w rite inward reinsurance business should have an underwriting policy for underwriting r einsurance business, which should be filed with the Authorit y stating the classes of business, geographical scope, underwriting limits and pr ofit objective. Where there is a positive enactment of the Indian legislature, the language of the statute is applied t o the facts of the case. However, the common law of England is often relied upon in consider ation of justice, equit y and good conscience.

A contract of insurance is a contract uberrimea fidei i.e. a contract of utmost good f aith. This is a fundamental principle of insurance law. Both the parties t o the contract are required to observe utmost good faith and should disclose every material fact known to them. There is no difference between a contract of insurance and any other contract except that in a contract of insurance there is a requirement of utmost good faith. The burden of proof to show non-disclosure or misrepresentation is on the insurance company and the onus is a heavy one. The duty of good faith is of a continuing nature in as much no material alteration can be made to the terms of the contract without the mutual consent of the parties. Just as the assured has a dut y to disclose all .the material facts, the insurer is also under an obligation to do the same. The insurer cannot subsequently demand additional premium nor can he escape liability by contending that the situation does not warrant the insurance cover.

The Insurance Act lays down that an insurance policy cannot be called in question two years af ter it has been in force for two years. This was done to obv iate the hardships of the insured w hen the insurance company tried to avoid a policy, which has been in force for a long time, on the ground of misrepresentation. However, this provision is not applicable when the statement was made fraudulently. The Marine Insurance Act, 1963 ("Marine Insurance Act") lays down that the insured must disclose all the material facts before the contract is concluded. The disclosures by the assured or by his agent should be true. The insured is should be paid as to whether such represent ations are wilful or innocent and whether they ar e preliminary or for part of the contract. The Insurance Act lays down thr ee conditions to establish that the misrepresentation was wilful; (a) the statement must be on a material mat ter or must suppress facts which it was material to disclose; (b) t he suppression must be fraudulently madc by the policy holder; and (c) the policy-holder must have known at the time of making the st atement that it was false or that it suppressed facts which it was mat erial to disclose. The burden of proof of est ablishing that the insured had in fact suppressed mater ial facts in obtaining insurance is on the insurer and all the aforesaid conditions are requir ed to be proved cumulatively. In determining whether there has been suppression of a material fact it is necessary to examine whether the suppression relat es to a fact which is in the exclusive knowledge of the person intending to take the policy and also that it could not be ascer tained by reasonable enquiry by a prudent person.

A warranty may be distinguished from a representation in as much a representation may be equitably and substantially answered but a warrant y must be strictly complied with. A breach of warranty will avoid the policy, although it may not relat e to a matter mater ial to the risk insured. Warranties may be express or implied, if it is condition implied by law. However, implied warranties are mostly confined t o marine insurance. The Marine Insurance Act defines a warrant y as a promise whereby the assured under takes that some particular t hing shall or shall not be done, or that some condition shall be fulfilled, or affir ms or negatives the existence of a par ticular state of facts.

The statements must be true in fact wit hout any qualification of judgement, opinion or belief. The warranty should be in the policy or must be incorporated by reference. If any of the s tatements or representations made by the assured in the proposal have been made the "basis" of the deemed to know every circums tance, which in the o course of business, ought to be known by him. The may avoid the contr act-if the assured fails to mak disclosure or if the representation made is untrue. Ho circumstances which diminish the risk, or whic presumed to be known by the insurer or information is waived by the insurer or any circumstance wh superfluous to disclose by reason of any express or im warrant y need not be disclosed, in absence of any enq

In India the post contractual dut y of good faith is strict. The situat ion, though, has changed in Eng through a recent decision of the House of Lords. The deci in the Star Sea Case lays down that the duty of good f in insurance contracts continues af ter the inception of policy, but the duty is far less s trict than it was prio the commencement of the contract. This is because it wo enable the insurers to avoid the whole policy ab init io a post-contractual breach, which had no effect when t policy was dr awn initially. However, this position has y to be accepted by the Indian courts. Representations a statements, made by one part y to the other, either pri to or while entering into an insurance contract, of som matter or circumstances relating t o it and which is not a integral part of the contract. These statements are said t have fulf illed their obligations when the final acceptance on the policy is conveyed.

A mere recital of represent ations made at the time of entering int o the contact will not make then warranties. However, if representations are made an int egral part of the contract they become warranties, and, in case of their being untrue, the policy can be avoided, even if the loss does not arise from the fact concealed or misrepresented. A policy of life insurance cannot be called in question on the ground of misrepresentat ion after a period of two years fr om the commencement of the policy. In dealing with representations as circumstances invalidating a contract, consideration contract and they are found to be untrue, the contract of insur ance would be void and unenforceable in law, irrespective of the question w hether the statement, concerned is of a material nature or not. However, non-compliance of a warranty is excused w hen, by reason of a change of circumstances, the warranty ceases t o be applicable to the circumstances of the contract, or when compliance with the warranty is r endered unlawful by any subsequent law or when such a warrant y has not been mentioned in the policy. Conditions are terms which pr escribe the limitations under which an insur ance policy is granted and which specify the duties of the assured. They can be either conditions precedent or subsequent. Conditions precedent are those, which ar e essential for the creation of a valid contract, the non-satisfaction of which makes the contract void ab initio. Conditions subsequent relate to the continuance of a valid contract, the non-fulfilment of which leads t o the avoidance of the contract from the date of the breach.

They can be further classified into expr ess conditions and implied conditions. Implied conditions are those, which are implied by law to apply t o every contract of insurance irrespective of any specific inclusion or reference to them such as insurable int erest, good faith etc. A condition, which seeks to reduce or curtail the per iod of limitation and prescribes a shor ter period than that prescribed by law is void. However, the insured is absolved once it is shown that he has done everyt hing in his power to keep, honour and fulfil the promise and he himself is not guilt y of a deliberate breach. An insurer cannot take recourse to a condition, w hich has not been mentioned in the policy to reduce his liability. However, an insurance policy may not curtail the right but may mer ely provide for forfeiture or waiver of any such right and such a right would be enforceable against either party. Most kinds of insurance policies other than life and personal accident insurance are contr acts of indemnity wher eby the insurer undertakes to indemnify the insured for the actual loss suf fered by him as a result of the occurring of the event insured against. Even wit hin the maximum limit, the insured cannot recover more than what he es tablishes to be his actual loss. A contract of marine insurance is an agreement whereby the insurer undertakes to indemnif y the insured to the extent agreed upon. Although the insured is to be placed in the same position as if t he loss has not occurred, the amount of indemnity may be limited by cer tain conditions:

- Injury or loss sustained by the insur ed has to be proved.
- The indemnity is limited to the amount specified in the policy
- The insured is indemnified only for the proximat e causes.
- The market value of the propert y determines the amount of indemnity.

Indemnity is a fundamental principle of insurance law, and the principle of Subrogation is a corollary of this principle in as much the insured is precluded from obtaining more than the loss he has sustained. The most common form of subrogation is when an insurance company pays a claim caused by the negligence of another. The doctrine of subrogation confers two specific rights on the insurer. Firstly, the insurer is entitled to all the remedies which the insured has against the third part y incidental to the subject matt er of the loss, such that the insurer can take advant age of any means available to extinguish or diminish, the loss for which the insurer has indemnified the insured.

Secondly, the insurer is entitled to the benefits received by the assured from the thir d part y with a view to compensate himself for the loss. The fact that an insurer is subrogated to the rights and remedies of the insured does not ipso jure enable him to sue third part ies in his own name. It will only entitle the insurer to sue in the name of insured, it being an obligation of the insured to lend his name and assis tance to such an action. An insurance policy may contain a special clause whereby the insur ed assigns all his rights, against third parties, in f avour of the insurer. In case of subrogation, which vest by operation of law rather than as the product of express agreement, the insur ed would be entitled to only to the extent of his loss. The excess amount, if any, would be returned to the insured.

The doctrine of proximate cause is expressed in the maxim 'Causa Proxima non remota spectator', which means that the proximate and not t he remote cause, shall be taken as the cause of loss. The insurer is thus has to make good the loss of the insured that clearly and proximately results, whether directly or indirectly, from the event insured against in the policy. The burden of proof that the loss occurred on account of the proximate cause, lies on the insured. As per the Marine Insurance Act, unless the insurance policy stat es otherwise, the insurer is liable for any loss proximately caused by a peril insured against, but he is not liable for any loss which is not proximately caused by a peril insured against. An insurer would therefore be exempted from liability when the cause of loss falls within the except ions of the policy. The Marine Insurance Act further states that the insur er is not liable for any wilful misconduct of the insured i.e. the assured cannot recover for a loss where his own deliberat e act is the proximate cause of it. Further, in the event of loss caused by the delay of the ship, the insurer cannot be held liable, irrespect ive of the proximity of the cause.

The Consumer Protection Act, 1986 ("Consumer Protection Act") is one of the most important socio-economic legislation for the protect ion of consumers in India. The provisions of this Act are compensatory in nature, unlike other laws, w hich are either punitive or preventive. Insurance services fall within the purview of the Consumer Prot ection Act, in as much, any deficiency in service of the insurance company would enable the aggrieved to make a complaint. Disputes between policyholders and insurers generally pert ain to repudiation of the insurance claim or the mat ters connected with admission of the claim or computation of the amount of claim. In the case of assignment of all rights by the insured to the insurer, the consumer forum and he courts generally refuse to accept the locus standi of the insured. The courts have held that insurance companies do not fall under the def inition of "consumer" under the Consumer Protection Act, as no serv ice is rendered to them directly. Neither the subrogation nor the transfer of the right of action would confer the legal status of a 'consumer' on the insurer, nor can the insurer be regarded as any beneficiar y of any service. Therefore, the remedy available to the insurer is to file a suit in a civil court for recovery of the loss To constitute insurable interest, it must be an interest such that the risk would by its proximate effect cause damage to the assured, that is to say, cause him to lose a benefit or incur a liability. The validity of an insurance contract, in India, is dependent on the existence of an insurable interes t in the subject matter. The person seeking an insurance policy must establish some kind of interest in the life or property to be insured, in the absence of which, the insur ance policy would amount to a wager and consequently void in nature.

The test for determining if ther e is an insurable interest is whet her the insured will in case of damage to the life or proper ty being insured, suf fer pecuniary loss. A person having a limited interes t can also insure such interest. Insurable interest varies depending on the nature of the insurance. The controversy as to the existence of an insurable interest between spouses was settled by the cour t, which held that such an interest could exist as neither was likel y to indulge in any 'mischievous game'. The same analogy may be extended to parents and children. Further, the courts have also held that such an insurable interest would exist for a creditor (in a debtor) and for an employee (in an employer) to the ext ent of the debt incurred and the remuneration due, respectively. The existence of insurable interest at the time of happening of the event is another important consideration. In case of life and personal accident insurance it is suff icient if the insurable interest is present at the time of taking the policy. However, in the case of fire and motor accident insurance the insurable interest has to be present both at the time of taking the policy and at the time of the accident. The case is completely different with marine insurance wherein there need not be any insurable interest at the time of taking the policy.

The general rule on the formation of a contract, as per the Indian Contract Act, is that the part y to whom the offer has been made should accept it uncondit ionally and communicate his acceptance to the person making the offer. Whether the final acceptance is to be made by the insur ed or insurer really depends on the negotiations of the policy. Acceptance should be signified by some act as agreed upon by the part ies or from which the law raises a presumption of acceptance. The mere receipt or retention of premium until after the death of the applicant or the mere preparation of the policy document is not acceptance. Nonetheless, acceptance may be presumed upon the retention of the premium. However, mere delay in giving an answer cannot be construed as acceptance. Also, silence does not denote consent and no binding contract arises until the person to whom an offer is made says or does something to signify his acceptance.

When the policy is of a particular date, it would cover the liability of the insur er from the previous midnight preceding the same date. However, where there is a special contract to the contrary in the policy, the terms of the contract would prevail. Hence where the time of the issue of the insurance policy is mentioned, then the liabilit y would be covered only from the time w hen it was issued.

11

PROPOSAL FOR COMMUNITY HEALTH INSURANCE-BROADENING OF COVERAGE TO INCLUDE HIV/AIDS

BACKGROUND

The need for effective community health insurance schemes for people living in economically challenged circumstances emerged out of several recent studies, and the impact of a Community Health Insurance program has been substantial. In countries like India, where close to 30% live below the poverty line, with close to no health security, such schemes will bring about a significant increase in both the health and the economic situation of the community.

Poverty along with poor nutrition and harsh living conditions makes the rural poor extremely vulnerable to ill health and diseases. This affects the economy of the village and hence the state, and in turn establishes a 'vicious cycle'.

Community based insurance schemes are important as they cover primary and secondary care, which is difficult for private insurance to administer. An insurance scheme that is mediated through the Primary Health Centres and the government health care system will bring health security under the purview of primary health care and will increase service delivery from Primary Health Centres, as opposed to private, profit-making agencies.

Considering the heavy burden that ill health imposes on resource-poor communities, which are a majority in rural India, HIV/AIDS tips the balance to the dangerous side. The disease hits at an individual, familial and at the community level, and results in social boycott, neglect and unbearable economic burden on the family. The latest figures show a prevalence of 1.5% in Antenatal clinics in 2004. This indicates the spread of the disease in the general population, and it is no more restricted to high risk groups.

The earlier focus of the program was only on IEC. Now, in view of the changed situation, there is a need for intensive IEC in addition to provision of effective curative and rehabilitative services at the level of the Primary Health Centre. The project proposes to integrate HIV/AIDS in primary care all over the state through the network of Primary Health Centres of Karuna Trust, and provide preventive, curative and rehabilitative services for HIV/AIDS at the primary level. It is proposed to evolve a unique insurance scheme to cover HIV/AIDS including investigations and treatment (Anti-retroviral Therapy and treatment of opportunistic infections).

PAST EXPERIENCE

A UNDP sponsored pilot project on the development of a possible and replicable model for community health insurance was taken up in Karnataka state. This project was implemented in 2 phases and covered the whole of Chamarajanagar district and T Narsipura Taluks. In Belgaum, the government was the implementing agency, and the second phase of the project is under way there. In effect, a replicable and workable model for community health insurance with:

- o Low premium
- o Immediate claim settlement
- o No exclusion policy
- o Coverage for wage loss and 'out-of-pocket' expenditure
- o Collaboration with the public-sector (National Insurance Corporation)

The 2 phases have been successfully completed. The results have shown increasing access to government health services and improvement in the access to services by women and children. The model has effectively brought in more than 1 lakh people under the health security blanket. The next phase involves the application of the experience gained in these 2 phases in up-scaling the program to 20 PHCs in various districts of the state and coverage of all aspects of HIV/AIDS under the program. The proposal addresses the sustainability issue and will use a network of Self-help groups (SHGs) for this purpose. The fact sheets with the details of the 2 phases are appended to the proposal.

Objectives

- o Increase access to medical care to rural poor and low income group
- o Health security to the rural poor at the primary level
- o Strengthen the primary care system to brace up to the new challenge of HIV/AIDS
- o To develop and test a model for incorporation of all aspects of HIV/AIDS in Community Health Insurance-IEC activities, case detection, counselling and treatment
- o Evolution of a sustainable community health insurance program in one PHC of every district of the state based on the CHI insurance in T N Pura and Yelandur.

- o Capacity building of existing health workers in PHCs to implement the HIV/AIDS program.

METHODOLOGY

In view of its wide ranging health implications, AIDS touches all aspects of primary health care, including mother and child health, family planning and education. It is important therefore that AIDS control programs are not developed in The project is to be implemented in the 19 PHCs being run by Karuna Trust in 14 districts of the state, 2 health centres in Mandya district and in 5 more districts where the process of taking over the PHC is on. The experience gained in running the project in T Narsipura and Yelandur will be useful in the implementation of the program in the aforementioned PHCs. In addition, a key aspect of the program will be the integration of all aspects of HIV/AIDS in primary care.

HIV/AIDS has traditionally been associated with high risk groups. The present prevalence rates in the state show its spread in the general population. The previous concept of provision of treatment and counselling at secondary level is no more tenable in this changed scenario. Hence, we advocate the implementation of all aspects of HIV/AIDS at the primary level-from prevention to rehabilitation. There is a need to undertake capacity building of the ANMs for:

- o Impressing upon them the concept of Community Health Insurance
- o Build up a network of Self-help groups who will be central to the sustainability of the CHI program
- o Identification of high-risk groups and bringing them under insurance cover
- o Pre and post test counselling

The PHCs shall be equipped with 3 different kits as per the NACO guidelines for testing for HIV/AIDS.

Counselling is an essential part of voluntary and confidential HIV antibody testing programs. It also plays a very valuable role in reducing the risk of infection, family planning, relationships, sexuality and sexual problems. Counselling is a vital part of caring for people who are dying, and supporting those who are taking care of them. The impact of HIV goes far beyond HIV-positive individuals. It has great implications for their sexual partners and family members-including future children. People with HIV or AIDS live in a perpetual state of fear, not so much of dying, but of being rejected by society if their HIV status becomes known to others. Rejection is often linked to feeling of extreme anxiety and helplessness, and fear that life is finished. Over the time and with continued counselling this may change. The counsellor can help the client to view HIV infection as something that can be managed, and develop a positive attitude about life with HIV.

Counselling

Capacity building of ANMs and lab technicians as counsellors, provision of pre and post test counselling

Prevention

Awareness generation with IEC materials, Focus group discussions with SHGs, social mapping and identification of high risk groups, Promotion of safe sexual practices and stress on Adolescent education program in schools Case detection-3 The insurance will be distributed through the self-help groups. Also, the ANM will be trained in social mapping to identify risk groups. The risk groups will be the special focus for the ANM.

The SHGs shall receive a corpus fund thus ensuring sustainability of the project. 6 priority PHCs will be identified amongst the 20 based on the HIV prevalence and access to government established VCTCs.

BIBLIOGRAPHY

Arrow, Kenneth J.: *Social Choice and Individual Values*, New York, Wiley, 1951.

Campbell, J.Y., Lo, A.W.: *The Econometrics of Financial Markets,* Princeton University Press, 1996.

Chaudhuri, Pramit: *The Indian Economy: Poverty and Development*, New York, St. Martin's Press, 1979.

Dhingra, C.: *The Indian Economy: Resources, Planning, Development, and Problems*, Delhi, Sultan Chand, 1983.

Greer, Douglas F.: *Industrial Organization and Public Policy*, MacMillan Publishing Company, 1992.

Ishwar, C.: *The Indian Economy: Resources, Planning, Development, and Problems*, Delhi, Sultan Chand, 1983.

Little, I.M.D.: *India: Macroeconomics and Political Economy, 1964-1991*, Washington, World Bank, 1994.

Mongia, J.N.: *India's Economic Development Strategies, 1951-2000 A.D.*. New Delhi, Allied, 1986.

Pranab, K.: *The Political Economy of Development in India*, Delhi, Oxford University Press, 1984.

Sargent, Thomas J.: *Dynamic Macroeconomic Theory*, Harvard University Press, 1987.

Tirole, Jean: *The Theory of Industrial Organization*, MIT Press, 1988.

Williamson, Jeffrey G.: *American Inequality: A Macroeconomic History*, New York, Academic Press, 1980.

Xavier Sala-i-Martin: *Economic Growth*. McGraw-Hill, 1995.

INDEX

◆◆◆